Charles Carleton Coffin

Daughters of the Revolution and their Times

1769-1776

Charles Carleton Coffin

Daughters of the Revolution and their Times
1769-1776

ISBN/EAN: 9783337227586

Printed in Europe, USA, Canada, Australia, Japan

Cover: Foto ©Andreas Hilbeck / pixelio.de

More available books at **www.hansebooks.com**

DAUGHTERS OF THE REVOLUTION AND THEIR TIMES

1769 — 1776

A Historical Romance

BY

CHARLES CARLETON COFFIN

BOSTON AND NEW YORK
HOUGHTON, MIFFLIN AND COMPANY
The Riverside Press, Cambridge
1896

INTRODUCTION.

No period in the history of our country surpasses in interest that immediately preceding and including the beginning of the Revolutionary War. Many volumes have been written setting forth the patriotism and heroism of the fathers of the Republic, but the devotion of the mothers and daughters has received far less attention. *This* volume is designed, therefore, to portray in some degree their influence in the struggle of the Colonies to attain their independence. The narration of events takes the form of a story — a slight thread of romance being employed, rather than didactic narrative, to more vividly picture the scenes and the parts performed by the actors in the great historic drama. It will not be difficult for the reader to discern between the facts of history and the imaginative parts of the story.

Eminent educators have expressed the opinion that history may be more successfully taught through the medium of fiction than by any other form of diction. The novels of Sir Walter Scott, notably " Waverley," "Ivanhoe," are cited as presenting pictures of the times more effectively than any purely historic volume. The same may be said of "Uncle Tom's Cabin," as illustrating the state of affairs in our own country preceding the War of the Rebellion. It may be questioned whether any work of fiction in the world's history has been so far-reaching in its influence as that portrayal of the institution of slavery by Mrs. Stowe. Believing that the spirit of the times can be best pictured by the employment of romance, I have adopted that form of narrative.

The story opens in the fall of 1769. The Stamp Act had been repealed, and the irritation produced by that act had been allayed. It was a period of quiet and rest. The colonists still regarded themselves as Englishmen and loyal to the crown. Information came that His Majesty George III. was determined to maintain his right to tax the Colonies by imposing an export duty on tea, to be paid by the exporter, who, in turn, would charge it to the consumer. The first resistance to that claim was the agreement of all but six of the merchants of Boston not to import tea from England, and the agreement of their wives and daughters not to drink tea so imported. It was a resistance which had its outcome in the destruction of three cargoes of tea by the historic "Tea-Party," — a resistance which became equally effective in the other Colonies, if less dramatic than in Boston. The determination of the mothers and daughters to abstain from its use brought about a change in social life, and was influential in awakening a public sentiment which had its legitimate outcome in the events at Lexington, Concord. and Bunker Hill.

There were causes other than the Stamp Act, Writs of Assistance, and the Tax on Tea, which brought about the Revolution.

"Whoever would comprehend the causes which led to the struggle of the Colonies for independence," says

John Adams, " must study the Acts of the Board of Trade."

In this volume I have endeavored to briefly present some of those acts, in the conversation of Sam Adams with Robert Walden, that the school children of the country may have a comprehension of the underlying causes which brought about resistance to the tyranny of the mother country. The injustice of the laws had its legitimate result in a disregard of moral obligations, so that smuggling was regarded as a virtuous act.

In no history have I been able to find an account of the tragic death and dramatic burial of the schoolboy Christopher Snider, given in chapter VIII. It was the expression of sympathy by the people in following the body of the murdered boy from the Liberty Tree to the burial-place that intensified the antagonism between the citizens and the soldiers of the Fourteenth and Twenty - ninth regiments of the king's troops, which led, the following week, to the Massacre of March 5, 1770. Bancroft barely mentions the name of Snider ; other historians make no account of the event.

To explain the motives and the play of forces which brought about the Revolution, I have endeavored to set forth society as it was not only in Boston but in Parliament and at the Court of George III. Most historians of the Revolutionary period regard the debt incurred by Great Britain in the conquest of Canada as the chief cause of the war, through the attempt of the mother country, subsequently, to obtain revenue from the Colonies ; but a study of the times gives conclusive evidence that a large portion of the indebtedness was caused by mismanagement and the venality and corruption of Parliament.

To set forth the extravagance and frivolity of society surrounding King George, I have employed Lord Upperton and his companion, Mr. Dapper, as narrators. The student of history by turning to Jessee's " Life and Times of George III.," Molloy's " Court Life Below Stairs," Waldegrave's " Memoirs," Horace Walpole's writings, and many other volumes, will find ample corroboration of any statement made in this volume.

The period was characterized by sublime enthusiasm, self - sacrifice, and devotion, not only by the patriots but by loyalists who conscientiously adhered to the crown. In our admiration of those who secured the independence of the Colonies, we have overlooked the sacrifices and sufferings of the loyalists; — their distress during the siege of Boston, the agony of the hour when suddenly confronted with the appalling fact that they must become aliens, exiles, and wanderers, leaving behind all their possessions and estates, — an hour when there was a sundering of tender ties, the breaking of hearts.

I have endeavored to make the recital of events strictly conformable with historic facts by consulting newspapers, documents, almanacs, diaries, genealogical records, and family histories.

It was my great privilege in boyhood to hear the story of the battle of Bunker Hill told by three men who participated in the fight. — Eliakim Walker, who was in the redoubt under Prescott. Nathaniel Atkinson and David Flanders, who were under Stark, by the rail fence. They were near neighbors, pensioners of the government, and found pleasure in rehearsing the events of the Revolutionary War. My grandfather, Eliphalet Kilburn, was at Winter Hill at the time of the battle.

It was also my privilege to walk over Bunker Hill with Richard Frothingham, author of the "Siege of Boston," whose home was on the spot where Pigot's brigade was cut down by the withering fire from the redoubt. Mr. Frothingham had conversed with many old pensioners who were in the redoubt at the time of the battle. In my account of the engagement I have endeavored to picture it in accordance with the various narratives.

I hardly need say that Ruth Newville, Berinthia Brandon, and Mary Shrimpton are typical characters, representing the young women of the period, — a period in which families were divided, parents adhering to King George, sons and daughters giving their allegiance to Liberty.

I am under obligations to the proprietors of the "Memorial History of Boston" for the portrait of Mrs. Joseph Warren. The portrait of Dorothy Quincy is from that in possession of the Bostonian Society; that of Mrs. John Adams from her "Life and Letters."

The historic houses are from recent photographs.

I trust the reader will not regard this volume wholly as a romance, but rather as a presentation of the events, scenes, incidents, and spirit of the people at the beginning of the Revolution.

CHARLES CARLETON COFFIN.

CONTENTS.

ILLUSTRATIONS.

DAUGHTERS OF THE REVOLUTION.

I.

JOSHUA WALDEN, of Rumford, Province of New Hampshire, was receiving letters from Samuel Adams and Doctor Joseph Warren in relation to the course pursued by King George III. and his ministers in collecting revenue from the Colonies. Mr. Walden had fought the French and Indians at Ticonderoga and Crown Point in the war with France. The gun and powder-horn which he carried under Captain John Stark were hanging over the door in his kitchen. His farm was on the banks of the Merrimac. The stately forest trees had fallen beneath the sturdy blows of his axe, and the sun was shining on intervale and upland, meadow and pasture which he had cleared. His neighbors said he was getting fore-handed. Several times during the year he made a journey to Boston with his cheeses, beef, pigs, turkeys, geese, chickens, a barrel of apple-sauce, bags filled with wool, together with webs of linsey-woolsey spun and woven by his wife and daughter. He never failed to have a talk with Mr. Adams and Doctor Warren, John Hancock, and others foremost in resisting the aggressions of the mother country upon the rights and liberties of the Colonies. When at home he was up early in the morning, building 'the fire, feeding the cattle, and milking the cows. Mrs. Walden, the while, was stirring the corn meal for a johnny-cake, putting the potatoes in the ashes, placing the Dutch oven on the coals, hanging the pots and kettles on the hooks and trammels.

Robert, their only son, twenty years old, would be glad to take another nap after being called by his father, but felt it would not be manly for one who had mowed all the hired men out of their swaths in the hayfield, and who had put the best wrestler in Rumford on his back, to lie in bed and let his father do all the chores, with the cows lowing to get to the pasture. With a spring he was on his feet and slipping on his clothes. He was soon on his way to the barn, drumming on the tin pail and whistling as he walked to the milking.

The cows turned into pasture, he rubbed down the mare Jenny and the colt Paul, fed the pigs, washed his face and hands, and was ready for breakfast.

It would not have been like Rachel Walden, the only daughter, eighteen years old, to lie in bed and let her mother do all the work about the house. She came from her chamber with tripping steps, as if it were a pleasure to be wide awake after a good sleep. She fed the chickens, set the table, raked the potatoes from the ashes, drew a mug of cider for her father. When breakfast was ready, they stood by their chairs while Mr. Walden asked a blessing. The meal finished, he read a chapter in the Bible and offered prayer. When the "Amen" was said, Mr. Walden and Robert put on their hats and went about their work. Mrs. Walden passed upstairs to throw the shuttle of the loom. Rachel washed the dishes, wheyed the curd, and prepared it for the press, turned the cheeses and rubbed them with fat. That done, she set the kitchen to rights, made the beds, sprinkled clean sand upon the floor, wet the web of linen bleaching on the grass in the orchard, then slipped upstairs and set the spinning-wheel to humming. His neighbors said that Mr. Walden was thrifty and could afford to wear a broadcloth blue coat with bright brass buttons on grand occasions, and that Mrs. Walden was warranted in having a satin gown.

Haying was over. The rye was reaped, the wheat and oats were harvested, and the flax was pulled. September had come, — the time when Mr. Walden usually went to Boston with the cheese.

"Father," said Rachel at dinner, "I wish you would take the cheeses to market. It is hard work to turn so many every day."

Mr. Walden sat in silence awhile. "Robert," he said at length, "how would you like to try your hand at truck and dicker?"

"If you think I can do it I will try," Robert replied, surprised at the question, yet gratified.

"Of course you can do it. You can figure up how much a cheese that tips the steelyard at twenty pounds and three ounces will come to at three pence ha'penny per pound. You know, or you ought to know, the difference between a pistareen and a smooth-faced shilling. When you truck and dicker, you've

got to remember that the other feller is doing it all
the time, while you will be as green as a pumpkin in
August. When you are tasting 'lasses, you must run
a stick into the bung-hole of the barrel clear down to
the bottom and then lift it up and see if it is thick or
thin. T' other feller will want you to taste it at the
spiggot, where it will be almost sugar. When you
are selecting dried codfish, look sharp and not let
him give you all damp ones from the bottom of the
pile, neither the little scrimped ones from the top.
Of course you will get cheated, but you have got to
begin knocking about some time. You're old enough
to have your eye teeth cut. You can put Jenny up
at the Green Dragon and visit Cousin Jedidiah Brandon on Copp's Hill, see the ships he is building, visit
with Tom and Berinthia. Tom, I guess, is going to
be a chip of the old block, and Berinthia is a nice girl.
Take your good clothes along in your trunk, so after
you get through handling the cheese you can dress
like a gentleman. I want you to pick out the best
cheese of the lot and give it to Samuel Adams, also
another to Doctor Warren, with my compliments.
You can say to Mr. Adams I would like any information he can give about what is going on in London
relative to taxing the Colonies. He is very kind, and
possibly may ask you to call upon him of an evening,
for he is very busy during the day. Doctor Warren
is one of the kindest-hearted men in the world, and
chuck full of patriotism. He will give a hearty shake
to your hand.

" You had better mouse round the market awhile
before trading. John Hancock bought my last load.

His store is close by Faneuil Hall. He is rich, inherited his property from his uncle. He lives in style in a stone house on Beacon Hill. He is liberal with his money, and is one of the few rich men in Boston who take sides with the people against the aggressions of King George and his ministers. Mr. Adams begins to be gray, but Warren and Hancock are both young men. They are doing grand things in maintaining the rights of the Colonies. I want you to make their acquaintance. By seeing and talking with such men you will be worth more to yourself and everybody else. Your going to market and meeting such gentlemen •will be as good as several months of school. You'll see more people than you ever saw on the muster-field; ships from foreign lands will be moored in the harbor. You'll see houses by the thousand, meetinghouses with tall steeples, and will hear the bells ring at five o'clock in the morning, getting-up time, at noon for dinner, and at nine in the evening, bed-time. Two regiments of red-coats are there. The latest news is that they are getting sassy. I can believe it. At Ticonderoga and Crown Point they used to put on airs, and call the Provincials " string-beans," " polly-pods," " slam bangs." They turned up their noses at our buckskin breeches, but when it came to fighting we showed 'em what stuff we were made of. Don't let 'm pick a quarrel, but don't take any sass from 'em. Do right by everybody."

" I will try to do right," Robert replied.

The sun was rising the next morning when Robert gathered up the reins and stood ready to step into the wagon which had been loaded for the market.

" You have three dozen new milk cheeses," said
Rachel, "and two and one half dozen of four meal. I
have marked the four meals with a cross in the centre,
so you 'll know them from the new milk. There are
sixteen greened with sage. They look real pretty. I
have put in half a dozen skims; somebody may want
'em for toasting."

" You will find," said Mrs. Walden, "a web of
linsey-woolsey in your trunk with your best clothes,
and a dozen skeins of wool yarn. It is lamb's wool.
I 've doubled and twisted it, and I don't believe the
women will find in all Boston anything softer or nicer
for stockings."

" I have put up six quarts of caraway seed," said
Rachel. " I guess the bakers will want it to put into
gingerbread. And I have packed ten dozen eggs in
oats, in a basket. They are all fresh. You can use
the oats to bait Jenny with on your way home."

" There are two bushels of beans," said Mr. Walden, " in that bag, — the one-hundred-and-one kind, —
and a bushel and three pecks of clover seed in the other
bag. You can get a barrel of 'lasses, half a quintal of
codfish, half a barrel of mackerel, and a bag of Turk's
Island salt."

" Don't forget," said Mrs. Walden, " that we want
some pepper, spice, cinnamon, nutmegs, cloves, and
some of the very best Maccaboy snuff. Oh, let me
see! I want a new foot-stove. Our old one is all
banged up, and I am ashamed to be seen filling it at
noon in winter in Deacon Stonegood's kitchen, with
all the women looking on, and theirs spick and span
new."

"Father and mother have told me what they want, and now what shall I get for you, Rachel?" Robert asked of his sister.

"Anything you please, Rob," Rachel replied with such tender love in her eyes that he had half a mind to kiss her. But kissing was not common in Rumford or anywhere else in New England. Never had he seen his father give his mother such a token of affection. He had a dim recollection that his mother sometimes kissed him when he was a little fellow in frock and trousers, sitting in her lap. He never had kissed Rachel, but he would now, and gave her a hearty smack. He saw an unusual brightness in her eyes and a richer bloom upon her cheek as he stepped into the wagon.

"I'll get something nice for her," he said to himself as he rode away.

Besides the other articles in the wagon, there was a bag of wool, sheared from his own flock. Years before his father had given him a cosset lamb, and now he was the owner of a dozen sheep. Yes, he would get something for her.

The morning air was fresh and pure. He whistled a tune and watched the wild pigeons flying in great flocks here and there, and the red-winged blackbirds sweeping past him from their roosting in the alders along the meadow brook to the stubble field where the wheat had been harvested. Gray squirrels were barking in the woods, and their cousins the reds, less shy, were scurrying along the fence rails and up the chestnut-trees to send the prickly burrs to the ground. The first tinge of autumn was on the elms and maples. Jenny had been to market so many times she could be

trusted to take the right road, and he could lie upon
his sack of wool and enjoy the changing landscape.

Mrs. Stark was blowing the horn for dinner at
· John Stark's tavern in Derryfield when Jenny came
to a standstill by the stable door.[1] Robert put her in
the stall, washed his face and hands in the basin on
the bench by the bar-room door, and was ready for
dinner. Captain Stark shook hands with him. Robert beheld a tall, broad-shouldered man, with a high
forehead, bright blue eyes, and pleasant countenance,
but with lines in his cheek indicating that he could be
very firm and resolute. This was he under whom his
father served at Ticonderoga and Crown Point.

"So you are the son of Josh Walden, eh? Well,
you have your father's eyes, nose, and mouth. If you
have got the grit he had at Ti, I'll bet on you."

Many times Robert had heard his father tell the
story of the Rifle Rangers, the service they performed,
the hardships they endured, and the bravery and cool-
ness of John Stark in battle.

Through the afternoon the mare trotted on, halting
at sunset at Jacob Abbott's stable in Andover.

It was noon the next day when Robert reached Cambridge. He had heard about Harvard College ; now
he saw the buildings. The students were having a
game of football after dinner. The houses along the
streets were larger than any he had ever seen before, —
stately mansions with porticoes, pillars, pilasters, carved
cornices, and verandas. The gardens were still bright

[1] John Stark, tavern-keeper in Derryfield, was the renowned Indian
fighter and captain of the corps of Rifle Rangers in the war with
France. (See Biography by Jared Sparks.) The tavern is still standing in the suburbs of the city of Manchester. N. H.

with the flowers of autumn. Reaching Roxbury, he came across a man slowly making his way along the road with a cane.

"Let me give you a lift, sir," Robert said.

"Thank you. I have been down with the rheumatiz, and can't skip round quite as lively as I could once," said the man as he climbed into the wagon. "'Spect you are from the country and on your way to market, eh?"

Robert replied that he was from New Hampshire.

"Ever been this way before?"

"No, this is my first trip."

"Well, then, perhaps I can p'int out some things that may interest ye."

Robert thanked him.

"This little strip of land we are on is the 'Neck.' This water on our left is Charles River, — this on our right is Gallows Bay. Ye see that thing out there, don't ye?"

The man pointed with his cane. "Well, that's the gallows, where pirates and murderers are hung. Lots of 'em have been swung off there, with thousands of people looking to see 'em have their necks stretched. 'T ain't a pretty sight, though."

The man took a chew of tobacco, and renewed the conversation.

"My name is Peter Bushwick, and yours may be — ?"

"Robert Walden."

"Thank ye, Mr. Walden. So ye took the road through Cambridge instead of Charlestown."

"I let Jenny pick the road. That through Charles-

town would have been nearer, but I should have to
cross the ferry. My father usually comes this way." [1]
"Mighty fine mare, Mr. Walden; ye can see she's
a knowing critter. She's got the right kind of an ear;
she knows what she's about."

They were at the narrowest part of the peninsula,
and Mr. Bushwick told about the barricade built by
the first settlers at that point to protect the town from
the Indians, and pointed to a large elm-tree which
they could see quite a distance ahead.

"That is the Liberty Tree," [2] he said.

"Why do you call it the Liberty Tree?"

"Because it is where the Sons of Liberty meet. It
is a mighty fine tree, and, as near as we can make out,
is more than one hundred years old. We hang the
Pope there on Guy Fawkes' day, and traitors to liberty
on other days."

"I have heard you have jolly good times on Gunpowder Plot days."

"You may believe we do. You would have laughed
if you'd been here Gunpowder day seven years ago
this coming November, when the Pope, Admiral Byng,

---

[1] No bridge from Charlestown had been constructed across Charles
Rivers (1769), and the only avenue leading into Boston was from Roxbury.

[2] The elm-tree stood at the junction of Orange and Essex streets
and Frog Lane, now Washington, Essex and Boylston streets. In 1766,
upon the repeal of the Stamp Act, a large copper plate was nailed upon
the tree with the following inscription: "This tree was planted in
the year 1646 and pruned by the Order of the Sons of Liberty February 14, 1766." Other trees stood near it, furnishing a grateful shade.
The locality before 1767 was known as Hanover Square, but after the
repeal of the Stamp Act, as Liberty Hall. In August, 1767, a flagstaff was raised above its branches; the hoisting of a flag upon the
staff was a signal for the assembling of the Sons of Liberty.

Nancy Dawson,[1] and the Devil, all were found hanging on the old elm."

" I don't think I ever heard about Admiral Byng and Nancy Dawson."

" Well, then, I must tell ye.   Byng did n't fight the French and Spaniards at Minorca, but sailed away and sort o' showed the white feather, and so was court-martialed and shot on his own ship."

" What did Nancy do ? "

" Oh, Nancy never did anything except kick up her heels ; she 's the best dancer in London, so they say. We have n't any theatre in this 'ere town, and don't have much dancing.   We have the Thursday lecture instead."

Robert wondered whether the allusion to the lecture was said soberly or in sarcasm.

" In London they go wild over dancing.   Maybe I might sing a song about her if ye would like to hear it."

" I would like very much to hear it."

Mr. Bushwick took the quid of tobacco from his mouth, cleared his throat, and sang, —

> " 'Of all the girls in our town,
> The black, the fair, the red, the brown,

---

[1] Nancy Dawson, when a little girl, was employed in setting up skittles for players in High Street, Mary-le-bone, London. She was agile, graceful, and had an attractive figure. She first appeared as a dancer at Sadler's Wells theatre, where she soon attracted much attention, and in a short time became a great favorite. A rhymster wrote a song for her which was introduced (1764) into the play, " Love in a Valley."   It was also arranged as a hornpipe for the harpsichord and sung by young ladies throughout England.   Children sang it in the play, " Here we go round the Mulberry bush."   The popularity of Nancy Dawson was at its height in 1769.

That dance and prance it up and down,
There 's none like Nancy Dawson.

" ' Her easy mien, her shape, so neat,
She foots, she trips, she looks so sweet,
Her every motion so complete, —
There 's none like Nancy Dawson.

" ' See how she comes to give surprise,
With joy and pleasure in her eyes ;
To give delight she always tries, —
There 's none like Nancy Dawson.' "

" That 's a good song," said Robert.   Mr. Bushwick put the quid once more in his mouth, and went on
with the story.

" On that night a great crowd gathered around the
tree ; the boys who go to Master Lovell's school came
with an old knocked-kneed horse and a rickety wagon
with a platform in it.   They fixed the effigies on the
platform with cords and pulleys, so that the arms and
legs would be lifted when the boys under it pulled the
strings.   We lighted our torches and formed in procession.   The fifers played the Rogue's March, and the
bellman went ahead singing a song.

" ' Don't you remember
The fifth of November —
The gunpowder treason plot ?
I see no reason
Why gunpowder treason
Should ever be forgot.

" ' From the city of Rome
The Pope has come
Amid ten thousand fears,
With fiery serpents to be seen
At eyes, nose, mouth, and ears.

> " ' Don't you hear my little bell
> Go chinking, chinking, chink ?
> Please give me a little money
> To buy my Pope a drink.'

" The streets were filled with people, who tossed pennies into the bellman's hat. Everybody laughed to see the Pope lifting his hands and working his under jaw as if preaching, Byng rolling his goggle eyes, Nancy kicking with both legs, and the Devil wriggling his tail. We marched awhile, then put the Pope and the devil into the stocks, Nancy in the pillory, tied Byng to the whipping-post and gave him a flogging, then kindled a bonfire in King Street, pitched the effigies into it, and went into the Tun and Bacchus, Bunch of Grapes, and Admiral Vernon, and drank flip, egg-nogg, punch, and black strap." [1]

Mr. Bushwick chuckled merrily, and took a fresh quid of tobacco. Robert also laughed at the vivacious description.

" But I don't quite see why it should be called the Liberty Tree," Robert said.

" I was coming to that." You know that Lord Bute brought forward the Stamp Act a few years ago : well, this old elm being so near the White Lamb and the White Horse, it was a convenient place for the citizens to meet to talk about the proposition to tax us. One evening Ben Edes, who publishes the ' Gazette and News - Letter,' read what Ike Barre said in Parliament in opposition to the Stamp Act, in which he called us Americans Sons

---

[1] Black strap was composed of rum and molasses, and was often drunk by those who could not afford more expensive beverages.

of Liberty, and as that was our meeting-place, we christened the place Liberty Hall and the old elm Liberty Tree. · That was in July, 1765, just after Parliament passed the Stamp Act. The king had appointed Andrew Oliver stamp-master, and one morning his effigy was dangling from the tree, and a paper pinned to it writ large : —

> " ' Fair Freedom's glorious Cause I 've meanly quitted
> For the sake of pelf ;
> But ah, the Devil has me outwitted ;
> Instead of hanging others,
> I 've hanged myself.'

"Then there was a figure of a great boot, with the Devil peeping out of it, to represent the king's minister, Lord Bute. When night came, all hands of us formed in procession, laid the effigies on a bier, marched to the Province House so that the villain, Governor Bernard, could see us, went to Mackerel Lane, tore down the building Oliver was intending to use for the sale of the stamps, went to Fort Hill, ripped the boards from his barn, smashed in his front door, and burned the effigies to let him know we never would consent to be taxed in that way. A few days later Oliver came to the tree, held up his hand, and swore a solemn oath that he never would sell any stamps, so help him God ! And he never did, for ye see King George had to back down and repeal the bill. It was the next May when Shubael Coffin, master of the brigantine Harrison, brought the news. We set all the bells to ringing, fired cannon, and tossed up our hats. The rich people opened their purses and paid the debts of everybody in jail. We

hung lanterns on the tree in the evening, set off rock-
ets, and kindled bonfires. John Hancock kept open
house, with ladies and gentlemen feasting in his par-
lors, and pipes of wine on tap in the front yard for
everybody."

"It must have been a joyful day," said Robert.

"That's what it was. Everybody was generous.
Last year when the day came round a lot of us gathered under the old tree to celebrate it. Sam Adams
was there, James Otis, Doctor Warren, John Hancock, and ever so many more. We fired salutes, sang
songs, and drank fourteen toasts. That was at ten
o'clock. Just before noon we rode out to the Greyhound Tavern in Roxbury in carriages and chaises,
and had a dinner of fish, roast pig, sirloin, goose,
chickens and all the trimmings, topping off with plum-
pudding and apple-pie, sang Dickenson's Liberty Song,
drank thirty more toasts, forty-four in all, filling our
glasses with port, madeira, egg-nogg, flip, punch, and
brandy. Some of us, of course, were rather jolly, but
we got home all right," said Mr. Bushwick, laughing.

"You mean that some of you were a little weak in
the legs," said Robert.

"Yes, and that the streets were rather crooked,"
Mr. Bushwick replied, laughing once more.

They were abreast of the tree, and Robert reined in
Jenny while he admired its beautiful proportions.

"I think I must leave you at this point; my house
is down here, on Cow Lane,[1] not far from the house
of Sam Adams. I'm ever so much obliged to you for
the lift ye've given me," said Mr. Bushwick as he
shook hands with Robert.

---

[1] Cow Lane is the present High Street.

" I thank you for the information you have given me," Robert replied.

Jenny walked on, past the White Horse Inn and the Lamb Tavern. A little farther, and he beheld the Province House, a building with a cupola surmounted by a spire. The weather-vane was an Indian with bow and arrow. The king's arms, carved and gilded, were upon the balcony above the doorway. Chestnut-trees shaded the green plot of ground between the building and the street. A soldier with his musket on his shoulder was standing guard. Upon the other side of the way, a few steps farther, was a meetinghouse; he thought it must be the Old South. His father had informed him he would see a brick building with an apothecary's sign on the corner just beyond the Old South, and there it was.[1] Also, the Cromwell's Head Tavern on a cross street, and a schoolhouse, which he concluded must be Master Lovell's Latin School. He suddenly found Jenny quickening her pace, and understood the meaning when she plunged her nose into a watering trough by the town pump. While she was drinking Robert was startled by a bell tolling almost over his head; upon looking up he beheld the dial of a clock and remembered his father had said it was on the Old Brick Meetinghouse; that the building nearly opposite was the Town House.[2] He saw two cannon in the street

---

[1] The building known as the Old Corner Bookstore, at the junction of School and Washington streets. The Cromwell's Head Tavern was No. 19 School Street.

[2] The old brick meetinghouse of the First Church occupied the site of the present Rogers Building, nearly opposite the Old State House.

OLD BRICK MEETINGHOUSE

and a soldier keeping guard before the door. Negro
servants were filling their pails at the pump, and
kindly pumped water for the mare. Looking down
King Street toward the water, he saw the stocks and
pillory, the Custom House, and in the distance the
masts and yard-arms of ships. Up Queen Street he
could see the jail.

The mare, having finished drinking, jogged on. He

Latin School.

saw on the left-hand side of the street the shop of
Paul Revere, goldsmith.[1] The thought came that
possibly he might find something there that would be
nice and pretty for Rachel.

Jenny, knowing she was nearing the end of her journey, trotted through Union Street, stopping at last in

[1] The shop of Paul Revere stood on Cornhill, now No. 169 Washington Street.

front of a building where an iron rod projected from the wall, supporting a green dragon with wings, open jaws, teeth, and a tongue shaped like a dart.[1] The red-faced landlord was standing in the doorway.

Green Dragon Tavern.

"Well Jenny, old girl, how do you do?" he said, addressing the mare. "So it is the son and not the father? I hope you are well. And how's your dad?"

Robert replied that his father was well.

"Here. Joe; put this mare in the stable, and give her a good rubbing down. She's as nice a piece as ever went on four legs."

[1] The Green Dragon Tavern stood in Green Dragon Lane, now Union street. The lane in 1769 terminated at the mill-pond, a few rods from the tavern. In front it showed two stories, but had three stories and a basement in the rear. The hall was in the second story. The sign was of sheet copper, hanging from an iron rod projecting from the building. The rooms were named Devonshire. Somerset, Norfolk, respectively. for the shires of Old England. The building was about one hundred years old. and was occupied. 1695, by Alexander Smith as a tavern. The estate at one time was owned by Lieut.-Governor William Stoughton. who was acting governor and took a prominent part in persecuting those accused of witchcraft. He was a man of large wealth. and devised a portion of his property to Harvard College, Stoughton Hall being named for him.

The hostler took the reins and Robert stepped from the wagon.

"Pete Augustus, take this gentleman's trunk up to Devonshire. It will be your room, Mr. Walden."

Robert followed the negro upstairs, and discovered that each room had its distinctive name. He could have carried the trunk, but as he was to be a gentleman, it would not be dignified were he to shoulder it. He knew he must be in the market early in the morning, and went to bed soon after supper. He might have gone at once to Copp's Hill, assured of a hearty welcome in the Brandon home, but preferred to make the Green Dragon his abiding-place till through with the business that brought him to Boston.

II.

FARMERS from the towns around Boston were already in the market-place around Faneuil Hall the next morning when Robert drove down from the Green Dragon.[1] Those who had quarters of beef and lamb for sale were cutting the meat upon heavy oaken tables. Fishermen were bringing baskets filled with mackerel and cod from their boats moored in the dock. An old man was pushing a wheelbarrow before him filled with lobsters. Housewives followed by negro servants were purchasing meats and vegetables, holding eggs to the light to see if they were fresh, tasting pats of butter, handling chickens, and haggling with the farmers about the prices of what they had to sell.

The town-crier was jingling his bell and shouting that Thomas Russell at the auction room on Queen Street would sell a great variety of plain and spotted, lilac, scarlet, strawberry-colored, and yellow paduasoys, bellandine silks, sateens, galloons, ferrets, grograms, and barratines at half past ten o'clock.

Robert tied Jenny to the hitching-rail, and walked amid the hucksters to see what they had to sell; by

[1] The market was held in the open space around Faneuil Hall, in which were rails where the farmers from the surrounding towns hitched their horses. It was bounded on one side by the dock where the fishermen moored their boats.

observation he could ascertain the state of the market, and govern himself accordingly. After interviewing the hucksters he entered a store.

" No, I don't want any cheese," said the first on whom he called.

Faneuil Hall.

" The market is glutted," replied the second.

" If it were a little later in the season I would talk with you," was the answer of the third.

" I 've got more on hand now than I know what to do with," said the fourth.

Robert began to think he might have to take them back to Rumford. He saw a sign, " John Hancock, Successor to Thomas Hancock," and remembered that his father had traded there, and that John Hancock was associated with Sam Adams and Doctor Warren in resisting the aggressions of the king's ministers. Mr. Hancock was not in the store, but would soon be there. The clerk said he would look at what Robert had to sell, put on his hat, stepped to the wagon, stood upon the thills, held a cheese to his nose, pressed it with his thumb, tapped it with a gimlet, tasted it, and smacked his lips.

" Your mother makes good cheese," he said.

" My sister made them."

" Your sister, eh.   Older than yourself? "

" No, younger; only seventeen."

" Indeed ! Well, you may tell her she is a dabster at cheese-making. Do you want cash? If you do I'm afeard we shall not be able to trade, because cash is cash these days; but if you are willing to barter I guess we can dicker, for Mr. Hancock is going to freight a ship to the West Indias and wants something to send in her, and it strikes me the sugar planters at Porto Rico might like a bit of cheese," the clerk said.

" I shall want some sugar, coffee, molasses, codfish, and other things."

" I'll give you the market price for all your cheeses, and make fair rates on what you want from us."

" I can't let you have all. I must reserve two of the best."

" May I ask why you withhold two? "

" Because my father wishes to present one to Mr. Samuel Adams and the other to Doctor Joseph Warren, who are doing so much to preserve the rights of the Colonies."

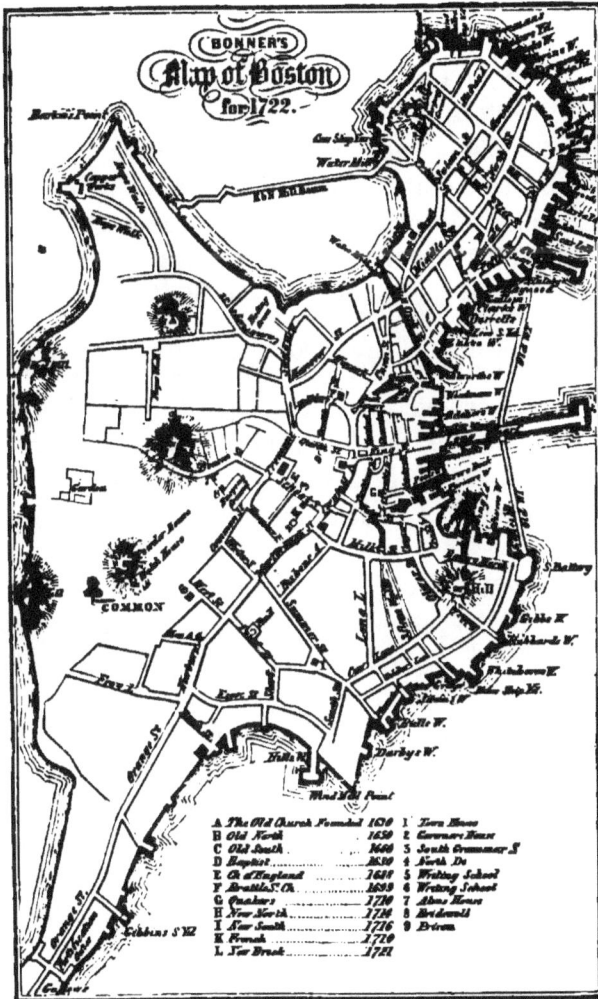

" Your father's name is " —

" Joshua Walden," said Robert.

" Oh yes, I remember him well. He was down here last winter and I bought his load. He had a barrel of apple-sauce, and Mr. Hancock liked it so well he took it for his own table. There is Mr. Hancock, now," said the clerk, as a chaise drove up and halted before the door.

Robert saw a tall young man, wearing a saffron colored velvet coat, ruffled shirt, buff satin breeches, black silk stockings, and shining shoe-buckles, step in a dignified manner from the chaise and hand the reins to a gray-headed negro, who lifted his hat as he took them.

" Good-morning, Mr. Ledger," he said to the clerk.

" Good-morning," the clerk replied, lifting his hat.

" Well, how is the Mary Jane getting on? Have you found anything in the market on which we can turn a penny? I want to get her off as soon as possible."

" I was just having a talk with this young gentleman about his cheeses. This is Mr. Walden from Rumford. You perhaps may remember his father, with whom we traded last year."

" Oh yes. I remember Mr. Joshua Walden. I hope your father is well. I have not forgotten his earnestness in all matters relating to the welfare of the Colonies. Nor have I forgotten that barrel of apple-sauce he brought to market, and I want to make a bargain for another barrel just like it. All my guests pronounced it superb. Step into the store, Mr. Walden, and, Mr. Ledger, a bottle of madeira, if you please."

The clerk stepped down cellar and returned with a bottle of wine, took from a cupboard a salver and glasses and filled them.

" Shall we have the pleasure of drinking the health

of your father?" said Mr. Hancock, courteously touching his glass to Robert's. "Please give him my compliments and say to him that we expect New Hampshire to stand shoulder to shoulder with Massachusetts in the cause of liberty."

Mr. Hancock drank his wine slowly. Robert saw that he stood erect, and remembered he was captain of a military company — the Cadets.

"Will you allow me to take a glass with you for your own health?" he said, refilling the glasses and bowing with dignity and again slowly drinking.

"Mr. Ledger, you will please do what you can to accommodate Mr. Walden in the way of trade. You are right in thinking the planters of Jamaica will like some cheese from our New England dairies, and you may as well unload them at the dock; it will save rehandling them. We must have Mary Jane scudding away as soon as possible."

Mr. Hancock bowed once more and sat down to his writing-desk.

Robert drove his wagon alongside the ship and unloaded the cheeses, then called at the stores around Faneuil Hall to find a market for the yarn and cloth and his wool. Few were ready to pay him money, but at last all was sold.

"Can you direct me to the house of Mr. Samuel Adams?" he asked of the town crier.

"Oh yes, you go through Mackerel Lane[1] to Cow Lane and through that to Purchase Street, and you will see an orchard with apple and pear trees and a big house with stairs outside leading up to a plat-

---

[1] Mackerel Lane is the present Kilby Street.

form on the roof; that's the house.   Do you know
Sam?"

"No, I never have seen Mr. Adams."

"Well, if you run across a tall, good-looking man
between forty-five and fifty, with blue eyes, who wears

Samuel Adams.

a red cloak and cocked hat, and who looks as if he
wasn't afear'd of the king, the devil, or any of his
imps, that is Maltster Sam.   We call him Maltster
Sam because he once made malt for a living, but didn't
live by it because it didn't pay.   He's a master hand
in town meetings.   He made it red hot for Bernard,

and he 'll make it hotter for Sammy Hutchinson if he don't mind his p's and q's. Sam is a buster, now, I tell you."

Robert drove through Cow Lane and came to the house. He rapped at the front door, which was opened by a tall man, with a pleasant but resolute countenance, whose clothes were plain and getting threadbare. His hair was beginning to be gray about the temples, and he wore a gray tie wig.

"This is Mr. Adams, is it not?" Robert asked.

"That is my name; what can I do for you?"

"I am Robert Walden from Rumford. I think you know my father."

"Yes, indeed. Please walk in. Son of my friend Joshua Walden? I am glad to see you," said Mr. Adams with a hearty shake of the hand.

"I have brought you a cheese which my father wishes you to accept with his compliments."

"That is just like him; he always brings us something. Please say to him that Mrs. Adams and myself greatly appreciate his kind remembrance of us."

A tall lady with a comely countenance was descending the hall stairs.

"Wife, this is Mr. Walden, son of our old friend; just see what he has brought us."

Robert lifted his hat and was recognized by a gracious courtesy.

"How good everybody is to us. The ravens fed Elijah, but I don't believe they brought cheese to him. We shall be reminded of your kindness every time we sit down to a meal." said Mrs. Adams.

Robert thought he never had seen a smile more gracious than that upon her pale, careworn countenance.[1] He noticed that everything about the room was plain, but neat and tidy. Upon a shelf were the Bible, Bunyan's Pilgrim's Progress, and a volume of Reverend Mr. South's sermons. Robert remembered his father said Mrs. Adams was the daughter of Reverend Mr. Checkley, minister of the New South Meetinghouse, and that Mr. Adams went to meeting there. Upon the table were law books, pamphlets, papers, letters, and newspapers. He saw that some of the letters bore the London postmark. He remembered his father said Mr. Adams had not much money; that he was so dead in earnest in maintaining the rights of the people he had little time to attend to his own affairs.

"Will you be in town through the week and over the Sabbath?" Mr. Adams asked.

Robert replied that he intended to visit his relatives, Mr. and Mrs. Brandon, on Copp's Hill.

"Oh yes, my friend the shipbuilder — a very worthy gentleman, and his wife an estimable lady. They have an energetic and noble daughter and a promising son. I have an engagement to-night, another to-morrow, but shall be at home to-morrow evening, and I would like to have you and your young friends take supper with us. I will tell you something that your father would like to know."

Robert thanked him, and took his departure. Thinking that Doctor Warren probably would be visiting his patients at that hour of the day, he drove to

---

[1] Mrs. Adams was the daughter of Reverend Samuel Checkley, pastor of the New South Church, which stood on Church Green at the junction of Summer and Bedford streets. She was a woman of much refinement and intelligence, and greatly beloved.

the Green Dragon, and put Jenny in her stall, and after dinner made his way to the goldsmith's shop to find a present for Rachel.

Mr. Paul Revere, who had gold beads, brooches, silver spoons, shoe and knee buckles, clocks, and a great variety of articles for sale, was sitting on a bench engraving a copper plate. He laid down his graving-tool and came to the counter. Robert saw he had a benevolent face; that he was hale and hearty.

"I would like to look at what you have that is pretty for a girl of eighteen," said Robert.

Mr. Revere smiled as if he understood that the young man before him wanted something that would delight his sweetheart.

"I want it for my sister," Robert added.

Mr. Revere smiled again as he took a bag filled with gold beads from the showcase.

"I think you cannot find anything prettier for your sister than a string of beads," he said. "Women and girls like them better than anything else. They are always in fashion. You will not make any mistake, I am sure, in selecting them."

He held up several strings to the light, that Robert might see how beautiful they were.

"I would like to look at your brooches."

While the goldsmith was taking them from the showcase, he glanced at the pictures on the walls, printed from plates which Mr. Revere had engraved.

The brooches were beautiful — ruby, onyx, sapphire, emerald, but after examining them he turned once more to the beads.

"They are eighteen carats fine, and will not grow

dim with use. I think your sister will be delighted with them."

Robert thought so too, and felt a glow of pleasure when they were packed in soft paper and transferred from the case to his pocket.

With the afternoon before him he strolled the streets, looking at articles in the shop windows, at the clock on the Old Brick Meetinghouse, the barracks of the soldiers, — the king's Twenty-Ninth Regiment.[1] Some of the redcoats were polishing their gun barrels and bayonets, others smoking their pipes. Beyond the barracks a little distance he saw Mr. Gray's rope walk. He turned through Mackerel Lane and came to the Bunch of Grapes Tavern,[2] and just beyond it the Admiral Vernon. He strolled to Long Wharf. The king's warship, Romney, was riding at anchor near by, and a stately merchant ship was coming up the harbor. The fragrance of the sea was in the air. Upon the wharf were hogsheads of molasses unloaded from a vessel just arrived from Jamaica. Boys had knocked out a bung and were running a stick into the hole and lapping the molasses. The sailors lounging on the

---

[1] The troops were ordered to Boston in 1765, in consequence of the riots growing out of the passage of the Stamp Act, the mob having sacked the house of Chief Justice Thomas Hutchinson. Though the Stamp Act had been repealed, and though the citizens were orderly and law-abiding, the regiments remained.

[2] The Bunch of Grapes Tavern stood on the corner of Mackerel Lane and King Street, now Kilby and State streets. Its sign was three clusters of grapes. It was a noted tavern, often patronized by the royal governors. In July, 1776, the Declaration of Independence was read to the people from its balcony. After hearing it they tore the lion and unicorn, and all emblems of British authority, from the Custom House, Court House, and Town House, and made a bonfire of them in front of the tavern.

wharf were speaking a language he could not understand. For the first time in his life he was in touch, as it were, with the great world beyond the sea.

During the day he had met several of the king's soldiers, swaggering along the streets as if privileged to do as they pleased, regardless of the people. Two, whom he had seen drinking toddy in the Admiral Vernon, swayed against him.

"Hello, clodhopper! How's yer dad and marm?" said one.

Robert felt the hot blood mount to his brow.

"Say, bumpkin, how did ye get away from your ma's apron-string?" said the other.

"He hasn't got the pluck of a goslin," said the first.

Robert set his teeth together, but made no reply, and walked away. He felt like pitching them headforemost into the dock, and was fearful he might do something which, in cooler blood, he would wish he had not done.

By what right were they strolling the streets of an orderly town? Those who supported the king said they were there to maintain the dignity of the crown. True, a mob had battered the door of Thomas Hutchinson, but that had been settled. The people were quiet, orderly, law-abiding. The sentinel by the Town House glared at him as he walked up King Street, as if ready to dispute his right to do so. He saw a bookstore on the corner of the street, and with a light heart entered it. A tall, broad-shouldered young man welcomed him.

"May I look at your books?" Robert asked.

"Certainly; we have all those recently published in London, and a great many pamphlets printed here in the Colonies," the young man replied.

"I live in the country. We do not have many books in New Hampshire," said Robert.

"Oh, from New Hampshire? Please make yourself at home, and look at any book you please. My name is Henry Knox,"[1] said the young man.

"I am Robert Walden."

"I am pleased to make your acquaintance, Mr. Walden, and shall be glad to render you any service in my power. Is this your first visit to town?"

Robert said it was. He could only gaze in wonder at the books upon the shelves. He had not thought there could be so many in the world. Mr. Knox saw the growing look of astonishment.

"What can I show you? Perhaps you do not care for sermons. We have a good many; ministers like to see their sermons in print. I think perhaps you will like this better," said Mr. Knox, taking down a copy of the Arabian Nights' Entertainments. "You will find it very interesting: just sit down and look at it."

Robert seated himself in a chair and read the story of the Forty Thieves.

"Do you think these are true stories?" he asked when he had finished it.

---

[1] Mr. Knox was clerk in the bookstore kept by Daniel Henchman. In 1773 he began business on his own account on Cornhill now Washington Street, upon the site now occupied by the *Globe* newspaper. His store was frequented by the officers of the regiments, and doubtless he obtained from them information that he turned to good account during the war.

Mr. Knox replied they were true in so far as they described the˙manners and customs of the people of Arabia and Persia. He did not doubt the stories had been told in Babylon, Nineveh, and Damascus, and he might think of the people in those cities sitting in the calm evenings under the almond-trees on the banks of the Euphrates or the river Abana listening to the story-teller, who probably did his best to make the story entertaining.

"Doubtless," said Mr. Knox, "we think. it would not be possible for things to happen as they are narrated, but I am not quite sure about that. One of the stories, for instance, tells how a man went through the air on a carpet. We think it cannot be true, but here is a pamphlet which tells how Henry Cavendish, in England, a little while ago discovered a gas which he calls hydrogen. It is ten times lighter than air — so light that another gentleman, Mr. Black, filled a bag with it which took him off his feet and carried him round the room, to the astonishment of all who beheld it. I should n't be surprised if by and by we shall be able to travel through the air by a bag filled with such gas."

Robert listened with intense interest, not being able to comprehend how anything could be lighter than air. He was not quite sure that his father and mother would approve of his reading a book that was not strictly true, and he was sure that the good minister and deacons of the church would shake their heads solemnly were they to know it; but he could read it on his way home and hide it in the haymow and read it on rainy days in the barn. But that would not be manly. No, he could not do that. He would tell his father and mother and Rachel about it, and read it to them by the kitchen fire. Hit or miss, he would purchase the book.

Mr. Knox kindly offered to show him the Town House. They crossed the street, and entered the council chamber. Lieutenant-Governor Hutchinson and the members of the council were sitting in their armchairs, wearing white wigs and scarlet cloaks. Their gold-laced hats were lying on their desks. Lieutenant-Colonel Dalrymple, commanding the king's troops, was seated by the side of Governor Hutchinson as a visitor. Upon the walls were portraits of Kings Charles II. and James II. in gilded frames; also portraits of Governors Winthrop, Endicott, and Bradstreet.

Thanking Mr. Knox for his kindness, Robert passed into the street, took a look at the stocks and pillory, and wondered if that was the best way to punish those who had committed petty offenses.

He saw a girl tripping along the street. A young lieutenant in command of the sentinels around the Town House stared rudely at her. In contrast to the leering look of the officer, the negro servants filling their pails at the pump were very respectful in giving her room to pass. He saw the two soldiers who had attempted to pick a quarrel with him on the wharf, emerge from an alley. One chucked the young lady under the chin; the other threw his arm around her and attempted to steal a kiss. Robert heard a wild cry, and saw her struggle to be free. With a bound he was by her side. His right arm swung through the air, and his clenched fist came down like a sledge-hammer upon the head of the ruffian, felling him to the earth. The next moment the other was picked up and plunged headforemost into the watering-trough. No word had been spoken. The girl, as if not comprehending what had happened, stood amazed before him.

"Thank you, sir; I never shall forget your kindness," she said, dropping a low courtesy and walking rapidly up Queen Street.

Never before had he seen a face like hers, a countenance that would not fade from memory, although he saw it but a moment.

Suddenly he found himself confronted by the lieutenant, who came running from the Town House, with flashing eyes and drawn sword. Robert did not run, but looked him squarely in the face.

"What do you mean, you " —

The remainder of the sentence is not recorded: the printed page is cleaner without it.

"I meant to teach the villains not to insult a lady."

"I've a good mind to split your skull open," said the lieutenant, white with rage, but not knowing what to make of a man so calm and resolute.

"Let me get at him! Let me get at him! I 'll knock the daylight out of him," shouted the fellow whom Robert had felled to the ground, but who had risen and stood with clenched fists. The other, the while, was clambering from the trough, wiping the water from his face and ready to rush upon Robert, angered all the more by the jeers of the grinning negroes

" What is all this about? "

It was Lieutenant-Colonel Dalrymple speaking. He had seen the commotion from the window of the council chamber, and hastened to the scene. " Put up your sword," he said to the lieutenant.

" What have you been doing, sir? " he asked, turning sternly to Robert.

" Suppose you first ask those two fellows what they 've been doing? Nevertheless, Colonel, lest you might not get a true answer, allow me to say that they insulted a lady, that I knocked one down and tossed the other into the watering-trough, to teach them better manners. For doing it your lieutenant has seen fit to draw his sword and threaten to split my head open."

It was said quietly and calmly.

" What have you to say to that? " Colonel Dalrymple asked, addressing the soldiers, who made no reply.

" Lieutenant, take them to the guardhouse, and consider yourself under arrest till I can look into this matter. Don't you know better than to draw your sword against a citizen in this way? "

The lieutenant made no reply, but looked savagely at Robert, as if to say, " I 'll have it out with you sometime," sheathed his sword and turned away, following the crestfallen soldiers to the guardhouse.

Colonel Dalrymple bowed courteously, as if to apologize for the insult to the lady. Robert came to the conclusion that he was a gentleman.

The negroes were laughing and chuckling and telling the rapidly gathering crowd what had happened.

Robert, having no desire to be made conspicuous, walked up Queen Street. He tarried a moment to look at the iron-grated windows and double-bolted doors of the jail, then turned down Hanover Street and made his way to the Green Dragon.

III.

THE SONS OF LIBERTY.

"Is it far to Doctor Warren's house?" Robert asked of the landlord after supper.

"Oh no, only a few steps around the corner on Hanover Street. So you are going to call on him, just as your father always does. You will find him a nice gentleman. He is kind to the poor, charging little or nothing when they are sick and need doctoring. He isn't quite thirty years old, but there isn't a doctor in town that has a larger practice. He is a true patriot. I heard a man say the other day that if Joe Warren would only let politics alone he would soon be riding in his own coach. The rich Tories don't like him much. They say it was he who gave Governor Bernard such a scorching in Ben Edes's newspaper awhile ago. He is eloquent when he gets fired up. You ought to hear him in town meeting; you won't find him stuck up one mite; you can talk with him just as you do with me."

With the cheese under his arm Robert walked along Hanover Street to Doctor Warren's house.[1] It

---

[1] The home of Doctor Warren stood upon the spot now occupied by the American House. It was a plain structure and was surrounded by a garden. Mrs. Warren — Elizabeth Hooton before marriage — was the daughter of Richard Hooton, a merchant possessing large

was a wooden building standing end to the road.
Entering a small yard, he rattled the knocker on the
door. The doctor opened it.

"Good-evening; will you walk in?" he said. It
was a pleasant, cheery voice, one to make a sick person
feel well.

"Please step into the office."

Robert entered a room smelling of rhubarb, jalap,
ipecac, and other medicines in bottles and packages on
the shelves.

Sincere and hearty were the thanks of Doctor Warren for the present.

"I want Mrs. Warren to make your acquaintance,"
he said.

A beautiful woman entered and gave Robert a cordial greeting.

"It is very kind of you to bring us such a gift. It
is not the first time your father has made us happy,"
she said. "We must find some way, husband, to let
Mr. Walden know we appreciate his kindness."

"That is so, wife."

"We live so far away," said Robert, "we do not
know what is going on. Father wishes me especially
to learn the latest news from London in regard to the
proposed tax on tea, and what the Colonies are going
to do about it."

"That is a very important matter," the doctor re-

wealth. She was beautiful in person and character. She died May,
1773. The Boston *Gazette* contained an appreciative tribute to her
worth.

> "Good sense and modesty with virtue crowned ;
> A sober mind when fortune smiled or frowned.
> So keen a feeling for a friend distressed,
> She could not bear to see a man oppressed."

plied, " and we are to have a meeting of the Sons of Liberty this evening to consider what shall be done in case the bill now before Parliament becomes a law, as I have no doubt it will. I shall be pleased to have you go with me. Of course our meetings are somewhat secret. We do not care to have any mousing Tory know just what we intend to do. You will have a hearty welcome from the boys. It is only a few steps from here, at the Green Dragon."

" That is where I am stopping," Robert replied.

" You can say to your father," the doctor continued, " that the redcoats are becoming very insolent, and we fear there will be trouble."

Robert said nothing about his experience at the town pump.

"Tommy Hutchinson," the doctor went on, " is acting governor. He is not the hyena Bernard was. Hutchinson was born here. He is a gentleman, but loves office. I would not do him any injustice, but being in office he naturally sides with the ministry. He does not see which way the people are going. King George believes that he himself is chosen of God to rule us, and Lord North is ready to back him up. The people around the king are sycophants who are looking after their own personal advantage. The ministers know very little about affairs in the Colonies. They are misled by Bernard and others. They are determined to raise revenue from the Colonies, but will be disappointed. But we will go round to the Green Dragon."

They reached the tavern. Doctor Warren nodded to the landlord, and led the way up the stairs along

DOCTOR JOSEPH WARREN

the hall and gave four raps on a door. One of the panels swung open. A man on the other side said something which Robert could not understand, neither could he make out what the doctor said in reply. The panel closed, the door opened, and they passed into a large room dimly lighted by two tallow candles. A dozen or more young men were seated in chairs around a table smoking their pipes. At one end of the table was a large punch-bowl, a basket filled with lemons, a bottle of rum, a plate of crackers, and half a cheese. One young man was slicing lemons and making rum punch. All clapped their hands when they saw Doctor Warren.

" I have brought a young friend; he is from New Hampshire and as true as steel," said the doctor.

" Boys," said Amos Lincoln, " this is the gentleman I was telling you about; let's give him three cheers."

The room rang. Robert did not know what to make of it; neither did Doctor Warren till Amos Lincoln told how he had seen Mr. Walden at the town pump, knocking down one lobster, throwing another into the watering-trough, and calmly confronting the prig of a lieutenant. When Amos finished, all came and shook hands with Robert.

Mr. John Rowe called the meeting to order.

" Since our last meeting," he said, " a ship has arrived bringing the news that the king and ministers are determined to levy an export duty of three pence per pound on tea : that is, all tea exported from England will be taxed to that extent. Of course, we could pay it if we chose, but we shall not so choose."

The company clapped their hands.

" We have sent round papers for the merchants to sign an agreement that they will not sell any tea imported from England. All have signed it except Hutchinson's two sons, Governor Bernard's son-in-law, Theophilus Lillie, and two others. The agreement does not prevent the merchants from selling tea imported from Holland. The Tories, of course, will patronize the merchants who have not signed the agreement, and the question for us to consider is how we shall keep out the tea to be imported by the East India Company."

" We must make it hot for 'em," said Mr. Mackintosh.

" The tea, do you mean? " shouted several.

There was a ripple of laughter.

" I don't see but that we shall have to quit drinking tea," said Doctor Warren. "We drink altogether too much. It has become a dissipation. We drink it morning, noon, and night. Some of the old ladies of my acquaintance keep the teapot on the coals pretty much all the time. Our wives meet in the afternoon to sip tea and talk gossip. The girls getting ready to be married invite their mates to quiltings and serve them with Old Hyson. We have garden tea-parties on bright afternoons in summer and evening parties in winter. So much tea, such frequent use of an infusion of the herb, upsets our nerves, impairs healthful digestion, and brings on sleeplessness. I have several patients—old ladies, and those in middle life—whose nerves are so unstrung that I am obliged to dose them with opium occasionally, to enable them to sleep."

" Do you think we can induce the ladies to quit drinking it?" Mr. Molineux asked.

" I am quite sure Mrs. Warren will cheerfully give it up, as will Mrs. Molineux if her husband should set the example," Doctor Warren replied.

Mr. Molineux said he was ready to banish the tea-pot from his table.

" I believe," continued the doctor, " that the women of America will be ready to give up the grat-ification of their appetites to maintain a great prin-ciple. They will sacrifice all personal considerations to secure the rights of the Colonies. Parliament proposes to tax this country without our having a voice in the matter. It is a seductive and insidious proposition — this export duty. I suppose they think we are simpletons, and will be caught in the trap they are setting. They think we are so fond of tea we shall continue to purchase it, but the time has come when we must let them know there is nothing so precious to us as our rights and liberties; that we can be resolute in little as well as in great things. I dare say that some of you, like myself, have invita-tions to Mrs. Newville's garden party to-morrow after-noon. I expect to attend, but it will be the last tea-party for me, if the bill before Parliament becomes a law. Mrs. Newville is an estimable lady, a hospi-table hostess; having accepted an invitation to be present, it would be discourteous for me to inform her I could not drink a cup of tea from her hand, but I have made up my mind henceforth to stand resolutely for maintaining the principle underlying it all, — a great fundamental, political principle, — our freedom."

The room rang with applause.

"Sometimes, as some of you know, I try my hand at verse-making.   I will read a few lines."

FREE AMERICA.

That seat of Science, Athens,
    And earth's proud mistress, Rome:
Where now are all their glories ?
    We scarce can find their tomb.
Then guard your rights, Americans,
    Nor stoop to lawless sway;
Oppose, oppose, oppose,
    For North America.

We led fair Freedom hither,
    And lo, the desert smiled,
A paradise of pleasure
    Was opened in the wild.
Your harvest, bold Americans,
    No power shall snatch away.
Huzza, huzza, huzza,
    For free America.

Some future day shall crown us
    The masters of the main ;
Our fleets shall speak in thunder
    To England, France, and Spain.
And nations over ocean spread
    Shall tremble and obey
The sons, the sons, the sons,
    Of brave America.

Captain Mackintosh sang it. and the hall rang with cheers.

"It is pitiable," said Mr. Rowe, "that the people of England do not understand us better, but what can we expect when a member of Parliament makes a speech like that delivered by Mr. Stanley just before the last ship sailed. Hear it.

Mr. Rowe, taking a candle in one hand and snuffing it with his thumb and finger, read an extract from the speech : " What will become of that insolent town, Boston, when we deprive the inhabitants of the power of sending their molasses to the coast of Africa? The people of that town must be treated as aliens, and the charters of towns in Massachusetts must be changed so as to give the king the appointment of the councilors, and give the sheriffs the sole power of returning juries."

" The ignoramus," continued Mr. Rowe, " does not know that no molasses is made in these Colonies. He confounds this and the other Colonies with Jamaica. One would suppose Lord North would not be quite so bitter, but he said in a recent speech that America must be made to fear the king ; that he should go on with the king's plan until we were prostrate at his feet."

" Not much will we get down on our knees to him," said Peter Bushwick. " Since the war with France, to carry on which the Colonies contributed their full share, the throne is n't feared quite as much as it was. Americans are not in the habit of prostrating themselves."

Captain Mackintosh once more broke into a song.

" Come join hand in hand, Americans all ;
By uniting we stand, dividing we fall.
To die we can bear, but to serve we disdain,
For shame is to freedom more dreadful than pain.
In freedom we 're born, in freedom we 'll live.
Our purses are ready : steady, boys, steady,
Not as slaves but as freemen our money we 'll give."

The Sons again clapped their hands and resolved that they would drink no more tea. The formal business of the evening being ended, they broke into groups, helped themselves to crackers and cheese, and lighted their pipes.

A young man about Robert's age came and shook hands with him.

"Did I understand correctly that you are Robert Walden from Rumford?" he asked.

"That is my name, and I am from Rumford."

"Then we are cousins; I am Tom Brandon."

"I was intending to call upon you to-morrow."

"You must go with me to-night. Father and mother never would forgive me if I did not take you along, especially when I tell them how you rubbed it into the king's lobsters."

The bells were ringing for nine o'clock — the hour when everybody in Boston made preparations for going to bed. All the Sons of Liberty came and shook hands with Robert.

"It is the most wholesome lesson the villains have had since they landed at Long Wharf," said Doctor Warren, who hoped to have the pleasure of seeing more of Mr. Walden.

"We must rely upon such as you in the struggle which we are yet to have to maintain our liberties," said Mr. Molineux.

Tom Brandon took Robert with him to his home on Copp's Hill. Robert could see by the light of the moon that it was a large wooden house with a hipped roof, surmounted by a balustrade, fronting the burial ground and overlooking the harbor and a wide reach of surrounding country.

"Why, Robert Walden! where did you come from?" Mr. Brandon exclaimed as Tom ushered him into the sitting-room.

"What! stopping at the Green Dragon! Why didn't you come right here, you naughty boy?"

He tinkled a bell and a negro entered the room.

"Mark Antony, go up to the Green Dragon and get this gentleman's trunk. Tell the landlord I sent you. Hold on a moment: it is after nine o'clock, and the watchman may overhaul you and want to know what you are doing. You must have an order."

Mr. Brandon stepped to a writing-desk and wrote an order, receiving which Mark Antony bowed and took his departure.

Mr. Brandon was in the prime of life, hale, hearty, vigorous, a former ship captain, who had been to London many times, also through the Straits of Gibraltar, to Madeira, Jamaica, and round Cape of Good Hope to China. He had seen enough of ocean life and had become a builder of ships. He was accustomed to give orders, manage men, and was quick to act. He had accumulated wealth, and was living in a spacious mansion on the summit of the hill. On calm summer evenings he smoked his pipe upon the platform on the roof of his house, looking through a telescope at vessels making the harbor, reading the signals flying at the masthead, and saying to himself and friends that the approaching vessel was from London or the West Indias.

Robert admired the homelike residence, the paneled wainscoting, the fluted pilasters, elaborately carved mantel, glazed tiles, mahogany centre-table, armchairs, the beautifully carved writing-desk, the pictures on the walls of ships under full sail weathering rocky headlands.

Mrs. Brandon and her daughter Berinthia entered the room. Mrs. Brandon was very fair for a woman in middle life. Berinthia had light blue eyes, cherry ripe lips, and rosy cheeks.

" I have heard father speak of you often, and he is always holding up cousin Rachel as a model for me," said Berinthia, shaking hands with him.

Tom told of what had happened at the town pump.

" The soldiers are a vile set," said Mrs. Brandon.

" They are becoming very insolent, and I fear we shall have trouble with them," said Mr. Brandon.

Mark Antony came with the trunk, and Tom lighted a candle to show Robert to his chamber. Berinthia walked with him to the foot of the stairs.

" Good-night, cousin," she said ; " I want to thank you in behalf of all the girls in Boston for throwing that villain into the watering-trough."

IV.

"How beautiful!" Robert exclaimed, as he beheld the harbor, the town, and the surrounding country from the top of the house the following morning. Berinthia pointed out the localities. At their feet

Copp's Hill Burial Ground.

was Copp's Hill burial ground with its rows of head-stones and grass-grown mounds. Across the river, northward, was Charlestown village nestling at the foot of Bunker Hill. Ferryboats were crossing the stream. Farther away beyond fields, pastures, and marsh lands were the rocky bluffs of Malden, the wood-crowned heights russet and crimson with the first tinges of autumn. Eastward was the harbor with its wave-washed islands, and the blue ocean sparkling in the sunlight. White sails were fading and vanishing on the far distant horizon. Ships were riding at anchor between the town and castle. Southward were dwellings, stores, shops, and the spires of meetinghouses. Beyond the town were the Roxbury, Dorchester, and Milton hills — fields, pastures, orchards, and farmhouses. Westward rose Beacon Hill, its sunny slopes dotted with houses and gardens; farther away, across Charles River, he could see the steeple of Cambridge meetinghouse and the roof of the college.

"This is Christ Church," said Berinthia, pointing to the nearest steeple. "That beyond is the Old North Meetinghouse where Cotton Mather preached.[1] Of course you have heard of him."

Robert replied that the name seemed familiar.

"He was one of the ministers first settled," said Berinthia, "and wrote a curious book, the 'Magnalia.' When he was a boy he picked up Latin so quickly that when twelve years old he was able to enter college, graduating four years later. That stately mansion

---

[1] Historical writers have made a mistake in speaking of Christ Church as the Old North Meetinghouse. They were distinct edifices — Christ Church standing in Salem Street, the Old North fronting North Square. Christ Church is the historic edifice from whose steeple Robert Newman hung the lantern to give notice of the movement of the king's troops, April, 1775. The Old North was torn down during the siege of Boston.

near the meetinghouse was the home of Lieutenant-
Governor Hutchinson. A mob smashed the windows
in connection with the attempt to enforce the Stamp
Act; and it was that which induced the king to send
the two regiments of soldiers to Boston. The house
adjoining is the home of Lady Agnes Frankland."

She told the romantic story of Lady Frankland's
life; how Sir Henry, when a young man, came from
England to be the king's collector of customs. One
day he went to Marblehead, and while at the tavern
saw a girl scrubbing the floor. She was barefooted,
but had a beautiful face. He thought that so pretty
a girl ought not to go barefooted, and gave her money
to buy a pair of shoes. A few weeks passed, and
again he saw her barefooted, still scrubbing the floor.
She had purchased the shoes, but was keeping them
for Sunday. Sir Henry was so pleased with her that
he offered to give her an education. A good minister
took her into his family and she learned very rapidly.
She in return gave him her love, and after leaving
school went to live with him. He not only owned
the house in town, but a great estate in the country. He kept horses and hounds, and had good wines.
After a while he took Agnes to England with him,
and from thence to Portugal. He was in Lisbon in
1755, at the time of the great earthquake, and was
riding in his carriage when suddenly the earth began
to heave and tremble, and houses, churches, all came
tumbling down, burying thirty thousand people. Sir
Henry's horses and himself and carriage were beneath
the bricks and mortar. Agnes was not with him at
the moment, but showed her love by running as fast

as she could and digging away the bricks with her own hands, finding him badly mangled but alive. He thought he was going to die, and made a vow that if his life was spared Agnes should be his lawfully wedded wife. His wounds healed and he kept his word, making her Lady Frankland. They came once more to Boston, bought the house next to Chief Justice Hutchinson, and lived very happily."

" We will go down to father's shipyard," said Tom, "and you can see the carpenters at work building a ship."

They descended the hill and entered the yard. Robert hardly knew what to think as he listened to the clattering of axes and mallets. Some of the workmen were hewing timber and putting up the ribs of the vessel; others were bolting planks to the ribs. The size of the ship amazed him; it was larger than his father's barn. In a few weeks the hull would be finished, the masts put in, the rigging rove, and then the ship would be launched.

" Father is going to name her for me, and I am to be the figurehead; come to the carver's shop and see me." said Berinthia with sparkling eyes and merry laugh.

They went into a little shop where a good-looking young man, with chisels. gouges, and mallet, was fashioning the bust of a woman. Tom introduced him as Abraham Duncan. Robert noticed a lighting up of Mr. Duncan's eyes as he greeted Berinthia.

" Mr. Duncan is one of us. As for that matter, every man in the yard is a Son of Liberty," Tom said.

" That is me." said Berinthia. pointing to the figure-

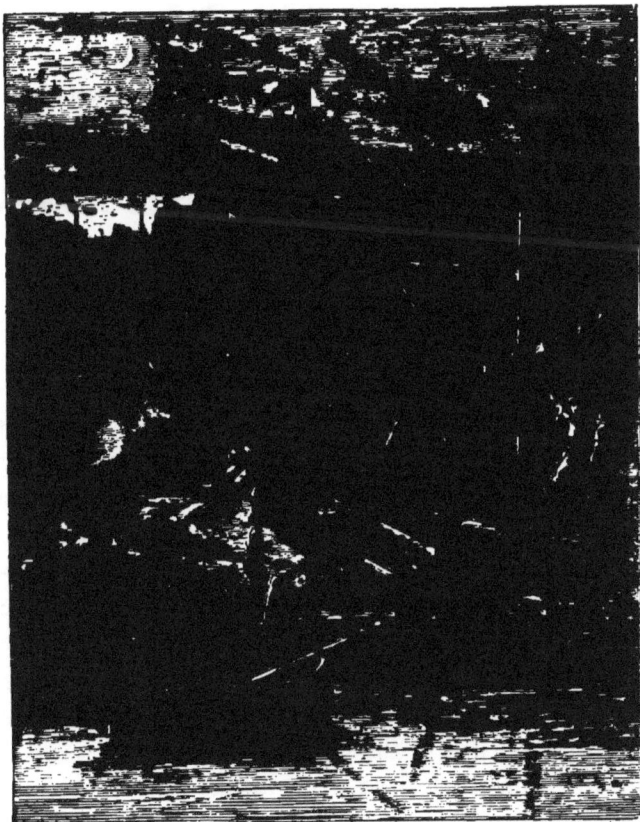

In the Shipyard.

head. " I am to be perched beneath the bowsprit to
look out upon the ocean and see which way the ship
ought to go. The waves will wet my hair, and the
tears will run down my cheeks when the storms are
on. My eyes will behold strange things. I shall see
the whales spout and the porpoises play, and poke my
nose into foreign parts," she said playfully.

Robert saw that the carver had fashioned the face

to look like her. She had been down to the shop
several times, that he might study her features. On
Saturday evenings after work for the week was over
he put on his best coat and called at the Brandon
house to look at her as she sat by the fireside with the
light from the hearth illumining her face. Although
Mr. Duncan usually went to hear Reverend Mr.
Checkley preach, he sometimes strayed away to Reverend Doctor Cooper's meetinghouse in Brattle Street,
and took a seat where he could see Berinthia's features in repose, as she listened to the sermon. Although the minister was very eloquent, Mr. Duncan
was more interested in looking at her than hearing
what was said in the pulpit. Robert noticed that she
seemed to enjoy talking with the carver, and when he
went to the other side of the building to get a port-
folio of drawings to show her how the cabin was to be
ornamented her eyes followed him.

" Father says Mr. Duncan is a very talented young
man, and one of the best artists in town," she said, as
they walked back to the house.

After dinner, Robert went to the Green Dragon,
obtained a chaise, harnessed Jenny, took in Berinthia,
and crossed the ferry to Charlestown, for a ride in the
country. They drove along a wide street at the foot
of Bunker Hill, and came to a narrow neck of land
between Charles River on the south and Mystic River
on the north. The tide was flowing in and covering
the marsh lands. They gained the summit of Winter
Hill, gazed upon the beautiful landscape, then turned
southward toward Cambridge. Reaching the college,
they entered the library and the room containing the

philosophical instruments. Robert rubbed his knife on a magnet so he could pick up a needle by touching it with the blade. They had little time to spare, for they were to take supper with Mr. Samuel Adams. Berinthia informed him that Mr. Adams was not rich, that he was very kind-hearted, and had lost his property through kindness to a friend.

" He lives very plainly," she said as they rode homeward. " We shall find simple fare, but he will give you a hearty shake of the hand. People have faith in him because he is true to his convictions."

It was supper time when they reached Mr. Adams's house.

" I am pleased to see you, and am glad to have an opportunity for a little talk," said Mr. Adams, welcoming them.

" We have very simple fare, only mush and milk, pandowdy,[1] and some Rumford cheese which is very delicious," said Mrs. Adams as she invited them to the supper table. They stood by their chairs while Mr. Adams asked a blessing, then took their seats.

" We have abolished tea from our table," he said. " I see no better way of thwarting the designs of the king and the ministry to overthrow the liberties of the Colonies than for the people to quit using it."

" Do you think the people will deny themselves for a principle ? " Robert asked.

" Yes; I have unbounded faith in the virtue of the American people. I do not know that we naturally

---

[1] Pandowdy was a compote of apples, with several layers of pastry made from rye meal, baked in a deep earthen dish and eaten with milk.

are more virtuous than the people of other lands, but
the course pursued by England ever since Cromwell's
time has been one of oppression.   Now tyranny,
when exercised towards a free and intelligent people,
is a process of education.   Away back when Cromwell
was administering the affairs of the nation a law was
passed, the design of which was to build up the commerce of England.   At that time Spain and Holland
were great maritime countries.   The ships of Spain
were bringing gold from Cuba, Mexico, and South
America to that country.   The ships of Holland were
bringing silks and tea from India and China.   Those
countries were doing pretty much all the carrying on
the ocean.   Cromwell, one of the greatest and most
far-sighted of all England's rulers, determined that
England should have her share of the trade.   The
law which was passed provided that no goods should
be imported into that country or exported from it
except in English vessels, and the master of every ship
and three fourths of the crew must be Englishmen,
under penalty of forfeiture of the ship and cargo.
The act was passed in 1651.   In a very short time
the commerce of England was twice what it had been.
The law was not designed to work any injury to the
Colonies, but for their benefit.   The great abundance
of timber in America, so much that farmers were
slashing down hundreds of acres and burning it, enabled the colonists to build ships very cheaply, and so
there was a swinging of axes in all our seaport towns.
When Charles II. came to the throne the royalists
determined there should be nothing left to remind the
people that a Commonwealth had ever existed.   All

the laws enacted during the period were repealed.
Their hatred was so great they could not let Cromwell's bones rest in peace, but dug them up, dragged
them through the streets of London, and set his skull
on Temple Bar. Well, that did not hurt Cromwell,
but it did hurt Charles II. and monarchy. I do not
imagine anybody in coming years will erect a statue to
the memory of that voluptuous king or hold him in
reverence, but the time will come when Oliver Cromwell will be held in grateful remembrance."

Mr. Adams passed his bowl for more pandowdy,
and then went on with the conversation.

"The meanness of human nature," he said, " is seen
in the action of Parliament immediately after Charles
II. came to the throne in repealing every law enacted
during the period of the Commonwealth. Having
wiped out every statute, what do you suppose Parliament did?"

Robert replied that he had not the remotest idea.

" Well, they reënacted them — put them right back
on the statute book. They were good laws, but the
Cromwellians had enacted them and they must be ex-
punged; having blotted them out, they must be put
back again because they were good laws."

Mr. Adams leaned back in his chair and laughed
heartily.

" Now we come to the iniquity of Parliament," he
continued. " Under the Commonwealth the Colonies
were kindly treated. Cromwell, at one time, together
with John Hampden, thought of emigrating to America, but he did not, and by staying in England rendered inestimable service to his fellow-men. The

iniquity was this: Parliament enacted a law which made each of these Colonies a distinct country, so far as commerce was concerned. Greed and selfishness prompted the passage of this act, which aimed to make England the distributor of all commerce, not only between the Colonies and other countries, but between this country and England, and, to cap the climax, England was to control the trade between the Colonies; that is, Massachusetts could not trade with New Hampshire, or New York with Connecticut, except by paying tribute to England. The people were no longer Englishmen, with the privileges of Englishmen, but outsiders, foreigners, so far as trade was concerned. If a Dutchman of Amsterdam wanted to find a market here in Boston he could not send his ship across the Atlantic, but only to England, that the goods might be taken across the ocean in an English ship. The merchants here in Boston who had anything to sell in Holland, France, Spain, or anywhere else, could not send it to those countries, but must ship it to England. The fishermen of Gloucester and Marblehead could not ship the codfish they had caught to Spain or Cuba. The people in Catholic countries cannot eat meat on Friday, but may eat fish. Spain and Cuba were good customers, but the fishermen must sell their fish to merchants in London or Bristol, instead of trading directly with the people of those countries. You see, Mr. Walden, that it was a cunningly devised plan to enrich England at our expense."

"It was unrighteous and wicked," Robert exclaimed.

"I do not wonder that it seems so to you, as it must to every one who believes in justice and fair dealing," Mr. Adams continued; "but human nature is apt to be selfish. In 1696 Parliament passed an act establishing the Lords of Trade, giving seven men, selected by the king, authority to control and regulate commerce.[1] The governors of the Colonies were to carry out the provisions of the act, which forbade all traffic between Ireland and the Colonies, and which repealed all the laws enacted by the colonial legislatures relating to trade and manufactures."

"Did not the people protest against such a law?" Robert asked.

"Yes, the Great and General Court sent a protest to London, but they might as well have whistled to the wind."

Mr. Adams turned partly round in his chair and took a paper from his desk.

"This is a copy," he continued, "of the protest. It represents that the people were already much cramped in their liberties and would be fools to consent to have their freedom further abridged. They were not bound to obey those laws, because they had no voice in making them. They stood on their natural rights. It would take many hours to tell you, Mr. Walden, the full story of oppression on the part of Parliament towards the Colonies, or to picture the greed of the merchants and manufacturers of England, who could not then, and who cannot now, bear to think of a spinning-wheel whirling or a shuttle flying anywhere outside of England, or of anybody selling anything unless for the benefit of the men who

---

[1] "The causes which brought about the American Revolution will be found in the acts of the Board of Trade." — JOHN ADAMS.

keep shop in the vicinity of Threadneedle Street or
Amen Corner.[1]   The course of England in selfishness and greed is like the prayer of the man who
said, —

> " ' O Lord, bless my wife and me,
> Son John and his she,
> We four,
> No more.' "

Robert, Berinthia, and Mrs. Adams laughed heartily. Mr. Adams finished his mush and milk, and while
Mrs. Adams was serving the pandowdy he went on : —
" Memory goes back to my boyhood.   When I was
ten years old or thereabouts, there were no less than
sixteen hat makers and possibly more in this one
town.   I used to pass several of the shops on my way
to school.   Beavers were plenty on all the streams in
New Hampshire and western Massachusetts, and the
hatters were doing a thriving business, sending their
hats to the West Indies and Holland.   One of the
merchants sent some to England.   The makers of felt
hats over there could not tolerate such a transaction.
There was a buzzing around the Lords of Trade ; a
complaint that the felters were being impoverished by
the hatters of America.   Parliament thereupon passed
a law to suppress the manufacture of hats.   Here is
the law."
Mr. Adams read from the paper : —
" No hats or felts, dyed or undyed, finished or unfinished, shall be put on board any vessel in any place
within any British plantations, nor be laden upon any

---

[1] Threadneedle Street and Amen Corner — noted localities in London.

horse or other carriage to the intent to be exported from thence to any other plantation, or to any other place, upon forfeiture thereof, and the offender shall likewise pay five hundred pounds for every such offense. Every person knowing thereof, and willingly aiding therein, shall forfeit forty pounds."

" That is diabolical," said Robert, his blood beginning to boil.

Mr. Adams saw the flush upon his cheek and smiled.

"I see that it stirs you up, as it does every lover of liberty. But I have not given you the full text of the iniquitous act: the law forbade any one from making a hat who had not served as an apprentice seven years, nor could a man employ more than two apprentices. Under that law no hatter up in Portsmouth could paddle across the Piscataqua and sell a hat to his neighbor in Kittery because the hat was made in New Hampshire. The hatter who had a shop in Providence could not carry a hat to his neighbor just over the line in Swansey, one town being in Rhode Island and the other in Massachusetts. The law, you see, was designed to crush out the manufacture of hats. The law applied to almost everything."

" I had no idea that such laws had been passed; they are abominable!" Robert replied with a vigor that brought a smile to Mr. Adams's face, who took a bit of cheese and smacked his lips.

" Every time I taste it I think of you and your father, mother, and sister who made it," he said.

"I hope to see them sometime," said Mrs. Adams.

" I am not quite through with the iniquity," continued Mr. Adams. " About forty years ago — it was

in 1737, I think — Parliament passed what is called the
Sugar Act, which imposed a duty on sugar and molasses, if imported from any of the West India Islands
other than those owned by Great Britain. Cuba, as
you know, is a dependency of Spain and St. Domingo
of France. The sugar plantations of Jamaica and
Guinea are owned by Englishmen, and the law was
passed to compel the Colonies to trade solely with the
Jamaica planters. The Great and General Court
protested that the act was a violation of the rights of
the Colonies, but no notice was taken of the protest —
it was thrown into the basket for waste paper. Since
the time of Charles II. not less than twenty-nine acts
have been passed, which, in one way or another, re-
strict trade and invade the rights of the Colonies. I
suppose, Mr. Walden, you leach the ashes, which you
scrape up from your fireplace ? ”

“ Oh yes,” Robert replied ; “ not only what we take
from the hearth in the kitchen, but when we have a
burning of a ten-acre lot, as we had a few weeks ago,
we scoop up several cart-loads of ashes which we leach,
and boil the lye to potash.” [1]

“ And what do you do with the potash ? ”

“ We shall probably bring it to Boston and sell it
to Mr. Hancock or some other merchant.”

“ Oh no, you can't do that legally, because you live
in New Hampshire, and the law prohibits trade of that
sort between the Colonies. You can take the potash
to Portsmouth, and if there is an English vessel in the

[1] The leaching of ashes and manufacture of potash was a large industry during the Colonial period. In some sections of the country
the article was known as “black salts.” There was one or more
potashery in every town.

Piscataqua you can send it to England and have it
shipped back to Boston; but it must be in an English
ship, not in one owned by my good friend John
Langdon, merchant in Portsmouth, who is ready to
stand resolutely against all oppression; or you may
pay the custom-house officer what it will cost to
transport it to England and back to Boston, and he
will give you permission to ship it direct to Boston.
That is the law; but it has been inoperative for several reasons — one, because it could not be enforced,
and another, because Great Britain has been compelled to rely upon the Colonies to aid in driving the
French from Canada. That has been accomplished,
and now King George, who is not remarkably intelligent, but pig-headed, and his short-sighted ministers
are determined to carry out measures, not only to
obtain revenue from the Colonies, but to repress
manufactures here for the benefit of the manufactures of England. Thanks to our spinning-school, a
stimulus has been given to our home manufactures
which will enable us to spin and weave a goodly
amount of plain cloth. Perhaps, Mr. Walden, you
may have noticed the spinning-school building in
Long Acre,[1] near the Common — a large brick building with the figure of a woman holding a distaff."

"Yes, I saw it yesterday, and wondered what it
might mean."

"Well, quite a number of years ago, the Great and
General Court passed a law for the encouragement of

[1] Long Acre extended from School Street to the Common, and
was sometimes called Common Street, now a section of Tremont
Street.

spinning, levying a tax on carriages and other luxuries for the establishment of the school. Its opening was celebrated on the Common. About one hundred women and girls came with their spinning-wheels and set them to humming beneath the trees. The court gave prizes for the best work. At present we buy our broadcloths and velvets in England, but the time will come when we shall make them this side of the Atlantic."

"The spinning-wheel and loom are going in our house from morning till night," Robert said.

"I am glad to hear it; the road to independence of the mother country lies in that direction. Industry will bring it about by and by, but I apprehend that other repressive and tyrannical measures will be passed. These arbitrary acts of Parliament have had one lamentable result, they have made the people of the Colonies a community of smugglers. I am pained to say that we are losing all correct sense of moral obligation in matters pertaining to the government. No one thinks it disreputable to smuggle goods into the country because everybody feels that the laws are unjust. The ministry undertook to enforce the laws against smuggling not long since, by issuing Writs of Assistance, as they were called. That attempt was more unjust than any of the laws that had been passed regulating trade. It gave the custom-house officers authority to enter not only stores, but private dwellings, break open chests, boxes, and closets in search of smuggled goods. Now if there is anything that Englishmen prize, it is the liberty secured by Magna Charta. Every man's house is his castle.

Writs of Assistance violated the fundamental principle of English liberty. Our great lawyer, Mr.
James Otis, has immortalized his name by his mas-
terly oration in opposition to the measure. The
writs have not prevented smuggling; on the contrary,
it is regarded as almost a virtue and a duty to circumvent a government which enacts unrighteous laws.
For instance, a little more than a year ago, John
Hancock's sloop, Liberty, arrived from Madeira with
a cargo of wine. The custom-house officer went on
board. He was followed by half a dozen seaman belonging to one of Hancock's other vessels, who locked
the officer into the cabin, unloaded the vessel, all except a few pipes of wine, and carted the cargo away.
The next morning the captain of the vessel made oath
that half a dozen casks was all the wine he had to
deliver for payment of duty. The collector, Mr.
Harrison, and the comptroller, Mr. Hallowell, resolved to seize the Liberty. Admiral Montague sent
a company of marines, who took possession of the
sloop and anchored her under the guns of the Romney. That incensed the people, who smashed in the
windows of the office, seized the collector's boat, carried it to the Common, and burned it. The revenue
officers, fearing for their safety, fled to the Castle,
where they remained till the troops arrived last October. Tyranny begets resistance on the part of the
people."

"What is to be the outcome of all this?" Robert
asked.

"I do not know," Mr. Adams replied thoughtfully,
"just what will come of it, but of one thing I am

sure, the people of America never will be slaves. At
present, we have an insolent soldiery walking our
streets, challenging and provoking the people. We
are treated as if under military law. The quiet of
the Sabbath is broken by the rattling of drums and
the shrill notes of the fife. The soldiers become in-
toxicated, and are ready to pick a quarrel with the
town's-people. No lady can appear on the street
unaccompanied by a gentleman without danger of
being insulted. I expect that collisions will occur
between the troops and people, and that sooner or
later blood will be shed. You can say to your father
that I have just received a letter from Colonel George
Washington of Virginia, who took command of the
troops after the wounding of General Braddock in the
battle near Fort Du Quesne. He agrees with me that
there must be united action on the part of the Colonies, and that we shall be warranted in using arms if
we cannot secure our liberties in any other way. Of
course, we shall not bring every one to stand up for
the rights and liberties of the Colonies. Those who
in any way are connected with the crown — the custom-house officials and their friends who are in re-
ceipt of salaries and perquisites — will support whatever measures the ministry may propose. Then there
are many gentlemen who naturally will maintain their
allegiance to the king, who think that an existing
government, no matter how unjust and tyrannical it
may be, stands for law and order, and that to resist it
in any way leads to revolution. Some of my old-time
friends are siding with the ministry. They think
we ought not to complain of so small a matter as

paying a tax of three pence per pound on tea. They lose sight of the great principle that taxation in any form without representation in Parliament is tyranny. We might willingly consent to pay it had we a voice in making it, but we will not consent to be taxed without such a voice. I am pleased, Mr. Walden, to have had this little conversation with you. I rely upon the young men of the country to stand resolutely for what is just and right, and I am equally sure," he said, turning to Berinthia, "that the young women will give all their influence to sustain the young men. Mrs. Adams is just as ready as I am to quit drinking tea, because by so doing she manifests her fealty to a great principle; if the mothers are ready to make sacrifices, I am sure the daughters will be equally ready."

The conversation of Mr. Adams was very attractive, he was so earnest, sincere, and truthful. Gladly would Robert have listened through the evening, but he reflected that such a man must have many letters to write, and he must not trespass upon his time.

"I am glad to have made your acquaintance, Mr. Walden; you must always come and see me when you are in town. I am sure you will do what you can to stir up the young men of Rumford to resist the aggressions of the king and his ministers. That there are lively times before us I do not doubt, but we shall maintain our liberties, cost what it may," he said, accompanying them to the door and bidding them good-by.

"I am invited to a garden tea-party to-morrow afternoon," said Berinthia, as they walked home. "Is n't it curious that while Mr. Adams wants us girls to leave off drinking tea for the sake of a great principle, I want you for my escort to the tea-party. It will be a grand affair and you will have a chance to see the best people of the town."

"I am at your service, and will do the best I can," Robert replied.

V

A GARDEN TEA-PARTY.

THE king's commissioner of imposts, Theodore Newville, had authority to collect for the crown three shillings per ton on all vessels of not more than two hundred tons burden, and four shillings per ton on vessels of larger dimensions. He also had authority to reserve the tallest, straightest, and largest pine-trees growing in the forests for the use of the royal navy. When the king's arrow was blazed upon a tree,[1] no man, not even the owner of the soil, could fell it to the ground. Every year, and at times as often as every six months, a ship arrived upon the New England coast for masts and spars.

Mr. Newville was provided with an office in the Custom House, but his home was on the sunny slope of Beacon Hill, a commodious mansion, with spacious rooms and ample hall. The fluted pilasters with Corinthians capitals, the modillions along the cornice, the semicircular balcony, were fitting adornments. The surrounding lawn was smoothly shaven. In the orchard were apples, pears, and melocotoons;[2] in the garden, roses, pinks, primroses, daffodils, bachelor's-buttons, and asters of every hue. The morning sun streaming

---

[1] The arrow was the sign of royal authority and ownership.

[2] The melocotoon was a variety of peach. The fruit was very large, beautifully colored, and of rich flavor.

into the dining-room illumined the richly cut decanters upon the shelves of the buffet. Very attractive, suggestive of ease, comfort, and culture, was the library, with its books and several portraits in gilded frames. The sun of the afternoon filled the richly furnished parlor with its mellow light. The front door opened to a wide hall and stairway, with carved baluster and polished mahogany rail. A clock stood upon the landing soberly counting the hours. Having inherited wealth, with a yearly stipend and many perquisites of office, Mr. Newville was abundantly able to live in a style befitting an officer of the crown. The knocker on the front door was so bright that Pompey could see his own white teeth and rolling eyeballs reflected from the shining brass. When through with the knocker he rubbed the fender, andirons, shovels, tongs, nozzle of the bellows, the hooks by the jams, candlesticks, snuffer, extinguisher, trays, and tinder-box, and wiped the dust from the glazed tiles of the hearth. It was the routine of every morning. Equally bright were the brass pots and pans in Phillis's realm. Pompey and Phillis were bondservants under the mild existing paternal form of slavery.

The king's commissioner of imposts perhaps would not have admitted he was passing the prime of life, but the crow's-feet were gathering in the corners of his eyes. His gray tie wig was in keeping with the white hairs upon his brow. He had a mild, blue eye, amiable countenance, and dignified deportment, as became an officer of the crown.

Time was in like manner beginning to turn its furrows upon the brow of the lady who sat opposite him at the table, but she was still very fair, as many a visitor had noticed while partaking of her hospitality.

When breakfast was finished Mr. Newville took his gold-headed cane from its place in the hall, adjusted his wig at the mirror under the sconce, put on his gold-laced hat and walked leisurely, as became his majesty's commissioner of imposts, along Tremont Street to Queen, thence past the jail, the Town House, the pillory and the stocks, to his office in the Custom House.

Mrs. Newville modeled her housekeeping on the last chapter of the Book of Proverbs. She began each morning with instructions to Phillis and Pompey. After breakfast, she walked to the market followed by Pompey at a respectful distance, with a basket to bring home the marketing. She was fastidious in her selection of meats; it must be a loin of beef, very tender, a chicken or duck, plump and fat; the freshest of eggs, and choicest butter. She found great pleasure in dispensing gracious hospitality, inviting the governor and lieutenant-governor of the Province, the justices, councilors, officers of the army and navy, strangers of distinction from other Provinces or from the other side of the sea; reverend doctors of divinity, lawyers, physicians, citizens of standing. She gave garden parties on summer afternoons, the guests sipping tea amid the flowers.

To such an entertainment Berinthia Brandon desired Robert's company. The barber on the corner of the street trimmed and powdered his hair, Mark Antony smoothed the wrinkles from his coat, and Berinthia fixed new ribbons in his knee-buckles.

"I am afraid I shall be so stiff and awkward you will be ashamed of me," he said, as she adjusted his ruffles.

"Oh no, I am sure your common sense will come to your aid."

"I shall not know anybody, and shall feel like a cat in a strange garret."

"But I will introduce you to some charming people."

"I shall make a fool of myself. I have never been in such society, and shall not know what to talk about. If it was like a quilting, such as we have at Rumford, I might get on, but I know I shall be the laughing-stock of the ladies."

"I am not afraid of it. Just be yourself, that's all."

The clock on the Old Brick Meetinghouse was striking three when they passed it on their way to the Newville mansion.

"You will find Mr. Newville a courtly, well-informed gentleman," said Berinthia. "Perhaps I ought to tell you that he is a Tory, which is quite natural, when we consider that he holds an office under the crown. He is very discreet, however, and is careful not to say or do anything offensive to the Sons of Liberty. Of course, political questions are not mentioned at these enjoyable gatherings. We say nothing about the Stamp Act; give all like topics the go-by, and just enjoy ourselves socially. You will find Mrs. Newville a delightful lady, and I know you will be charmed by Miss Ruth, a lovely girl, with gracious ways and a character all her own. I cannot describe her. Only intimate friends can know her goodness.

Few young ladies in Boston are more accomplished. Master Lovell [1] is her tutor, visiting her after school hours, to direct her course of study. She has been through the arithmetic, while most of us never have been beyond proportion. Having finished the accidence she has begun Latin; she can tambour, make

Master Lovell.

embroidery, draw, paint, play the harpsichord, and sing so charmingly that people passing along the street stop to listen to the enchanting music."

"You awaken my curiosity. But what will one who knows so much think of the awkward fellow keep-

[1] John Lovell was master of the Latin School, in School Street, from 1717 to 1776. He gave his sympathies to the crown, and became an exile upon the evacuation of Boston. His house was near the schoolhouse.

ing you company? Will she not regard me as a simpleton?"

"No, indeed; that would not be like Ruth Newville. Be assured, she will do what she can to make it a pleasant occasion to you."

"What can I say that will interest her, what talk about?"

"She will enable you to find your tongue. The chances are that you will fall in love with her just as everybody else does, — colonels, majors, captains, lieutenants of the army and navy, besides widowers and bachelors; but Ruth is too sensible a girl to throw herself away. Her mother would like her to marry some nobleman, or lord of ancient family. Ruth does not care much for coats-of-arms or titles, but would rather be sure of what a man is, rather than who were his ancestors. But we are almost there."

Many guests had already arrived. Ladies and gentlemen were strolling beneath the trees in the orchard, and along the garden paths. Pompey showing his white teeth, his dusky countenance beaming with pleasure, bowed very courteously as they entered the mansion.

"Massa and Missus Newville will welcome de ladies and genmens in de garding," he said.

Berinthia led the way and introduced Robert as her relative from New Hampshire.

"And so you are from that dependency of the crown? What news do you bring from that Province?" Mr. Newville asked.

"I do not know that there is anything particularly new or interesting. Not much is going on there. We have had a good crop of hay, the corn looks middling well; the rye is not much rusted. I think we shall not want for bread," Robert replied.

"It is excellent news. Bread is the staff of life, and I trust the people will be grateful for the bounties of Providence, and rest in peace and quiet under the rule of our gracious sovereign, King George."

"I hope we shall be truly thankful for all that is good," Robert replied.

"It is very kind in you to accompany our friend Miss Brandon to our entertainment this afternoon; we gladly welcome you, Mr. Walden," said Mrs. Newville, who ran her eyes over him, and, so far as Robert could judge, rather liking his stalwart form and figure, while saying to herself that he was no hawk or eagle to bear off her chicken.

"Ruth, daughter, this way, please," said Mrs. Newville.

Robert saw a young lady wearing a white muslin dress turn towards them from a group of ladies and gentlemen; but it was not the snowy whiteness of the garment, neither her dark brown unpowdered hair in contrast to that of the ladies around her, that attracted his attention, but the hazel eyes and the lips that had said, "I never shall forget your kindness, sir."

"Mr. Walden, allow me to introduce my daughter," said Mrs. Newville.

There was a startled, wondering look in the hazel eyes. She courtesied, with the fresh blood suffusing her cheeks.

"I am pleased to make your acquaintance, Mr. Walden," she said.

" I took the liberty of bringing him," said Berin-thia.   " I was sure you would extend to him the same cordial welcome you give to everybody."

" Certainly, anybody whom you may invite will always be welcome. Mr. Walden, shall I serve you with a cup of tea? What kind will you take — shall it be Old Hyson, Bohea, or Twankey?"

She stood with a salver ready to serve him.

" I will take Old Hyson, if you please," he said.

The pink slippers tripped across the lawn to a table where Phillis in white apron and cap, with smiling countenance, was pouring tea from silver urns into dainty cups. So this was the young lady whom he had rescued from the clutches of the villains. What should he say to her? By no word or look must she know that he was conscious of having be-friended her.

The sun was shining through the branches of the melocotoon tree beneath which she was standing. It seemed to him that the rich bloom of the ripening fruit by some subtle process of nature was being transmuted to her face. He recalled the description of the pure-hearted damsel that welcomed the Pilgrim of Bunyan's allegory to the beautiful palace in the land of Beulah. She soon returned bringing with steady hand the salver with the tea, sugar-bowl, and pitcher of cream.

" Shall I serve you with the sugar and cream, Mr. Walden?"

He could but notice the graceful movement of her deft fingers as she picked the sugar from the bowl with the silver tongs, and poured the cream.

" I will bring you some confections," she said, and tripped away once more, returning with a plate of cake and bonbons.

" I hope you find the tea to your taste ? " she said.

" It could not be better," he replied.

He could see she was scanning his face with an inquiring look, as if endeavoring to solve a perplexing question — whether the stranger in working clothes who rescued her from the arms of the assaulting soldiers and this gentleman in fitting costume for genteel society were one and the same. " Can it be he ? " was the question revolving in her thoughts. The countryman was tall, stout, and broad-shouldered; so was Mr. Walden. She saw resolution and indignation in the face of the stranger. Could not the face before her exhibit like qualities under like provocation? She must find out during the afternoon, if possible, whether or not Mr. Walden was her benefactor. If so, what should she say to him — how make known her gratitude ?

" And so you are from New Hampshire, Mr. Walden ? " she said inquiringly.

" Yes, and this is my first visit to Boston."

" I dare say you find things somewhat different here from what they are there."

" Oh yes. In Rumford the houses are scattered; but here they are as thick as spatter. There is n't near so many things going on there as here."

" I think it must be delightful to live in the country, among the green fields and pastures, and have chickens and goslins, and see the lambs play."

"Yes; but we have to look sharp, to see that the foxes, and hawks, and weasels don't get 'em."

Their conversation was interrupted by Berinthia, who introduced him to Miss Lucy Flucker,[1] daughter of the secretary of the Province, Miss Dorothy Quincy, Miss Mary Shrimpton, and to Isaac and John Coffin,[2] sons of his majesty's receiver-general.

"Do you have garden tea-parties in Rumford?" Miss Flucker asked.

"No, not garden parties, but the ladies get together in a parlor, sip their tea, take pinches of snuff from each other's boxes, talk about the number of cheeses they have made, how much salt they put into the curd, how much yarn they have spun, how many yards of linen they have woven."

[1] Miss Flucker received the attentions of Henry Knox the bookseller, and became his wife. While her father remained loyal to the king, she became an ardent patriot, and married the man of her choice. Soon after the battle of Lexington and Concord, Mr. Knox escaped from Boston. Mrs. Knox received a permit to join him, from General Gage, who had issued an order prohibiting any one from taking arms from the town. The patriotic wife concealed her husband's sword in her underskirts, and successfully eluded the vigilance of the sentinels.

[2] Isaac Coffin obtained an appointment in his majesty's navy in 1773. Upon the outbreak of the war he proffered his resignation, not being willing to fight against his countrymen, but being assured he would not be sent to North America remained in the service of the king, rising by merit to the position of rear-admiral. He retained through life a deep affection for his countrymen, and endowed a school on the island of Nantucket.

His younger brother John, from the outset, sided with the king. He joined the British forces, became captain of a company of loyalists, served under Colonel Tarleton in South Carolina, becoming major, colonel, and after the war a major-general. He received a grant of several thousand acres of land in Nova Scotia. Though maintaining allegiance to the king, he had great respect and admiration for those who espoused the patriotic cause.

"Such a party must be very enjoyable," said Miss Quincy.

"Yes, I think they like to find out what everybody else is doing, and how they do it. Their tongues wag lively when they get to talking about what has happened and what they expect will happen; who was cried the Sunday before, and who probably will be the next Sunday."

The ladies smiled at Robert's vivacious conversation.

"Does the town clerk cry the proposed marriages?" Miss Shrimpton asked.

"Yes. The moment the minister finishes the benediction Sunday afternoon, Squire Fellows breaks in, shouting that marriage is intended between Hezekiah and Mehitable. Of course there are blushes on Mehitable's face, while Hezekiah looks kinder sheepish."

Again the ladies laughed.

"Do all the ladies take snuff?"

Miss Flucker asked the question.

"Nearly all the old ladies carry their snuff-boxes in their pockets or work-bags. There's one lady, however, who does not — Aunt Hipsy Jenkins. Perhaps I ought to say she is well along in years, and that the town clerk never has cried her. She carries her nose as she pleases. She says if the Lord had intended it for a dust-hole, he would have put it on the other end up."

A merry peal of laughter rang through the garden — so joyful that several ladies and gentlemen joined the group, to hear what the young man from the country was saying.

"Her name," said Robert, by way of explanation, "is Hepsibah, but everybody calls her Hipsy."

"Evidently," said Isaac Coffin, "she is a lady who is up to snuff."

Again the company laughed.

"You may be sure she never minces things, but speaks her mind, whether anybody likes it or not," Robert replied.

"Are the gentlemen invited to the tea-parties?" John Coffin asked.

"Not to the afternoon parties, neither are the young ladies; the old ladies like to be by themselves while sipping their tea. Perhaps they think it would not be dignified on the part of the gentlemen to devote the afternoons to gossip," Robert replied.

"Do not the young ladies meet?" Miss Shrimpton asked.

"Not as do our mothers, but they have their own good times, — their quilting parties. In the country every girl as soon as she can sew begins to make patchwork. When they get enough for a quilt, they invite their acquaintances to the quilting, and spend the afternoon in talking about — well, I can't exactly say what they do talk about. Perhaps you ladies can tell better than I."

The ladies smiled at his pleasant way of indicating what was uppermost in the thoughts of young maidens on such delightful occasions.

"Do not the gentlemen participate in some way?" Miss Quincy inquired.

"Oh yes: we join them in the evening, after they are through with the quilting, and try to make things

lively. We play blindman's-buff, hide the handkerchief, roast beef behind your back, come Philander,
stage-coach, and other games, and have a jolly time.
The ladies serve us with bread and butter, doughnuts,
cookies, tarts, gingerbread, and tea. We guess riddles and tell ghost stories."

"How delightful!" Miss Newville exclaimed.

"A little later than this we have huskings in the
barns, seated around a heap of corn. Husking over,
we eat pudding, baked beans, mince, apple, and pumpkin pie, and top off with pop-corn, apples, and cider.
After supper the girls clear away the dishes; then we
push the table into one corner of the kitchen, Julius
Cæsar mounts it with his fiddle, and we dance jigs
and quicksteps. The girl who first found a red ear
while husking, and was kissed before she could throw
it into the basket, is privileged to lead the dance."

"How I should enjoy it," said Miss Shrimpton.

"Finding the red ear?" queried Isaac Coffin.

"Oh no, — you know I did n't mean that; but
having such a jolly time with nobody saying it is n't
proper," Miss Shrimpton replied with a blush man-
tling her cheek.

"Ruth, daughter," — it was Mrs. Newville calling
her to meet other guests, and Miss Newville turned
regretfully away, for it was a pleasure to talk with
Mr. Walden, and she hoped he would drop a word
which would enable her to make sure it was he who
had befriended her.

Robert, with Berinthia and the ladies whose acquaintance he had made, sauntered along the garden
walks. The midsummer flowers were gone, but those of

autumn were in bloom, — marigolds, asters, and sunflowers.   Picturesque the scene : ladies in paduasoys, taffetas, and brocades, gentlemen in purple, russet, and crimson coats, white satin waistcoats, buff breeches, and silk stockings.   Officers of the king's regiments in scarlet with silver-starred epaulets, clergymen in suits of black, lawyers and doctors in white wigs, loitering along the paths, gathered in groups beneath the trees, young ladies serving them with syllabubs.   From the vine-clad arbor the music of the orchestra floated upon the air.

Robert saw a gentleman and lady shaking hands with Mr. and Mrs. Newville.

"That is John Adams, one of the smartest lawyers in town," said Berinthia.   "That is his wife Abigail; she is the daughter of Reverend Mr. Smith, the minister of Braintree.   She knows Latin and Greek, and is one of the nicest women in town.   She writes beautiful letters, and knows — oh, so much!   I'll introduce you to them.   I know you will be charmed with her."

Mr. Adams courteously greeted Robert, and very gracious was the recognition by Mrs. Adams.   She asked him if he had ever been in Boston before; who was the minister in Rumford; if he had many books to read. So pleasant and agreeable was her conversation, she seemed to Robert to be an old friend.

Robert was pleased to meet Doctor Warren, and received a cordial greeting.

"And are you acquainted?" Miss Newville inquired wonderingly.

"I am happy to claim Mr. Walden as my friend. I have long known his father," the doctor replied.

ABIGAIL SMITH ADAMS

Robert was pleased, also, to meet Mr. Knox, the bookseller, who was polite and affable to all, particularly to Miss Flucker.

When Berinthia and Robert were by themselves she informed him that Mr. Knox was attentive to Miss Flucker; that her parents opposed the match, Mr. Knox being a Whig and her father a Tory. Berinthia was sure that the more her father opposed the bookseller, the better Miss Lucy liked him.

Mr. Hancock's House.

Mr. John Hancock, though living but a short distance from Mr. Newville, came in his coach with driver and footmen in blue livery. He bowed politely to Mr. and Mrs. Newville, took a pinch of snuff from

Mr. Newville's gold box, and graciously greeted Miss Dorothy Quincy. Berinthia whispered to Robert that they were engaged to be married.[1]

"If Miss Newville and Miss Brandon will excuse us, Mr. Walden and myself will take a turn through the grounds," said Doctor Warren, locking arms with Robert.

"I am glad to meet you once more, Mr. Walden. I want to thank you for the good work you did yesterday afternoon. I have heard of it several times; the people are chuckling over it. But the soldiers of the Twenty-Ninth Regiment are as mad as hornets and threaten retaliation. They are anxious to get hold of that fellow from the country who did it. I thought I would put you on your guard. I wish I knew who the young lady was, but no one can find out. Neither she nor her friends have made complaint to the selectmen, and of course you could not know."

Robert thanked him. He said he did not anticipate any trouble; if attacked he would try and give a good account of himself.

They had strolled to the farthest part of the grounds. Returning, they saw Miss Newville surrounded by ladies and gentlemen ; young and old alike were finding pleasure in her society. Major Evelyn, to whom Robert had been introduced, was telling how jolly it was in old England to follow the hounds in a fox hunt, leaping ditches, walls, and hedges, running

---

[1] The Dorothy Quincy who married John Hancock is not to be confounded with the Dorothy Q. of Holmes's poem : —

> "Grandmother's mother, her age I guess,
> Thirteen summers, or something less."

DOROTHY QUINCY

Reynard to cover. Although courteously listening, her eyes glanced towards Robert and Doctor Warren.

"Pardon me, Major, but I must have a word with my good doctor who gives me pills and powders when I am sick," she said graciously, tripping across the lawn.

"I have not served you with tea, doctor; what kind would you prefer?" she said.

"Well, let it be Old Hyson, if you please."

"And yours, Mr. Walden : it was the Old you had before. Will you not try a cup of Young Hyson for variety ? "

"If you please, Miss Newville."

A few moments and she was with them again.

"Old Hyson for old friendship, Young, for new acquaintance," said the doctor, as he took the cup from her hand. "You see, Mr. Walden, Miss Newville and I are old friends, and our relations at times are quite intimate. I am privileged to hold her hand, feel her pulse, and look at her tongue."

"Do you not think, Mr. Walden, that the doctor is very rude to take a young lady's hand when she cannot help herself?"

"Of course it is rude, but I apprehend you do not object, under the circumstances," Robert replied.

"Oh no, she likes it so well that she often asks when I will come again," said the doctor.

Merry was the laughter.

"This is delicious tea," he said, sipping the beverage.

"I am glad you like it."

"It is all the more delicious, Miss Ruth, because I

have it from your own gracious hand, and because it is probably the last I shall drink for many months."

She gazed at him wonderingly.

"You know I am firm in my convictions as to what is right and just, and I have decided to quit drinking tea as a protest against what the king and Lord North are preparing to do. So this will be a memorial day for me. Pardon me, I did not mean to allude to it."

"One need not beg pardon for having a conviction of what is right and just. If it is to be your last cup I'm glad I have the privilege of serving it," she said.

One by one guests joined them, charmed by her presence, Major Evelyn hovering around her. More than once the eyes of Robert and Miss Newville met. Would she not think him rude? But how could he help looking at her?

While Miss Newville was serving other guests, with Berinthia and Miss Shrimpton Robert walked the garden once more, the great shaggy watch-dog trotting in advance, as if they were guests to be honored by an escort.

The afternoon was waning. Guests were leaving, and it was time for Berinthia and Robert to take their departure.

"Oh, you are not going now. I have not had an opportunity to speak a dozen words with you, Berinthia, and I have shamefully neglected Mr. Walden. I have not had a chance to drink a cup of tea with him. I am sure you will excuse me, Major Evelyn, while I redeem myself. You will find Miss Brandon delightful company," said Miss Newville.

Major Evelyn, being thus politely waved one side, could but acquiesce.

"Shall we sit, Mr. Walden?" she asked, leading the way to seats and bringing tea and cake.

"I enjoyed your description of life in the country, and the young ladies were delighted," she said.

"We have pretty good times with the quiltings, huskings, and sleighing parties, when we pile into a double pung, ride in the moonlight, have supper, and a dance."

"How delightful! Have you brothers and sisters?"

"Only a sister, Rachel, two years younger than I."

"Does she love flowers?"

"Yes, she is very fond of them. I make up beds in the garden for her and she sows bachelor's-buttons, flytraps, pansies, marigolds, hollyhocks, and has morning-glories running over strings around the sitting-room window."

"They must make your home very pleasant in summer."

"Yes, and she has asters and sweet peas. I try to keep the weeds down for her as she has so many things to look after, — the chickens, goslins, young turkeys, besides washing dishes, spinning, and wetting the cloth bleaching on the grass. I help a little by drawing the water."

"It must be very beautiful in the country these September days."

"It is not quite late enough for the woods to put on their brightest colors; that will be in October."

"Which season do you like best?"

"I hardly know. Sometimes, when the country is covered with snow and the air is fresh and keen and healthful, I think there is no part of the year more enjoyable than winter; then when spring comes, and the buds start and the leaves are growing, I feel like a young colt ready to caper and kick up my heels. When the flowers are in bloom and the birds are singing I think there is no season like summer. At this time of the year, when we are gathering the harvests and the woods are more beautiful than our Queen Charlotte in her coronation robes, I think there is no period of the year so delightful as autumn."

"Living in the town," Miss Newville said, "I lose much that I should enjoy in the country. Sometimes I ride with my father to Roxbury, Dorchester, and Cambridge. He sits in his chaise while I pick the flowers by the roadside. A few weeks ago we went sailing down the harbor, and saw the waves rolling on the beach at Nantasket and breaking on the rocks around the lighthouse. Oh, it was beautiful!"

"I do not doubt it. As you love the country so much, I am sure you would be charmed with the view from our home, Miss Newville, especially at this season of the year."

"Please tell me about it. I am sure from your description I shall be able to picture the scene."

"You would see a broad valley, fields, pastures, meadows, uplands, the river flowing between banks fringed with elms and willows, hills farther away, and in the distance blue mountains; the forest all scarlet, russet, yellow, and crimson. That would be the view. You would hear the crickets chirping, crows cawing, and squirrels barking in the woods."

"How delightful! I know I should revel in such beauty."

"You asked me, Miss Newville, which season I liked best. I think, all things considered, I enjoy autumn more than any other portion of the year."

"May I ask why you like it best?"

"Because it is the harvest-time, when we gather the gifts of Providence; and it sets me to thinking I ought to be doing something for somebody in return for what Providence is doing for me."

Her eyes were watching his lips.

"Oh, go on, please, Mr. Walden, and tell me what the seasons say to you."

"I hardly know what they say, but the change from the brightness of summer to the russet of autumn, the falling leaves, ripening fruits, fading flowers, shortening days, the going of the birds are like a sermon to me."

"And why are they like a sermon?" she asked.

"Because the birds will come, the flowers bloom again, but the summer that has gone never will return; the opportunities of to-day will not be here to-morrow. I must make the most of the present, not only for myself but for others. Providence bestows rich gifts; I must give to others."

"Thank you, Mr. Walden."

She was silent. None of the officers, not Major Evelyn or any of the captains of his majesty's troops, ever had uttered such words in her presence. Oh, could she but know if he were the one who rescued her from the hands of the miscreants! She must know.

"Mr. Walden, may I ask if we have not met before?"

" I think we have, Miss Newville."

" I thought so, but was not sure. May I say I cannot tell you how grateful I am for the service you rendered me yesterday. I never shall forget it. I have not mentioned it, not even to my parents, for I would not have them concerned in the future for my welfare."

" I can understand how anxious they might be, and I appreciate your prudence. The incident, I understand, is making some stir in town, especially among the soldiers. Doctor Warren has just informed me of it, and was kind enough to say it would be well for me to be on my guard, as the soldiers threaten retaliation. I learn, also, that no one as yet has been able to discover who the young lady was. People are wondering that no complaint has been made to the proper authorities by her or her friends."

" Oh, I am so glad that no one knows it except ourselves. May I not ask that it shall be our secret, and ours only ? "

" Most certainly, Miss Newville."

" I cannot express my obligation to you, Mr. Walden. It is very honorable in you, and you will not let the soldiers injure you ? " she said inquiringly.

" I do not think they will molest me. I shall not put myself in their way, neither shall I avoid them. I am a free citizen : this is my country. I know my rights, and I trust I shall ever be enough of a man to resent an insult to myself, and most certainly to a lady."

" Do you remain long in town ? " she asked.

" No : only a day or two — over Sunday. I shall start from the Green Dragon for home next Monday morning."

" Do you have melocotoons in Rumford?" she asked,
looking up to the luscious fruit, ripening above them.

"Not yet; we have some young trees, but they are
not in bearing."

" I should like to send a basket of fruit to your sister, if agreeable to you. Pompey will take it to the
tavern Monday morning."

" You are very kind. I will take it with pleasure,
and you may be sure Rachel will appreciate your goodness."

He comprehended her proposition, — that it was her
delicate way of giving emphasis to her thanks for what
he had done.

" Mr. Walden, I shall always be pleased to see you.
I would like to hear more about what you see in nature, and the sermons that are preached to you."

Berinthia and Major Evelyn joined them. The
band had ceased playing, and the last of the guests
were departing.

" I hope you have had an enjoyable afternoon,"
said Mr. Newville.

" I have enjoyed myself very much, and cannot express my thanks for your hospitality," Robert replied.

" It was very kind in you to honor us with your
company," said Mrs. Newville with a charming grace
and dignity.

Miss Newville went with them to the gate, Major
Evelyn improving the opportunity to walk by her side.
Robert thought there was a shade of vexation on her
face.

" Excuse me, gentlemen, while I talk with Miss
Brandon a moment," she said, dropping behind.

Robert walked on a few steps and waited for Berinthia. Major Evelyn lingered a moment as if to have a last word with Miss Newville, but politeness would not admit his further tarrying; he lifted his hat and walked away.

" Oh, Mr. Walden, what do you think your good cousin has been saying ? " said Miss Newville, calling him once more to the gate.

" Possibly that she has had an agreeable chat with one of his majesty's brilliant officers," Robert replied.

" Instead of being brilliant, he was positively stupid. I don't like epaulets," said Berinthia.

" Not those sent to protect us ? " Miss Newville asked.

" No."

" Neither do I."

The words were spoken firmly, with an emphasis which Robert alone could understand.

Miss Newville locked her arm in Berinthia's as if loath to have her go. They lingered by the gate, how long Robert could not say. Just what was said he could not recall. He only knew it was delightful to stand there, to hear her voice, to see the smiles rippling upon her face, and the loving eyes that turned towards him at times. When at last the good-night was spoken, when himself and Berinthia were quite a distance, looking backward he saw her white handkerchief waving them farewell.

VI.

CHRIST CHURCH CHIMES.

CALM and peaceful was the Sabbath morning in Rumford, where the stillness was broken only by lowing cattle and singing birds, but in Boston Robert heard the rattling of drums, — a prolonged roll, as if the drummers found special pleasure in disturbing the slumbers of the people. It was the reveille arousing the troops. Mr. Brandon said the officers of the king's regiments seemed to take delight in having extra drills on Sunday for the purpose of annoying the people. A few of the officers, he said, were gentlemen, but others were vile, and not to be admitted into decent society.

The drums ceased and there was a period of quiet ; then suddenly the air was melodious with the music of bells. Berinthia saw the wonder on Robert's face.

" It is Christ Church chimes," she said.

He heard " Old Hundred," sweet and enchanting.

" If you would like, we will go to Christ Church this morning."

Robert replied he would gladly go with her.

" The sexton is a Son of Liberty, Robert Newman ; you saw him the other night at the Green Dragon ; his brother plays the organ," said Tom.

The sexton welcomed them and gave them seats. Robert gazed in wonder at the fluted columns, the high arched ceiling, the pillars supporting the galleries, the great windows, the recess behind the pulpit, the painting of the Last Supper. He read the words, "This is none other than the House of God; this is the Gate of Heaven."

The bells ceased their pealing, but suddenly delightful music filled the church.

Christ Church.

"That is John Newman at the organ," Berinthia whispered.

It began soft and faint, as if far away — a flute, then a clarinet, a trumpet, growing louder, nearer, deeper, heavier, the loud notes rolling like far-off thunder, then dying into melody as sweet as the song of a bird. Never had Robert heard any music so delightful. Looking towards the loft, he saw the gilded pipes of the instrument. Upon the railing around it were figures of angels with trumpets.

" They were captured from a French ship in 1746 by Captain Grushea of the Queen of Hungary privateer," Tom whispered. " They were designed for a Romish church in Canada, but the captain brought them to Boston and presented them to the wardens of this church."

Berinthia said the Bible and prayer-book were given by King George II. at the request of Governor Belcher. She found the places in the prayer-book for him. He thought the prayers very beautiful, but could not quite see the need of getting up and sitting down so often. He never had taken part in meeting before, but when all the others read felt he too must let his voice be heard, otherwise the people would think he did not know how to read. He was startled at the sound of his own voice, but soon got over it, and rather liked the idea of the people taking some part in the service instead of having it all done by the minister. It was very delightful when the choir came in with the organ, in contrast to the singing in Rumford meetinghouse where the deacon lined the Psalms, two lines at a time, and set the tune with his pitch-pipe.

When the service was over and the people were going out, the organ began to play. The sexton took them upstairs to see his brother John handle it. Robert was surprised to see him using his feet as well as his hands, fingering two sets of keys, pushing in and pulling out what Tom said were "stops." When through with the piece, the organist explained the mechanism of the instrument, playing softly and then making the windows rattle.

An hour at noon, and then the meetinghouse bells were tolling for the afternoon service.

"We will go to our own meeting; I want you to hear Reverend Doctor Cooper,"[1] said Berinthia. The meetinghouse was in Brattle Street, close by the barracks. The soldiers were lounging around the building staring at the people, laughing, smoking their pipes, and making rude remarks. When meeting was over the soldiers gathered around the door and leered at the girls. Robert clenched his fist and felt his blood grow hot. A lieutenant started to walk beside Berinthia.

"My cousin will not need your escort, sir," said Robert touching his elbow.

The officer grew red in the face and disappeared in the barracks.

On Monday morning Robert bade his friends good-by. Peter Augustus had something for him at the Green Dragon : a basket filled with fruit — melocotoons, pears, and plums — and a neatly written note.

---

[1] The meetinghouse in Brattle Street at the time of the opening of this story was a large unpainted wooden structure which was torn down in 1772, and replaced by an elegant edifice of brick with quoins of freestone. John Hancock gave one thousand pounds and a bell. The pastor, Reverend Samuel Cooper, was an earnest advocate for the rights of the Colonies, and without doubt his influence, combined with that of Samuel Adams, had much to do in attaching Hancock to the patriots' side.

" Will Mr. Walden kindly take a basket of fruit to his sister, Miss Rachel, from Ruth Newville."

That was all. What a surprise it would be to Rachel! Why was Miss Newville sending it? She never had met Rachel; knew nothing of her, except what little he had said, yet the gift!

The sun was going down the following evening when he reached the turn of the road bringing him in sight of home. ·He was yet half a mile away, but Rachel was standing in the doorway waving her apron. She could not wait for Jenny to trot home, but came down the road bareheaded, climbed into the wagon, put her arms around his neck, and gave him a hug and a kiss. There was a look of wonder on her face when he uncovered the basket of fruit and told her who had sent it, — a beautiful girl, one of Berinthia's friends, whom he had rescued from the king's soldiers. There were tears in Rachel's eyes when he put the beads around her neck.

" Oh, Rob! how good you are! "

It was all she could say.

November came, and Berinthia Brandon was sitting in her chamber. From its eastern window she looked across the burial ground with its rows of headstones. The leafless trees were swaying in the breeze. She was thinking of what Samuel Adams had said to her, that life is worth living just in proportion to the service we can render to others. What had she ever done for anybody? Not much. A feeling of sadness came over her. The afternoon sun was lengthening the shadows of the headstones across the grass-grown mounds. The first snow of approaching winter was lying white and pure above the sleeping forms of those who had finished their earthly work. Beyond the burial ground she beheld the harbor. The tide had been at its flood, and was sweeping towards the sea. A ship was sailing down the roadstead to begin its adventurous voyage to a distant land.

"Why can I not do something for somebody instead of idling my time away?" she said to herself, recalling what Mr. Adams had said — that it was the duty of every woman to forego personal comfort and pleasure for the promotion of the public good; that everybody should leave off using tea to let the king, the ministry, and the people of England know that the men and women of the Colonies could stand resolutely and unflinchingly for a great principle. With her father, mother, and Tom she had quit drinking tea; why should she not persuade others to banish it from their tables? A thought came to her, and she opened her writing-desk, a gift from her father, beautifully inlaid with ivory, which he had obtained in a foreign country. She dipped her pen into the ink, reflected a moment, and then wrote her thought: "*We, the daughters of patriots, who have stood and do now stand for the public interest, with pleasure engage with them in denying ourselves the drinking of foreign tea, in hope to frustrate a plan that tends to deprive the community of its rights.*" [1]

In her enthusiasm she walked the floor, thinking of those whom she would ask to sign it. She would not

---

[1] The agreement signed by the mothers and daughters may be found in the *Boston News-Letter*, February 15, 1770.

subject herself to ridicule by calling upon those who sided with the king, but upon those who she knew were ready to make sacrifices for justice and right.

"I am glad you have written it, daughter," Mr. Brandon said when she informed him of what she had done and was intending to do; "I see no reason, wife, why you should not do what you can in the same way among the women, to let people on the other side of the sea understand the Colonies are in earnest. Already there has been a great falling off in trade between the Colonies and England, and if we can stop this tea trade it will not be long before the merchants will be swarming around Parliament demanding something to be done. We must arouse public sentiment on this question, and you, daughter, are just the girl to begin it."

Mr. Brandon reached out his hand and took Berinthia's and gave it a squeeze to let her know he had faith in her.

"I will do what I can to persuade others," she said, returning the pressure.

Through the night Berinthia was thinking over what she had started to accomplish, and what arguments she should use to influence those whom she would ask to sign the agreement. The great idea, with a moral principle behind it, took possession of her mind and drove sleep from her eyes and aroused the energies of the soul. Why undertake the arduous task alone? Why not ask Doctor Cooper to preach about it? If she could but get the ministers enlisted, they could awaken public sentiment.

"Ah! I have it. Week after next is Thanksgiv-

ing, and I will get them to preach sermons that will
stir up the people," she said to herself.

Thanksgiving Day came. Very eloquent were the
words spoken for Justice, Right, and Liberty by Reverend Doctor Cooper, Reverend Doctor Eliot, Reverend Doctor Checkley, and nearly all the other ministers, excepting Reverend Mr. Coner, rector of King's
Chapel, and Reverend Mather Byles of Christ Church,
whose sympathies were with the king.[1]

In every household fathers and mothers, sons and
daughters and grandchildren, gathered in the old home,
and had a great deal to say, while partaking of the
roast turkey and plum-pudding, of the sermons they
had heard in the different meetinghouses. All the
ministers preached about the proposal of Parliament
to levy a tax upon tea, and that if it could not be de-
feated in any other way it was the patriotic duty of
the people to quit using the herb. They must deny
themselves the luxury, that they might maintain
their freedom. Little did they know that a blue-eyed
girl had called upon Doctor Cooper and read to him
what she had written, an agreement to drink no more
tea ; how his soul had been set on fire and he had gone
with her to the houses of other ministers, that they
might look into her eyes and see the flashing of a
resolute spirit in behalf of justice, righteousness, and
liberty.

[1] Reverend Andrew Eliot was pastor of the New North Church,
an edifice still standing at the corner of Hanover and Clark streets,
and used by the Roman Catholics. Reverend Samuel Checkley was
pastor of the New South Church, and Reverend Samuel Blair of the
Old South. These pastors were outspoken in denunciation of the
offensive measures of the king and his ministers.

Although the snow was deep in the streets, the drifts did not deter Berinthia from calling upon her friends. Many of the good ladies were ready to sign an agreement to drink no more tea; others hesitated. She was warmly welcomed by Mrs. Abigail Adams, who at once saw how great would be the influence of the women upon their husbands.

"But what shall we drink instead of tea?" asked Dorothy Quincy.

"When summer comes, we will go out into the fields and gather strawberry leaves, and call them Hyperion, or some other elegant name. I think it quite as pretty a name as Old Hyson, and I am not sure that they will not be more healthful," Berinthia replied.

Miss Dorothy laughed heartily. "Yes, and we can, upon a pinch, drink cold water from the town pump and flavor it with peppermint," she said, as she wrote her name.

After leaving Miss Quincy, Berinthia lifted the knocker of the Newville mansion, not to ask Ruth to sign the agreement; she could not do that, for Mr. Newville was a Tory, and the signers were daughters of patriots.

"How good it is to see you once more. It is a very long time since I have looked upon your face," Ruth exclaimed, embracing her.

"The snow has been so deep and I have had so much to do, I have not found time to call till now, and I don't know as I should be here to-day only I am spinning street-yarn for a particular purpose."

Ruth was at a loss to understand her.

"I am calling on my acquaintances, and I was not quite sure whether I ought to skip you or not."

"Skip me! What have I done that you should think of dropping me from your acquaintance?"

Berinthia saw a wondering and injured look in the loving eyes.

"Oh, you have n't done anything; it is what the king, Lord North, and Parliament are doing. They intend to make us pay taxes against our will, and we girls are signing an agreement not to drink any more tea, and I am calling on my friends for that purpose."

The look of wonder and grief disappeared, and Ruth's face brightened once more. She read the agreement and the list of names.

"I did n't call, dear Ruth, to ask you to sign it. I have no right to do so. It is an agreement to be signed by the daughters of those who are opposed to being taxed in this way. Your father, doubtless, may be willing to pay the tax; my father is not. You may not think as we do, but that shall not disturb our friendship. I shall love you just as I have ever since we were children."

"How good you are! I appreciate your kindness. My father and mother stand for the king, but I have my own opinion. Under the terms of the agreement, I cannot sign it, but I am with you in spirit. I can see the course taken by the king is not right or just, and it will fail. Nothing can succeed in the end that is not right."

"Oh, Ruth, how you shame me. Here I have been fidgeting over the cutting things some of the girls and their mothers have been saying. One asked if I expected to bankrupt the East India Company. Another wanted to know if I was going to wear trousers and vote in town meeting."

" So mother's afternoon tea-party stands a chance of being the last, for the present, at least. By the way, do you ever hear from your cousin, Mr. Walden ? "

" No, I have not heard a word since he left us. I should not be surprised, however, if he were to drop in upon us any day, for I have written him that the ship is to be launched soon. Father intends to make it a grand occasion when the Berinthia Brandon glides into the water. I shall have all my friends present, Ruth Newville chief among them."

" Count upon me to do whatever I can to make it a happy day," said Ruth.

VII.

LAUNCHING OF THE BERINTHIA BRANDON.

THE pigs had been fattening through the winter, and it was quite time to send them to market.

"You did so well with the cheese, you may see what you can do with the shoats," said Mr. Walden to Robert. "It is good sleighing. You can harness the colt and Jenny, and go with the pung. I want you to take Rachel along. You can stay a couple of weeks and have a good visit."

There was a glow upon Rachel's face. It would be her first journey. She would see new things, and make new acquaintances. During the evenings she had been knitting a hood and mittens of the finest wool, and would present them to Miss Newville.

It was a resplendent morning, with the eastern sky like molten gold in the light of the rising sun, and the hoar-frost upon the twigs of the leafless trees changing to glittering diamonds. The colt, sleek and plump, was champing his bit and shaking his head in his impatience to be off. Jenny was staid and sober, but when Robert said, " Now, lad and lady," the colt pranced a few steps, then settled to a steady trot, learning a lesson from Jenny.

An hour before lunch-time they whirled up to Captain Stark's tavern in Derryfield, and before sunset came to a halt in the dooryard of a relative in Andover. Before noon the next day Rachel was looking with wondering eyes upon the gleaming spires of the meetinghouses and the crooked streets of Boston.

" You have come just at the right time," said Berinthia, welcoming her with a kiss, " for I am to be launched day after to-morrow."

Seeing by the look of wonder on Rachel's face that she was not understood, Berinthia explained that the ship her father was building was to bear her name, and that everything was ready for the launching.

"Oh, it will be so delightful to have you here!" she added. "We will be on the deck, ever so many of us, — my friends, papa's and mamma's and Tom's. Ruth Newville will be here; and Tom's classmate in Harvard College, Roger Stanley, who lives out beyond Lexington, is coming. He's a real nice young man, and I am sure you will like him. Tom's girl will be here, Mary Shrimpton; she is out in the kitchen now. She has been helping us make crumpets, crullers, gingerbread, and cake. Father and mother intend to make it a grand affair, and have invited half of the town, — doctors, lawyers, ministers, and their wives; everybody that is anybody. Tom has invited his friends, and I mine, because the ship is to bear my name."

Rachel said she was glad she had come to see and enjoy it all.

"We will have a jolly time while you are here; it is vacation at college, and I shan't have to study," said Tom.

A young lady with a pleasant face, light blue eyes,

and soft brown hair, entered the room and was introduced as Miss Shrimpton.

" She has been helping us get ready, and has rolled out a bushel of crullers," said Tom.

" Not quite so many," said Miss Shrimpton, smiling. Robert thought her very attractive and pleasing.

" I think I will go home now; father and mother will be expecting me, but I will be round to-morrow," said Miss Shrimpton.

Tom put on his hat and escorted her. When he returned, and he and Robert were by themselves, he said that she was the best girl in Boston.

" Her father," he went on, " is a redhot Tory. He lives in a fine house, owns thousands of acres of land out in the country, thinks King George a saint, ordained of God to rule us; that Sam Adams and Doctor Warren are tricksters fooling the people for their own benefit. But Mary is just the nicest girl you ever saw. She has no mother, runs the house for her father, keeps everything as neat as a pin, and by and by, after I get through at Harvard and am in possession of my sheepskin with A. B. on it, she will be Mrs. Tom Brandon."

Robert congratulated Tom upon his engagement.

The next morning saw Robert in the market disposing of what he had to sell, while Berinthia with Rachel called upon Miss Newville.

" It was very kind of you to send such a basket of fruit to me, a stranger; will you please accept a little gift in return? It is not much, but it will let you know that I appreciate your goodness," said Rachel, placing a bundle in Miss Newville's hands. When it was opened Ruth beheld a close-fitting hood of the softest lamb's wool, made beautiful with pink ribbons; there was also a pair of mittens.

" Oh, Miss Walden! How good you are! How soft and nice! And they are of your own carding, spinning, and knitting? And you have done it for me, whom you never had seen, and of whom you never heard except through your brother. And is he well? " Miss Newville asked.

" Quite well. You will see him to-morrow at the launching."

" Is n't it delightful that they have come in the nick of time? " said Berinthia.

" How fortunate! And you are to have such a nice party. I will wear the hood and be the envy of everybody," said Miss Newville, putting it on, praising its beauty, and calling in her mother to make Rachel's acquaintance and admire the gift.

The launching of the ship was to be at flood-tide, eleven o'clock in the forenoon. Though in midwinter, the air was mild, as if a warm breath had been wafted landward from the Gulf Stream. There was a fever of excitement and preparation in the Brandon home. Dinah in the kitchen was taking pots of baked beans and loaves of brown bread smoking hot from the oven, filling baskets with crumpets and crullers. Mark Antony was taking them to the shipyard. Mrs. Brandon, Berinthia, Rachel, and Mary Shrimpton were preparing the cakes and pies. Tom and Robert on board the ship were arranging for the collation.

Never before had Rachel beheld anything so enchanting as the scene in the shipyard, — the ship with

its tall and tapering masts, its spars and yardarms;
the multitudes of ropes like the threads of a spider's
web; flags, streamers, red, white, green, blue, yellow,
with devices of lions, unicorns, dragons, eagles, fluttering from bowsprit to fore-royal mast, from taffrail to
mizzen.   Beneath the bowsprit was the bust of Berinthia, the heart and soul of the man who carved it in
every feature, for to Abraham Duncan there was no
face on earth so beautiful as that of the shipmaster's
daughter.

The guests were assembling on the deck: the commissioner of imposts, Theodore Newville, Mrs. Newville, and their daughter, Ruth; his majesty's receiver-
general, Nathaniel Coffin, and his two sons, Isaac and
John; Reverend Doctor Samuel Cooper, minister of
the church in Brattle Street; Doctor Warren, physician
to the family of the shipmaster; Lieutenant-Colonel
Dalrymple, commanding the king's troops, — for Mr.
Brandon, though deprecating the presence of the
troops in Boston, determined to be courteous to the
representatives of his majesty; Admiral Montague,
who came in his gig rowed by six sailors from his flag-
ship, Romney; William Molineux [1] and John Rowe,
merchants; Richard Dana and Edmund Quincy, magistrates; John Adams, a young lawyer; honored citizens and their wives; Master Lovell; and Tom's classmate, Roger Stanley, who had walked from Lexington

[1] William Molineux was a prominent merchant who gave his sympathies to the cause of the people. He was one of the committee who
demanded the removal of the troops after the Massacre of March 5,
1770. He was one of the "Indians" composing the "Tea-party."
He was also one of the promoters of the spinning-school in Long
Acre. He died before the outbreak of hostilities.

in the early morning. Among the many ladies, most
attractive was Ruth Newville, wearing a close-fitting
hood of soft lamb's wool, trimmed with bright ribbon,
all her friends admiring it.

Berinthia introduced Rachel and Robert to Mrs.
Adams. They found her a very charming lady; she
had brought her little boy, John Quincy, to see the
launching of the ship.

Picturesque the scene: gentlemen wearing white
wigs, blue, crimson, and scarlet cloaks, carrying gold-
headed canes, taking pinches of snuff from silver-
mounted boxes; young gentlemen with handsome
figures and manly faces; ladies with tippets and
muffs; girls in hoods, — all congratulating Berinthia,
admiring the beauty and tidiness of the ship, and the
lovely figure of herself. All praised Abraham Duncan, who blushed like a schoolboy.

They could hear the clattering of mallets and axes
beneath them, and knew the carpenters were knocking
away the props. The ways had been slushed with
grease. The tide was at the flood. Ruth Newville
was to break the bottle of wine. She had shaken
hands with Robert Walden, and given expression of her
pleasure at meeting him once more. Her eyes had
followed him; even when not looking towards him she
had seen him. Once more she thanked Rachel for
her gift. Her mates were asking her where she had
found a hood so beautiful and becoming. They stood
upon the quarter-deck, Berinthia the queen of the hour,
Ruth, radiant and lovely, by her side. They heard the
bell striking the hour of eleven. A great crowd had
assembled to see the launching. Men, women, boys,

and girls were in the yard, flocking the street, gazing from doors and windows of neighboring houses.

" Are you ready there?"

Launching the Ship.

It was the builder of the ship, Mr. Brandon, shouting over the taffrail to those beneath.

" Aye, aye, sir."

" Then knock it away."

They heard a blow from an axe. The stately ship quivered a moment, then glided with increasing speed down the ways.

Mr. Brandon raised his hand, and a ball of bunting at the topmast fluttered out into the Cross of St. George. Ruth lifted the bottle of wine, broke it upon the rail, and poured the contents into the river. A huzza rose from the quarter-deck. Handkerchiefs fluttered in the air. The people tossed up their hats. From street, doorway, and window came an answering shout.

Out from the shore drifted the Berinthia till the anchor dropped from her bow, and she lay a thing of beauty, swinging with the ebbing tide.

In the cabin the guests were partaking of the bountiful and appetizing repast.

"I remember, Miss Newville, that you once graciously served me at an afternoon tea; shall I have the pleasure of waiting upon you?" Robert asked.

"I shall be pleased to be served by you. The fresh air has sharpened my appetite, and I will begin with a plate of beans, if you please."

He brought what she desired, served himself, and took a chair by her side. They talked of the successful launching, of the beauty of the ship, sitting as gracefully as a swan upon the water, of the almost perfect likeness of the figurehead to Berinthia.

"Possibly it is so beautiful because the engraver's heart has gone into it," she said with a smile.

Their eyes met. He thought hers very beautiful at the moment.

Roger Stanley found equal pleasure in serving

Rachel, and in listening to what she had to say about
the launching, her visit to Boston, and of things in
Rumford.

Robert talked with Isaac Coffin, who said he expected to have a commission in his majesty's navy.
Admiral Montague was very kind, and was using his
influence to secure an appointment.   His younger
brother, John, liked the army better.   Robert came
to the conclusion that they were not Sons of Liberty,
but were inclined to take sides with the ministry,
which was very natural, as their father was holding a
very important office under the crown.

There was a merry chattering of voices, a rattling
of knives and forks, and changing of plates.   Mark
Antony was master of ceremonies at the table, giving
directions to Cæsar and Pompey.

Although society was divided politically, neighbors
still were friends, accepting and giving hospitality, and
when meeting socially avoiding all allusion to the
proposed bill for taxing the Colonies.   All hoped that
nothing would be done by Parliament to interrupt
friendly relations between the Colonies and the mother country.   Doctor Warren made himself agreeable to bluff Admiral Montague.   William Molineux
cracked jokes with Colonel Dalrymple.   Richard Dana
and Nathaniel Coffin were friendly neighbors.   Mr.
Dana could look out from his front windows near
Frog Lane,[1] and see the spacious grounds of his
neighbor Coffin's "Fields," as the boys who played

[1] Frog Lane extended from Newbury, now Washington Street, to
the Common. It is now a part of Boylston Street. Mr. Dana's house
commanded an extensive view across the fields, gardens, and orchards
owned by Nathaniel Coffin, south of the present Summer Street.

ball called it. There was no reason why they should be at odds socially, just because Lord North and the king proposed to levy a tax of three pence a pound on tea.

With story and jest the company enjoyed the banquet and then were rowed to the shore, all shaking hands with Berinthia and congratulating her upon the successful launching of the vessel bearing her name.

"What can we do to round out the day for you, dear?"

It was Miss Newville addressing Berinthia.

"I don't know; what can we?" was the reply.

"How would you like a sleigh-ride?" Robert asked.

"Delightful!" exclaimed Miss Newville.

"Jenny and the colt are rested, and if you don't mind riding in a pung, I shall be pleased to take a little spin out of town."

"Oh, it will be so charming! I would rather go in a pung than in a sleigh; it is more romantic," Miss Newville said.

It was quickly arranged. Robert went to the Green Dragon, put new straw in the pung, and was soon back with the team. They were eight in number and quickly seated themselves. It was natural that Berinthia and Abraham Duncan, who had put his heart into his work while carving her features, should sit side by side, and that Tom Brandon and Mary Shrimpton should desire to be tucked under the same bearskin. It was a pleasure to Roger Stanley to ask Miss Walden to keep him company.

"They have decided, Mr. Walden, that we shall sit together," Miss Newville said as she stepped into the pung.

" I shall regard it an honor to have your company,"
was the reply.

When all were ready, the horses set the sleigh-bells
jingling.   Farmers plodding home from the market
gave them the road, and smiled as they listened to the
merry laughter.   They went at a brisk trot over the
Neck leading to Roxbury, and turned to the left, taking the Dorchester road.   At times the horses came
to a walk, but at a chirrup from Robert quickened
their pace, the colt throwing snowballs into Miss
Newville's face.

" You must excuse him, Miss Newville ; he is young,
and has not learned to be polite," Robert said, apolo-
gizing for the animal.

They gained the highlands of Dorchester, from
whence they could overlook the harbor and its islands,
and see the lighthouse rising from its rocky founda-
tion, with the white surf breaking around it.   A ship
which had left Charles River with the ebbing tide
had reached Nantasket Roads, and was spreading its
sails for a voyage across the sea.

" So the Berinthia will soon be sailing," said Miss
Newville, " and we shall all want to keep track of her ;
and whenever we read of her coming and going we
shall all recall this delightful day, made so enjoyable
for us this morning by Berinthia and so charming this
afternoon by your kindness."

She turned her face towards Robert.   The afternoon sun was illumining her countenance.   He had
seen in Mr. Henchman's bookstall a beautiful picture
of a Madonna.   Mr. Knox told him it was a steel engraving from a picture painted by the great artist

Raphael, and Robert wondered if the countenance was any more lovely than that which looked up to him at the moment.

They were riding towards the Milton Hills. The woodman's axe had left untouched the oaks, elms, maples, and birches; they were leafless in midwinter, but the pines and hemlocks were green and beautiful upon its rocky sides. The purple sky, changing into gold along the western horizon, the white robe of winter upon hill and dale, the windows of farmhouses reflecting the setting sun, made the view and landscape of marvelous beauty. Descending the hill, they came to the winding Neponset River, and rode along its banks beneath overhanging elms. The bending limbs, though leafless, were beautiful in their outlines against the sky. Turning westward, they reached the great road leading from Boston to Providence.

"We might go to Dedham, but I think we had better turn back towards Roxbury, let the horses rest a bit at the Greyhound Tavern, and have supper,"[1] said Tom, who was well acquainted with the road.

The sun had gone down when they whirled up to the tavern, whose swinging sign was ornamented with a rude picture of a greyhound. A bright fire was blazing in the parlor. They laid aside their outer garments and warmed themselves by its ruddy glow. The keen, fresh air had sharpened their appetites for supper. Chloe and Samson, cook and table-waiter, served them with beefsteak hot from the gridiron,

---

[1] The Greyhound was a much frequented tavern in Roxbury, with the figure of a greyhound upon its sign. It was in this tavern that the repeal of the Stamp Act was celebrated, 1767. Convivial parties were courteously entertained by the accommodating landlord.

swimming in butter; potatoes roasted in the ashes; shortcake steaming hot from the Dutch oven.

"Shall I brew Bohea, Hyson, or Hyperion [1] tea," the landlady asked, beginning with Miss Newville and glancing at each in turn.

"I will take Hyperion," Miss Newville replied, with a tact and grace that made her dearer than ever to Berinthia, and to them all, knowing as they did that Bohea and Hyson were still served in her own home.

Supper over, they returned to the parlor, where the bright flame on the hearth was setting their shadows to dancing on the walls. The feet of Mary Shrimpton were keeping time to the ticking of the clock.

"Why can't we have a dance?" she asked.

"Why not?" all responded.

"I'll see if we can find Uncle Brutus," said Tom.

Uncle Brutus was the white-haired old negro who did chores about the tavern.

"Yes, massa, I can play a jig, quickstep, minuet, and reel. De ladies and genmen say I can play de fiddle right smart." Brutus responded, rolling his eyes and showing his well-preserved white teeth.

"If de ladies and genmen will wait a little till old Brutus can make himself 'spectable, he'll make de fiddle sing."

While the old negro was getting ready to entertain them with his violin, they proposed conundrums and riddles and narrated stories.

There came at length a gentle rap on the door, and Brutus, with high standing collar, wearing a cast-

---

[1] Strawberry and other domestic teas were called by the high-sounding name, Hyperion.

off coat given him by his master, his round-bowed spectacles on the tip of his nose, entered the room, bowing very low. He took his stand in one corner and tuned his violin. The chairs and light-stand were removed to the hall.

" De ladies and genmen will please choose pardners for de minuet," said Brutus.

The choosing had been already done; the partners were as they had been. After the minuet came the reel and quickstep, danced with grace and due decorum.

The hour quickly flew. The horses had finished their provender and were rested. Once more they were on the road, not riding directly homeward, but turning into cross-roads to Jamaica Pond, where the boys were gliding over the gleaming ice on their skates. They had kindled fires which lighted up the surrounding objects, the dark foliage of pines and hemlocks, and the branches of the leafless elms and maples growing on the banks of the pond.

The full moon was shining in their faces as they rode homeward. The evening air was crisp, but the hot supper and the merry dance had warmed their blood. The jingling of the sleigh-bells and their joyous laughter made the air resonant with music.

At times the horses lagged to a walk, and Robert could let the reins lie loose and turn his face toward Miss Newville. Her eyes at times looked up to his. He could feel her arm against his own. The violet hood leaned towards him as if to find a resting-place. To Robert Walden and to Ruth Newville alike never had there been such a night, so full of beauty, so delightful.

The horses came to a standstill at last by the entrance to the Newville mansion.

"This has been the most enjoyable day of my life," Miss Newville said, as Robert gave her his hand to assist her from the pung.

"Good-night, all. Thank you, Mr. Walden, for all your kindness," her parting words.

VIII.

CHRISTOPHER SNIDER.

THE night-watchman of the North End of Boston, with overcoat buttoned to the chin and a muffler around his neck, a fur cap drawn down over his ears to exclude the biting frost of midwinter, was going his rounds. He saw no revelers in the streets, nor belated visitors returning to their homes.

If suitors were calling upon their ladies, the visits were ended long before the clock on the Old Brick struck the midnight hour. No voice broke the stillness of the night. The watchman scarcely heard his own footsteps in the newly fallen snow as he slowly made his way along Middle Street,[1] with his lantern and staff. He was not expecting to encounter a burglar, breaking and entering a shop, store, or residence. He heard the clock strike once more, and was just pursing his lips to cry, " Two o'clock, and all 's well," when he caught a glimpse of a figure in front of Theophilus Lillie's store.[2] Was it a burglar? The man was standing stock-still, as if scanning the premises. The

---

[1] The section of the present Hanover Street east of Blackstone Street was called Middle Street.

[2] Mr. Theophilus Lillie was one of the six merchants who refused to sign the association paper not to import goods from England, thereby making himself exceedingly obnoxious to the people. Other merchants had agreed not to make any importation, and had violated the agreement.

watchman dodged back behind the building on the corner of the street, hid his lantern, and peered slyly at the thief, who was still looking at the store. What was the meaning of such mysterious inaction? The watchman, instead of waiting to catch the culprit in the act of breaking and entering, stepped softly forward. Grasping his staff with a firm grip, to give a sudden whack, should the villain turn upon him, — "What ye 'bout, sir!'" he shouted.

The burglar did not reply, neither turn his head.

"Is the fellow dead, I wonder — frozen stiff, this bitter night, and standing still?" the question that flashed through the watchman's brain.

"Bless my soul! It's Mr. Lillie's head, — his nose, mouth, chin. Looks just like him. And the post is set in the ground. I'll bet that carving is Abe Duncan's work. Nobody can carve like him. But what is it here for? Ah! I see. Lillie has gone back on his agreement not to import tea. The Sons of Liberty have rigged it up to guy him. Ha, ha!"

The watchman laughed to himself as he examined the figure.

"Well, that's a cute job," he said reflectively. "The ground is frozen stiff a foot deep. They had to break it with a crowbar, but not a sound did I hear. Shall I say anything about it? Will not the selectmen make a fuss if I don't notify 'em at once? But what's the use of knocking 'em up at two o'clock in the morning? The thing's done. 'T ain't my business to pull it up. The post won't run away. I'll report what time I found it."

Remembering that he had not cried the hour, he shouted : --

" Two o'clock, all 's well ! "

He secreted himself in a doorway awhile, to see if any one would appear, but no one came.

The early risers — the milkmen and bakers' apprentices going their rounds, shop boys on their way to kindle fires in · stores — all stopped to look at the figure. The news quickly spread. People left their breakfast-tables to see the joke played on Mr. Lillie. Ebenezer Richardson, however, could not see the fun of the thing. The schoolboys called him " Poke Nose " because he was ever ready to poke into other people's affairs.[1] The officers of the custom house employed him to ferret out goods smuggled ashore by merchants, who, regarding the laws as unjust and oppressive, had no scruples in circumventing the customs officers. Richardson hated the Sons of Liberty, and haunted the Green Dragon to spy out their actions.

" This is their work," he said to those around the figure. " It 's outrageous. Mr. Lillie has just as good a right to sell tea as anything else, without having everybody pointing their fingers at him. It 's an insult. It 's disgraceful. Whoever did it ought to be trounced."

" Charcoal ! Charcoal ! Hard and soft charcoal ! "

---

[1] The offensive and unjust laws and acts and ordinances of the Board of Trade in enforcing the collection of customs dues had brought about systematic effort to circumvent the custom-house officials, who employed spies and informers to ferret out fraudulent transactions. Smuggling was regarded as a virtue, and outwitting the officials a duty rather than an offense. Ebenezer Richardson, by his service to the custom-house officials, made himself obnoxious to the community. An account of the incidents that led to the shooting of Christopher Snider may be found in the newspapers of March, 1770.

It was the cry of the charcoal-man, turning from Union into Middle Street.

"I'll get him to run his sled against it and knock it over," said Mr. Richardson to himself.

Slowly the charcoal vender advanced.

Seeing the post and the group of people around it, he reined in his old horse and looked at the figure.

"See here," said Mr. Richardson. "Just gee a little and run the nose of your sled agin it and knock it over, will ye? It's a tarnal fiendish outrage to set up such a thing in front of a gentleman's store."

"Do you own the figger?"

"No."

"Do you own the store?"

"No."

"Anybody ax ye to get it knocked down?"

"No; but it's an outrage which honest citizens ought to resent."

"Think so, do ye?"

"Yes, I do; and everybody else ought to, instead of laughing and chuckling over it."

"That may be, mister, but ye see you don't own it, and may be I'd get myself into trouble if I were to run my sled agin it purposely. Should like to oblege ye, neighbor, but guess I'd better not. Charcoal! Charcoal! Hard and soft charcoal!" he shouted, jerking the reins for the old horse to move on.

"Gee, Buck! Haw, Barry!"

It was a farmer driving his oxen drawing a load of wood, swinging his goad-stick, who shouted it. The team came to a standstill by the figure.

" What's up? " the farmer inquired.

" The Sons of Liberty have perpetrated a rascally trick, by setting this effigy in front of this gentleman's store," said Mr. Richardson.

" What'd they do that for? "

" 'Cause he agreed not to sell tea, and then, finding he'd made a bad bargain, backed out of it; and now I'd like to have ye hitch yer oxen to the thing and snake it to Jericho."

" 'Fraid I can't 'commodate ye; got to go down to widow Jenkins's with my wood. Gee, Buck! Haw, Barry! " said the farmer, as he started on.

" Rich, why don't ye pull it up yourself," said an apprentice.

" Better get an axe and chop it down, if it's such an eyesore to ye," said another.

" Get a crowbar and dig it up. A little exercise will be good for ye," said a third.

" Has Lillie engaged ye to get rid of the thing? " another asked.

" Did the Sons of Liberty smuggle it ashore during the night? "

Tom Brandon asked the question, which nettled Mr. Richardson exceedingly. Possibly the informer could not have said why he was so zealous for the removal of the effigy. He would not have been willing to admit that he was seeking to advance himself in the estimation of Hon. Theodore Newville, commissioner of imposts, and Hon. Nathaniel Coffin, his majesty's receiver-general. Quite likely he could not have given any very satisfactory reason for his activity in attempting to remove the figure. He knew that the selectmen would be obliged to clear the street of the obstruction, but a display of loyalty to the king might possibly inure to his benefit. Boys on their way to school began to chaff the informer.

"Say, Poke Nose; how much are ye going to get for the job?" shouted one of the boys.

"You mind your own business."

"That's what you don't do."

"Don't ye call me names, you little imp," shouted the informer, shaking his fist at the boy.

"Poke Nose! Poke Nose! Poke Nose!" the chorus of voices.

"Take that, Poke Nose!" said a boy as he threw a snowball.

Losing his temper, the informer threw a brickbat in return. He was but one against fifty lads pelting him with snowballs, which knocked off his hat, struck him in the face, compelling him to flee, the jeering boys following him to his own home.

Tom Brandon accompanied the boys. He saw the informer raise a window. There was a flash, a puff of smoke, the report of a gun, a shriek, and two of the boys were lying upon the ground and their blood spurting upon the snow. He helped carry them into a house, and then ran for Doctor Warren. It was but a few steps. The doctor came in haste.

"Samuel Gore is not much injured, but Christopher Snider is mortally wounded," he said.

Christ Church bells were ringing. Merchants were closing their stores: blacksmiths leaving their forges; carpenters throwing down their tools, — everybody hastening with buckets and ladders to put out the fire, finding instead the blood-stained snow and wounded schoolboys.

" Hang him ! Hang him ! " shouted the apprentices and journeymen. But the sheriff had the culprit in his keeping, and the law in its majesty was guarding him from the violence of the angered people.

" Christopher Snider is dead," said Doctor Warren, as he came from the house into which the boy had been carried by Tom Brandon and those who assisted him.

Thenceforth the widow's home in Frog Lane would be desolate, for an only child was gone.

An exasperated multitude, among others Tom Brandon and Robert Walden, gathered in Faneuil Hall, Tom as witness, attending the examination of Ebenezer Richardson,[1] charged with the murder of Christopher Snider. Upon the platform sat the justices, John Ruddock, Edmund Quincy, Richard Dana, and Samuel Pemberton, wearing their scarlet cloaks and white wigs. There was a murmuring of voices.

" I hope the spy will swing for it," Robert heard one citizen say.

" It's downright murder, this shooting of a boy only nine years old, who hadn't even been teasing Poke Nose," said another.

" This is what comes from customs nabobs trying to enforce wicked laws," said an old man.

---

[1] John Ruddock, Edmund Quincy, Richard Dana, and Samuel Pemberton were the principal magistrates of the town, and unitedly sat as a court. Richardson was committed to jail, tried, and condemned to death. As his crime grew from political troubles, Governor Hutchinson caused his execution to be delayed. He was kept in jail till the outbreak of the war, when he was set at liberty.

" Yes, and keeps two regiments of lobsters here to insult us."

" That's so," responded Peter Bushwick, whom Robert recognized. " If the laws were just the people wouldn't smuggle. If there was no smuggling there wouldn't be any spies, and Ebe Richardson, instead of being a sneaking informer, would have been earning an honest living. He wouldn't have been called Poke Nose; there wouldn't have been any snowballs nor brickbats nor shooting. Ever since I was a little boy Parliament has been passing laws to cripple us; that's what's brought on smuggling; that's what keeps the troops here. Ebe Richardson is part of the system."

There was a louder buzzing as the sheriff entered the hall and made his way through the crowd with his prisoner, who stood pale and trembling before the justices while the indictment was read. Witnesses were sworn and examined, and the sheriff ordered to commit the accused to the jail for trial.

" No other incident," said Mr. John Adams, " has so stirred the people as the shooting of this boy. Nothing has so brought to the consciousness of the community the meaning of the ministerial system. Instinctively they connect the death of Christopher with the attempt to enforce the unrighteous laws. Richardson is in the employ of the government. There is no evidence that Theodore Newville or Nathaniel Coffin or any of the officers of the customs engaged him to remove the effigy: he did it on his own account, and must suffer for it, but the obloquy falls, nevertheless, upon the officers of the crown, and especially upon the soldiers, who are a constant menace. I fear this is but the beginning of trouble."

Tom had been called upon to testify as a witness in regard to the shooting. He had heard the informer ask the peddler of charcoal and the farmer to run against the effigy with their teams; had seen the snowballs and brickbat fly, the shooting, and had assisted in caring for the wounded and summoning Doctor Warren.

"Have you any idea, Tom, who placed the effigy there?" Mrs. Brandon asked.

"I might have an idea, which might be correct or which might not be. A supposition isn't testimony. I don't think I'll say anything about it," said Tom.

"Can you guess who carved it?" Berinthia asked earnestly.

"Anybody can guess, Brinth, but the guess might not be worth anything; I'll not try."

"You Sons of Liberty don't let out your secrets," Berinthia said.

"If we did they wouldn't be secrets."

Never had there been such a funeral in the town as that of Christopher Snider. The schools were closed that the scholars might march in procession. Merchants put up the shutters of their stores; joiners, carpenters, ropemakers, blacksmiths, all trades and occupations laid down their tools and made their way to the Liberty-Tree, where the procession was to form. Mothers flocked to the little cottage in Frog Lane to weep with a mother bereft of her only child. Tom Brandon and five other young men were to carry the bier. The newspaper published by Benjamin Edes expressed the hope that none but friends of freedom would join in the procession.

Robert made his way to the Liberty Tree at the hour appointed. A great crowd had assembled. Somebody had nailed a board to the tree, upon which were painted texts from the Bible: —

" *Thou shalt take no satisfaction for the life of a murderer. He shall surely be put to death.*"

" *Though hand join in hand, the wicked shall not pass unpunished.*"   :

The clock was striking three when the bearers brought the coffin from the home of the mother in Frog Lane to the Liberty Tree. While the procession was forming Robert had an opportunity to look at the inscriptions upon the black velvet pall. They were in Latin, but a gentleman with a kindly face, Master Lovell, translated them to the people.

> " *Latet Anguis in Herba.*"
> " *Hæret Lateris lethalis Armada.*"
> " *Innocentia nusquam in tuta.*"

> The serpent is lurking in the grass.
> The fatal dart is thrown.
> Innocence is nowhere safe.

All the bells were tolling. Mothers and maidens along the street were weeping for the mother following the body of her boy. Old men uncovered their heads, and bared their snow-white locks to the wintry air, as the pall-bearers with slow and measured steps moved past them. Schoolboys, more than six hundred, two by two, hand in hand; apprentices, journeymen, citizens, three thousand in number; magistrates, ministers, merchants, lawyers, physicians in chaises and carriages, — composed the throng bearing the murdered boy to his burial.

Listen, my Lord Frederick North, to the mournful pealing of the bells of Boston! Listen, King George, to the tramping of the schoolmates of Christopher Snider, laying aside their books for the day to bear witness against your royal policy, — boys now, men ere long, — protesting with tears to-day, with muskets by and by! Listen, ye men who have purchased seats in parliament to satisfy your greed!

Lord North.

The assembled multitude, the tolling bells, the tramping feet, the emblems of mourning, are the indignant protest of an outraged community against tyranny and oppression, — the enforcement of law by the show of force, — by musket, sword, and bayonet. Listen, and take warning.[1]

[1] Historians have made little account of the shooting of Christopher Snider, but there can be no question that it led directly to the collision between the ropemakers and soldiers one week later, resulting in the Massacre of March 5, 1770.

IX.

THE LOBSTERS AND ROPEMAKERS.

ALTHOUGH March had come, the snow was still deep upon the ground. Robert and Rachel could prolong their stay in Boston and enjoy the hospitality of their friends. It was Monday evening the 5th of the month. Berinthia had invited Ruth Newville to tea.

"The soldiers and the ropemakers are at loggerheads," said Tom, as he came in and laid aside his coat.

"What is the trouble?" Robert asked.

"It seems that a negro hemp-stretcher, down in Gray's ropewalk,[1] last Friday asked a soldier if he wanted to work, and the red-coat replied he did. What the ropemaker told him to do wasn't very nice, and they had a set-to. The soldier got the worst of it, and swore vengeance. The redcoat went to the barracks, but was soon back again with eight others, armed with clubs, swearing they'd split the skulls of

---

[1] Edward Gray, in 1712, purchased a large tract of land on the westerly side of Hutchinson's Lane, now Pearl Street, and erected a ropewalk seven hundred and forty feet long. The large number of ships built in Boston and other New England towns made it a lucrative occupation. His son, Harrison Gray, was appointed treasurer of the Province. He was a loyalist, and took his departure from Boston upon its evacuation by the British. His property was confiscated to the state. He proceeded from Halifax to London, where he gave generous hospitality to his fellow exiles in that city.

the beggars. The ropemakers seized their woolding-sticks, and they had it hot and heavy, but the lobsters got a licking. You 'd better believe there was a buzzing in the barracks. Pretty soon between thirty and forty of the hirelings, armed with bayonets, clubs, and cutlasses, rushed down to the ropewalk. The ropemakers rallied, but all told they were only fourteen. They showed what stuff they were made of, though, and proved themselves the better men. They whacked the lobsters' skulls and drove them."

" Good for the ropemakers," said Berinthia, clapping her hands.

Robert saw a lighting up of Miss Newville's eyes, but no word fell from her lips.

" I fear," said Mr. Brandon, " there will be an outbreak between the soldiers and the people. Since the funeral of Snider, the soldiers have been growing more insolent. The long stay of the troops with nothing to do except the daily drill and parade, and drinking toddy, has demoralized them. The under-officers are but little better than the men, spending most of their time in the taverns playing cards. Discipline is lax. I shall not be surprised at whatever may happen."

Miss Newville and Robert sat down to a game of checkers. He debated with himself whether or not he would let her win the first game. Would it be gentlemanly to defeat her? Ought he not to allow her to win? But almost before he was aware of what had happened she was victor, and he was making apology for playing so badly. Again the men were set, and again, although he did his best to win, his men were swept from the board.

"I see I'm no match for you," he said.

"I am not so sure about that. I saw your mistake. You would soon learn to correct it," she said with a smile.

Although yet early in the evening, Miss Newville said she must be going home, as her parents might be concerned for her.

"I trust the soldiers will not molest you," said Mrs. Brandon, bidding Miss Newville farewell.

"I am sure I shall be safe with Mr. Walden," she replied. There was a meaning in her eyes which he alone understood, the silent reference to their first meeting.

The moon was at its full, its silver light gleaming upon the untrodden snow. There was no need for them to hasten their steps when the night was so lovely.

"Oh, look, Mr. Walden! see Christ Church!" Miss Newville exclaimed. "Tower, belfry, turret, and steeple are glazed with frozen sea-mist and driven snow."

The church loomed before them in the refulgent light, a mass of shining silver. Above all was the tapering spire and golden vane.

"It is the poetry of nature. Such beauty thrills me. I feel, but cannot express, my pleasure," she said.

"It is indeed very beautiful," he replied. "The snow, the silver, gold, light and shade, the steeple tapering to a point, make it a wonderful picture. Would that you could see on such a night as this the view from my own home, — upland and valley, meadow and forest, walls and fences, leafless oaks, elms, and maples in fields and pastures, pure white and shining like polished silver in the moonlight, and all the twigs and branches glittering with diamonds. On such nights, when the crust is hard and firm, we boys and girls pile ourselves on a sled and go like the wind from the top of the hill in the pasture down to the meadow, across the intervale, over the river bank, and out upon the gleaming ice. We wake the echoes with our laughter and have a jolly time."

"Oh, how I should enjoy it," she said.

Suddenly they heard other voices, and as they turned the corner of the street came upon a group of men and boys armed with cudgels.

"We'll give it to the lobsters," they heard one say.

"I fear there may be trouble," Robert remarked, recalling the conversation at the supper-table.

Passing the home of Doctor Warren, they saw a light burning in his office, and by the shadow on the window curtain knew he was seated at his writing-desk. Turning from Hanover towards Queen Street, they found several soldiers in earnest conversation blocking the way.

"I'd like to split the heads of the blackguards," said one, flourishing a cutlass.

"Will you please allow me to pass?" said Robert.

"When you take off your hat to us," the answer.

"This is the king's highway," said Robert.

He felt Miss Newville's arm clinging more firmly to his own.

"You can pass if your wench gives me a kiss," said the soldier with the cutlass.

Swiftly Robert's right arm and clenched fist sent the fellow headlong into the snow. He faced the others a moment, and then with Miss Newville walked leisurely away. He could feel her heart palpitating against his arm. He cast a glance behind, but the redcoats were not following him.

"It seems we are fated to meet ill-bred men," he said.

"Oh, Mr. Walden, how resolute and brave you are!"

"It is not difficult to be courageous when you know you are right."

"But they are so many."

"We are more than they," he replied, smiling.

"More than they! We are only two."

"He who is in the right has all of God's host with him. They knew they were in the wrong; that made them cowards."

Again he felt the warmth and pressure of her arm, as if she would say, "I know I shall be safe with you to protect me."

They were passing King's Chapel. Its gray walls never had seemed so picturesque as on that evening with the moon casting the shadows of pillar, cornice, roof, and tower upon the pure white snow that had fallen through the day. Beyond it were the young elms of Long Acre, twig and limb a mass of glittering diamonds. They stood at last beneath the portico of her home.

"I have been thinking," she said, "of the strange happenings that have come to us — how you have been my protector from insult. I cannot express my gratitude, Mr. Walden."

"Please do not mention it, Miss Newville. I

should indeed be a poltroon did I not resent an indignity to a lady, especially to you. I esteem it an honor to have made your acquaintance. May I say I cannot find words to express the pleasure I have had in your society? I do not know that I shall see you again before we start on our homeward journey."

"Must you go? Can you not prolong your stay?"

"We have already overstayed our time; but not to

King's Chapel, 1895.

our regret. I never shall forget, Miss Newville, these days and evenings which you, with Berinthia, Tom, Miss Shrimpton, and Roger Stanley have made so enjoyable."

"I trust we shall not be like ships that signal each other in mid-ocean, then sail away never to meet again," she replied.

She reached out her hand to bid him farewell. It rested willingly in his.

"I hope," she said. "I never shall be so ungrateful

as to forget what you have done for me. I certainly shall not forget the lesson you have taught me — to stand resolutely for the right. I shall always be pleased to see you."

"You may be sure, Miss Newville, I never shall fail to pay my respects to one whose very presence makes life more beautiful and worth the living."

The full moon was falling upon her face. Her eyes seemed to be looking far away. He saw for a moment a shade of sadness upon her countenance, succeeded by a smile. Her hand was still resting in his.

"Good-by till we meet again," her parting words.

Never before had he felt such an uplifting of spirit. "Till we meet again" would ever be like a strain of music. He lingered awhile, loath to leave the spot. A light was soon shining in her chamber. The curtains revealed her shadow. It was something to know she was there. Would she think of him when lying down to sleep? When would he again behold those loving eyes, that radiant face, that beauty of soul seen in every feature? What had the future in store for them? Ah! what had it? The light in the chamber was extinguished, and he turned away. Once more he lingered by the gray walls of King's Chapel to take a parting look at the white-curtained window, and then walked to Queen Street, past the jail and printing office. It would be a pleasure to stand once more upon the spot where first he met her.

He heard a commotion in the direction of Dock Square. — oaths and curses; and suddenly beheld citizens running, followed by soldiers, whose swords were flashing in the moonlight. They followed the fleeing people nearly to the town pump, then turned and disappeared in an alley.

"What has happened?" Robert asked of a man who had a pail of oysters in his hand.

"What? Just see what I've got from the hellish rascals," the man replied, setting down the pail and pointing to a gash on his shoulder. "The red-coated devils are cutting and slashing everybody. They are ripping and swearing they'll kill every blasted Son of Liberty."

While the oysterman was speaking, a little boy came along, piteously crying.

"What's the matter, my boy?" Robert asked.

Amid his sobs it was learned that the boy's father sent him on an errand; that while peacefully walking the street, a soldier rushed upon him swearing, aiming a blow, felling him to the ground with his sword.

"I'll kill every Yankee whelp in Boston," said the redcoat.

Again there was a commotion — soldiers rushing towards Dock Square.

"Where are the blackguards? let's kill 'em," they shouted.

"Come on, you dirty cowards; we are ready for ye," the answering shout.

Robert could hear oaths and vile words, and then the whacking of clubs, and saw the soldiers fleeing towards their barracks followed by the people. A man with a stout club came along the street.

"What's going on?" Robert asked.

"We are giving it to the poltroons. We'll drive 'em off Long Wharf. They rushed out upon us just now, with shovels, tongs, swords, and baggernets, and called us cowards. We whacked 'em with our clubs and drove the ruffians — blast their picters."

The commotion was increasing. Robert walked towards the barracks to learn the meaning of it. Reaching an alley, he saw a crowd of soldiers, and that the officers were trying to get them within the barrack gates. Towards Dock Square was a group of young men flourishing cudgels, and daring the lobsters to come on.

" Let 's set the bell ringing," he heard one say, and two apprentices rushed past him towards the meetinghouse.

The officers, the while, were closing the barrack gates.

" To the main guard! Let us clean out that viper's nest," shouted one; and the apprentices moved towards King Street.

The bell was ringing. Robert walked back to the pump, and past it to the meetinghouse. Citizens were coming with fire-buckets. He could see by the clock above him that it was ten minutes past nine. Mr. Knox, the bookseller, came, out of breath with running.

" It is not a fire, but there is trouble with the soldiers," said Robert.

Together they walked down King Street, and saw the sentinel at the Custom House loading his gun. Robert learned that a boy had hurled a snowball at him.

" Stand back, or I 'll shoot," said the soldier to those gathering round him.

" If you fire, you 'll die for it," said Mr. Knox.

" I don't care if I do," the sentinel replied with an oath.

" You dare n't fire," shouted a boy.

The redcoat raised his gun, and pulled the trigger. The lock clicked, but the powder did not flash.

" Spit in the pan ! " said another boy, chaffing him.

" Guard ! Guard ! " shouted the sentinel, calling the main guard.

Captain Preston, with a file of men, came from the guardhouse upon the run, in response to the call. The meetinghouse bell was still ringing, and other bells began to clang. The soldiers, nine in number, formed in front of the Custom House with their bayonets fixed, and brought their guns to a level as if to fire. Robert thought there were thirty or more young men and boys in the street. Among them was a burly negro leaning on a stick, and looking at the soldiers. The others called him Crisp.

" Are your guns loaded ? " asked a man of Captain Preston, commanding the soldiers.

" Yes."

" Are they going to fire? "

" They can't without my orders."

" For God's sake, captain, take your men back again, for if you fire your life must answer for it," said Mr. Knox, seizing the captain by the coat.

" I know what I 'm about," Captain Preston replied.

The bayonets of the soldiers almost touched the breasts of Crispus Attucks and Samuel Gray. The negro was still leaning upon his cudgel, and Gray stood proudly before them with folded arms, a free citizen, in the dignity of his manhood protesting against the system of government instituted by King George and his ministry.

" You don't dare to fire," he said.

Why should they fire? The jeering apprentices before them had no guns, only sticks and clubs; they were not fifty in number. What had they done? Thrown a snowball at the sentinel; called him names; pointed their fingers at him; dared him to fire. It was not this, however, which had brought the guns to a level; but the drubbing, the rope-makers had given them, and the funeral of Christopher Snider. These were not the beginning of the trouble, but rather the arrogance, greed, selfishness, and intolerance of the repressive measures of a bigot king, a servile ministry, and a venial Parliament.

Robert heard the clicking of gun-locks. He did not hear any order from Captain Preston, but a gun flashed, and then the entire file fired. He saw the negro, Samuel Gray, and several others reel to the ground, their warm blood spurting upon the newly fallen snow. There was a shriek from the fleeing apprentices. Robert, Mr. Knox, and several others ran to those who had been shot, lifted them tenderly, and carried them into a house. Doctor Warren, hearing the volley, came running to learn the meaning of it. He examined the wounded. "Crispus Attucks has been struck by two balls; either would have been fatal. He died instantly," the doctor said.

By the side of the negro lay Samuel Gray, who had stood so calmly with folded arms, the bayonets within a foot of his heart. In the bloom of youth,

Samuel Maverick, seventeen years old, who had come to find the fire, was lying upon the ground, his heart's blood oozing upon the snow. Patrick Carr and Samuel Caldwell, who also had come to put out a fire, were dying, and six others were wounded. The soldiers were reloading their guns, preparing for another volley. Robert heard the rat-a-tat of a drum, and saw the Twenty-Ninth Regiment march into the street from Pudding Lane, the front rank kneeling, the rear rank standing, with guns loaded, bayonets fixed, and ready to fire.

"To arms! To arms!"

He could hear the cry along Cornhill, and down in Dock Square. All the meetinghouse bells were clanging and people were gathering with guns, swords, clubs, shovels, crowbars, and pitchforks.

. Lieutenant-Governor Hutchinson came.[1]

[1] Thomas Hutchinson was a native of Boston. He graduated from Harvard College, 1727. He became a merchant, but was unsuccessful; studied law and opened an office in Boston. He was sent to London by the town as its agent, and upon his return was elected to the legislature several years in succession. He held the office of judge of probate, and was a councilor from 1749 to 1766, a lieutenant-governor from 1758 to 1771. He was also appointed chief justice, 1758. At the time this story opens he was holding four high offices under the crown. Upon the departure of Governor Francis Bernard for England in the autumn of 1769, Hutchinson became acting governor. He was commissioned as governor, 1771. In May, 1770, he issued his proclamation for the legislature to meet in Cambridge; but that body insisted that the terms of the charter required the General Court to assemble in Boston. A sharp and bitter controversy followed. Doctor Franklin was appointed agent of the Province to look after its welfare before Parliament. In 1773 he came into possession of a large number of letters written by Hutchinson to Mr. Whately, one of the under-secretaries, advising the ministry to take coercive measures with Massachusetts. Franklin sent the letters to Thomas Cushing, speaker of the House of Representatives. Their publication aroused

" Are you the officer who was in command of the troops ? " he asked, addressing Captain Preston.

" Yes, sir."

" Do you know you have no power to fire upon the people except by order of a magistrate ? "

" I was obliged to fire to save the sentry."

" That's a lie," shouted the crowd.

The surging multitude compelled the lieutenant-governor to enter the Town House.   A few moments later he appeared upon the balcony overlooking King Street.

" I am greatly grieved," he said, " at what has happened.   I pledge you my honor that this unhappy occurrence shall be inquired into.   The law shall have its course.   Now, fellow-citizens, let me urge you to retire to your homes."

" No, no!   Send the troops to their barracks. We won't go till they are gone ! " the shout from the people.

" I have no power to order them."

<hr/>

the indignation of the people. which was increased by the action of Hutchinson in connection with the arrival of the tea-ships. He became very unpopular and sailed for England, June 3, 1774. So eager was the king to see him that he was summoned into his royal presence before he had time to change his clothing. He assured King George that the bill closing the port of Boston to commerce was a wise and beneficent measure. and would compel the people to submit to royal authority. The conversation lasted two hours. Upon its conclusion the king expressed his great pleasure for the information and comfort Hutchinson had given him. He was created a baronet. and was consulted by Lord North and the other members of the ministry. That his opinions had great weight with the king and his ministers, and that he was largely instrumental in bringing about the Revolutionary War, cannot be questioned. He died at Brompton, near London, June 3. 1780.

The Town House.

" The troops to their barracks! to their barracks! "

" I cannot do it; I have no authority."

" Arrest Preston! Hang the villains! To the barracks! " shouted the angry multitude.

" I will consult with the officers," said Hutchinson.

He went into the council chamber. Louder the outcry of the indignant people. The troops were as they had been, drawn up in two lines, the front rank kneeling, ready to fire upon the gathering multitude. Robert felt that it was a critical moment. If the troops were to fire into the surging throng, the gutters would run with blood.

" The troops to their barracks!   Away with them!"
the cry.

" I will order them to their barracks," said Colonel
Dalrymple, who recognized the danger of the moment.

Robert breathed more freely when the front rank
rose, and the troops filed once more through Pudding
Lane to their quarters.

Tom Brandon had come with his gun ready to
fight.   A great crowd gathered around the Town
House where the governor was holding a court of
inquiry.   Robert and Tom edged themselves into the
room, and heard what was said and saw what was
going on.   It was nearly three o'clock in the morning when the magistrates directed the sheriff to put
Captain Preston and the soldiers who had fired the
volley in jail.   It was a great satisfaction to Robert
and Tom to go up Queen Street and see the redcoats
enter the jail and hear the key click in the lock behind
them.   Civil law was still supreme.

The night was far gone when Robert reached the
Brandon home.   Although retiring to his chamber, he
could not compose himself to sleep.   He was looking
into the future, wondering what would be the outcome
of the massacre.

Long before the rising of the sun the following
morning, the streets were swarming with people, hastening in from the country, with muskets on their
shoulders, with indignation and fierce determination
manifest in every feature, assembling in Faneuil Hall;
but only a few of the multitude could get into the
building.

" The Old South! Old South!" cried the people,

and the crowd surged through Dock Square and along
Cornhill to the Old South Meetinghouse. Samuel
Adams, John Hancock, Joseph Warren, and others
were chosen a committee to wait on the governor in
the council chamber.

" The inhabitants and soldiery can no longer live
together in safety; nothing can restore peace and prevent further carnage but the immediate removal of
the troops," said Mr. Adams, speaking for the committee.

Colonel Dalrymple informed Governor Hutchinson
that, as the Twenty-Ninth Regiment had done the
mischief, he was willing it should be sent down the
harbor to Fort William, and he would direct its
removal.

" The people," said Mr. Adams, " not only of this
town, but of all the surrounding towns, are determined
that all the troops shall be removed."

" To attack the king's troops would be high treason,
and every man concerned would forfeit his life and
estate," said Hutchinson.

" The people demand their immediate withdrawal,"
Mr. Adams replied, bowing, and taking his departure.

Cornhill, all the way from the Town House to the
Old South, was crowded with resolute and determined
citizens, equipped with muskets and powder-horns.
They saw Samuel Adams, loved and revered, descend
the steps of the Town House, followed by the other
members of the committee.

" Make way for the committee! " the cry.

" Hurrah for Sam Adams! " the shout.

They saw the man they loved lift his hat. They

knew King George wanted him sent to England to be tried for treason; that Lieutenant-Governor Hutchinson was ready to aid in such a plan; but there he was, more determined than ever to maintain the rights of the people.

Tom worked his way into the meetinghouse and heard Mr. Adams say the lieutenant-governor's answer was unsatisfactory.

"All the troops must go," shouted the citizens.

Once more Mr. Adams and six of his fellow-citizens made their way to the Town House. The lieutenant-governor and the council were assembled together with Colonel Dalrymple, Admiral Montague, and other officers in their scarlet uniforms. Robert edged his way into the building.

"It is the unanimous opinion," said Mr. Adams, "that the reply of your excellency is unsatisfactory. Nothing will satisfy the people other than the immediate removal of all the troops."

"The troops are not subject to my authority; I have no power to remove them," said Hutchinson.

Robert saw Mr. Adams raise his right arm towards Hutchinson. His words were clear and distinct: —

"Lieutenant-Governor Hutchinson, if you have power to remove one regiment, you have power to remove both. It is at your peril if you do not. The meeting is composed of three thousand people. They are impatient. One thousand men have arrived from the surrounding towns. The country is in motion. The people expect an immediate answer."

A whiteness came into the face of the lieutenant-governor. His hands began to tremble. One hundred years before, the people in their majesty and might had put Edmund Andros in prison. Might they not do the same with him?

"What shall be done?" he asked of the council, with trembling lips.

"It is not such people as injured your house who are asking you to remove the troops," said Councilman Tyler; "they are the best people of the town, men of property, supporters of religion. It is impossible, your excellency, for the troops to remain. If they do not go, ten thousand armed men will soon be here."

"Men will soon be here from Essex and Middlesex," said Councilman Bussell of Charlestown.

"Yes, and from Worcester and Connecticut," said Mr. Dexter of Dedham.

Every member said the same, and advised their removal. Colonel Dalrymple had consented that the regiment which began the disturbance should leave, but it would be very humiliating if all the troops were to go. The instructions from the king had put the military as superior to the civil authority.

"I cannot consent, your excellency, voluntarily to remove all the troops," said Dalrymple.

"You have asked the advice of the council," said Councilman Gray to Hutchinson; "it has been given; you are bound to conform to it."

Robert felt it was a home-thrust that Councilman Gray gave, who said further: —

"If mischief shall come, your excellency, by means of your not doing what the council has advised, you alone must bear the blame. If the commanding officer after that should refuse to remove the troops, the blame then will be at his door!"

"I will do what the council has advised," said Hutchinson.

"I shall obey the command of your excellency," said Dalrymple.

The victory was won. "The lobsters have got to go," the shout that went up in the Old South, when Mr. Adams informed the people.

Very galling it was to the king's troops to hear the drums of the citizens beating, and to see armed men patrolling the streets, while they were packing their equipments. It was exasperating to be cooped up in Fort William, with no opportunity to roam the streets, insult the people, drink toddy in the tap-rooms of the Tun and Bacchus and the White Horse taverns. No longer could the lieutenants and ensigns quarter themselves upon the people and be waited upon by negro servants, or spend their evenings with young ladies. They who came to maintain law and order had themselves become transgressors, and were being sent to what was little better than a prison, while Captain Preston and the men who fired upon the unarmed citizens were in jail as murderers. It was a humiliating, exasperating reflection.

X

MRS. NEWVILLE'S DINNER-PARTY.

His majesty's commissioner of imposts, Theodore
Newville, being an officer of the crown, dispensed generous hospitality. Gentlemen of position or culture
arriving in town were cordially entertained. His table
was abundantly supplied with meats and with wines
mellowed by age. He was loyal to his sovereign ;
gloried in being an Englishman, gave reverence to
King George, and was respected and honored by his
fellow-citizens. On Sunday, in King's Chapel, he
repeated with unction the prayer for their majesties
the king and queen, and for his royal highness the
Prince of Wales. Not only as a servant of the crown
but as a citizen it was his duty to be loyal to the king.
He was kind, courteous, and tolerant towards those
who did not agree with him in political affairs. He
thought Sam Adams, James Otis, and Doctor Warren
were rather hot-headed, but they were nevertheless
frequent guests at his table.

Mrs. Newville took pride in making her home attractive. Whether as hostess at the dinner-table or in
the parlor, she displayed tact and grace in conversation. She was ever solicitous for the welfare and
happiness of Ruth, her only child, and fondly hoped
a kind Providence would bring about an alliance with

some worthy son of an ancient and honorable family. Her day-dreams pictured a possible marriage of her beloved daughter to some lord, earl, or baronet from the mother country, owner of a great estate, a castle, or baronial hall.

It was an agreeable announcement which Mr. Newville made to Mrs. Newville, that the ship Robin Hood, sent out by the Admiralty to obtain masts, had arrived, bringing as passengers young Lord Upperton and his traveling companion, Mr. Dapper. His lordship had recently taken his seat with the peers, and was traveling for recreation and adventure in the Colonies. Not only was he a peer, but prospective Duke of Northfield. He was intimate with the nobility of the realm, and had kissed the hands of the king and queen in the drawing-room of Buckingham Palace:

Mr. Dapper was several years the senior of Lord Upperton, so intelligent, agreeable, polite, courteous, and of such humor, that he was ever welcomed in the drawing-room of my lady the Countess of Epsom, the Marquise of Biddeford, and at the tables of my Lady Stamford, and of her grace the Duchess of Alwington. The doors of the London clubs were always wide open to one who could keep the table in a roar by his wit. Lord Upperton had chosen him as his companion during his visit to his majesty's Colonies.

"It will indeed be an honor to entertain Lord Upperton and his friends," said Mrs. Newville, with sparkling eyes. It was not only the anticipated pleasure of their company at dinner that set her pulses throbbing, but the thought that it might in the end make her day-dreams a reality.

Mr. Newville thought it would be eminently fitting to invite the commander of his majesty's fleet, Admiral Montague, and also the rector of King's Chapel, Reverend Mr. Coner ; together they would represent the crown and the church.

Mrs. Newville did not intend that any bevy of beautiful girls should assemble around her table and be a cluster of diamonds to dazzle his lordship by their brilliancy. She would have but one brilliant, her own daughter. The other ladies should be of mature years. She would invite Miss Milford, who made it a point to read every new book ; Miss Artley, who could paint in oils, and Miss Chanson, who would sing a song after dinner, and accompany herself upon the harpsichord ; Mr. John Adams, the able lawyer, and his accomplished wife.

From her chamber window, Ruth saw a lumbering coach drive up the street. The footman in blue livery opened the coach door, and a young man, tall, handsome, wearing a blue velvet coat, the sleeves slashed with gold, an embroidered waistcoat, buff breeches, lace ruffles, and powdered wig, walked up the path accompanied by a gentleman several years his senior, faultlessly dressed, with crimson velvet coat and costly ruffles. The other guests had previously arrived. Ruth, in accordance with her mother's wishes, wore a rich brocaded silk of pure white. She needed no adornment of silver, gold, or precious stones to set forth her loveliness as she entered the parlor.

"My lord, shall I have the pleasure of presenting my daughter?" said her mother.

Lord Upperton bowed. Mrs. Newville saw a look of

surprise upon his face, as if he had not expected to find so sweet a flower in the wilderness of the Western world. He bowed again, very politely, and expressed his pleasure at making her acquaintance.

Pompey, bowing low, informed Mr. Newville that dinner was ready to be served.

" My lord, may I presume to assign my daughter to you? " said Mrs. Newville, giving her own arm to Admiral Montague.

Mr. Dapper solicited the favor of Mrs. Adams's company. As Miss Chanson sang in the choir at King's Chapel, Reverend Mr. Coner thought it becoming to offer her his arm, leaving Miss Artley to Mr. Newville, and Miss Milford to Mr. Adams.

" I presume, my lord, you find things quite different here from what you do in England," Ruth remarked, feeling it was incumbent upon her to open the conversation.

" Yes, Miss Newville, very different; for instance, in London, and in almost all our towns, the houses are mostly brick, with tiles or thatch; but here, they are built of wood, covered with shingles. Your churches are meetinghouses. Queer name." Lord Upperton laughed.

" Ha, ha! I had a funny experience the other day. I told the landlord of the Admiral Vernon I would like a chair for myself, and another for Mr. Dapper, — that we wanted to see the town. Well, what do you think happened? A little later, in came two niggers, each bringing a big rocking-chair. ' Dese be de cheers you axed for, Massa,' they said."

Miss Newville laughed heartily.

" The landlord evidently did not know you meant sedan-chairs; we do not have them here," she said.

" More than that, I told him I should want some links for the evening, as I was to be out late. He said I could get 'em in Faneuil Hall Market, if it was sausages I wanted."

Again Miss Newville gave way to laughter.

" I do not suppose," she said, " that the landlord ever had heard that a link-boy is a torch-bearer."

" I had the pleasure of attending services at your church last Sunday," said Lord Upperton to the rector, when they were seated at the table. " I noticed that you have a substantial stone edifice."

" Yes, my lord, and we regard it with what, I trust, is reverential pride. The Church of God is enduring, and the church's edifice should be firm and solid, and of material that the tooth of time will not gnaw," the rector answered.

" Ought it not to be beautiful as well? " Miss Newville inquired.

" Most certainly."

" I cannot say I think King's Chapel is beautiful in the architecture, with its stump of a tower, and no steeple or spire," Miss Newville replied.

" Perhaps by and by we shall have money enough to carry out the plan of the architect. I admit it is not as attractive as it might be," said the rector.

" I never look at the lower tier of windows without laughing over the wit of Reverend Mr. Byles [1] in regard to them," said Mr. Adams.

[1] Rev. Matthew Byles, the first pastor of Hollis Street Church, was born in Boston, 1706, descended from Reverend John Cotton, the

" What might it be ? " the rector asked.

" He said he had heard of the canons of the church, but never before had he seen the portholes."

The company laughed.

" Excellent! Excellent ! " exclaimed Mr. Dapper.

" The reverend gentleman, Mr. Byles, though dissenting from our Apostolic Church, I am happy to say is loyal to our most gracious King George," said the rector.

" Reverend Mr. Byles is very witty," Miss Newville remarked. " He asked the selectmen several times to give their attention to a quagmire in the road near his house. After long delay, they stepped into a chaise and rode to the spot. Suddenly they found themselves stuck in the mud. Mr. Byles opened his window and remarked that he was glad they were stirring in the matter at last."

Again the company laughed.

" Capital; he must be a genius," said Mr. Dapper.

Pompey served the oysters, large, fat, and juicy.

" Pardon me, madam, but may I inquire what these may be ? " Mr. Dapper inquired.

" They are oysters. I think you will find them quite palatable," Mrs. Newville replied.

Mr. Dapper put his glasses to his eyes, tilted an oyster on his fork, and examined it.

" Do you mean to say that you swallow these monsters ? "

first minister, and Richard Mather. He was minister of the parish more than forty years. He was a celebrated wit and punster. He maintained his allegiance to the king, and remained in Boston after the departure of the British. He died in 1788. His clock is preserved in the old State House, by the Bostonian Society.

" We think them fine eating," Mrs. Adams replied.

" My lord," said Mr. Dapper, turning to Upperton, " I 'm going to try one. I 've made my last will and testament. Tell 'em at Almack's, when you get home, that Dapper committed suicide by attempting to swallow an oyster."

" I will send Pompey for the coroner," exclaimed Mr. Newville, laughing.

" 'Pon my soul, madam, they are delicious. Bless me! It is worth crossing the Atlantic to eat one. Try one, my lord, and then you can torment the Macaronies[1] by telling them they don't know anything about fine eating," said Dapper, after gulping it down.

Lord Upperton ate one, smacked his lips, and testified his enjoyment by clearing his plate.

" I dare say, my lord, that you find many amusing things here in the Colonies," remarked Mrs. Adams.

" Indeed I do. Yesterday, as I was smoking my pipe in the tap-room of the Admiral Vernon, a countryman stepped up to me, and said, ' Mister, may I ax for a little pig-tail?' I told him I did n't keep little pigs and had n't any tails. I presumed he would find plenty of 'em in the market."

Lord Upperton was at a loss to know the meaning of the shout of laughter given by the company.

" The bumpkin replied if I had n't any pig-tail, a bit of plug would do just as well for a chaw."

Again the laughter.

---

[1] The derisive term "Macaronies" was applied to ladies and gentlemen who had visited Italy, and who upon returning to England aped foreign customs in the matter of dress.

"I expect I must have made a big bull, but, 'pon my soul, I can't make out where the fun comes in."

"He was asking you first for pig-tail tobacco for his pipe, and then for a bit of plug tobacco for chewing," Mrs. Adams explained.

"Oh ho! then that is it! What a stupid donkey I was," responded Lord Upperton, laughing heartily. "He wasn't at all bashful," he continued, "but was well behaved; asked me where I was from. I told him I was from London. 'Sho! is that so? Haow's King George and his wife?' he asked. I told him they were well. 'When you go hum,' said he, 'jes give 'em the 'spec's of Peter Bushwick, and tell George that Yankee Doodle ain't goin' to pay no tax on tea.'" Lord Upperton laughed heartily. "I rather like Peter Bushwick," he said. "I'd give a two-pound note to have him at Almack's for an evening. He'd set the table in a roar."

"My lord, shall I give you some cranberries?" Miss Newville asked, as she dished the sauce.

"Cranberries! What are they? I am ashamed to let you know how ignorant I am, but really I never heard of 'em before. Do they grow on trees?"

She explained that they were an uncultivated fruit, growing on vines in swamps and lowlands.

"'Pon my soul, they are delicious. And what a rich color. Indeed, you do have things good to eat," he added, smacking his lips.

"I trust you will relish a bit of wild turkey," said Mr. Newville, as he carved the fowl.

"Wild turkey, did you say?"

"Yes, my lord. They are plentiful in the forests."

Again Lord Upperton smacked his lips.

" By Jove, Dapper, it is superb ! " he exclaimed.

" Will you try some succotash, my lord ? " Ruth inquired.

" There you have me again. What a name ! "

" It is an Indian name, my lord," said Mrs. Adams.

" Oh ho ! Indian. They told me I should find the people lived like the savages. Succotash ! what is it ? "

" Succotash, my lord, is a mixture of beans and Indian corn."

" Beans ! beans ! Do you eat beans over here ? " his lordship asked.

" We do, my lord," Mrs. Adams replied, " and we think them very nutritious and palatable, notwithstanding the maxim, ' *Abstincto a fabis.*' Possibly you may be a disciple of Pythagoras, and believe that the souls of the dead are encased in beans, and so think it almost sacrilegious for us to use them as food."

Lord Upperton looked up in astonishment. Was it possible that ladies in the Colonies were acquainted with the classics ?

" In England we feed our sheep on beans," his lordship replied; " and may I ask what is Indian corn ? "

" Possibly you may call it maize in England. When our fathers came to this country they found the Indians used it for food, and so ever since it has been known as Indian corn."

" Beans for sheep ; corn for savages. Pardon me,

madam, but I am not a sheep, nor yet quite a savage with a tomahawk. Thank you, but I don't care for any succotash."

" Better take some, Upperton. It is positively delicious," said Mr. Dapper, after swallowing a spoonful.

Lord Upperton poked the mixture with his spoon and then tasted it.

" It isn't so very nasty," he said, and took a second spoonful. " By Jove, it isn't bad at all. Bless me, the more I eat the better I like it."

His plate was quickly cleaned.

" Pardon me, Miss Newville, but the succotash is so superb that I dare violate good manners, which I am sure you will overlook, and pass my plate for more."

" You see, my lord, what you have gained by trying it. If you had not tasted it, you would have gone back to England and told the nabobs that the people in the Colonies eat just such nasty things as the sheep-men feed to their flocks; but now you can torment them by describing the dainty delicacies of the Colonies."

" By Jove! That's a capital idea, Dapper. It will make the Macaronies mad as March hares.

" Please fill your glasses, ladies and gentlemen, and we will drink the health of our most gracious sovereign."[1] said Mr. Newville.

[1] George III. was grandson of George II., and son of Frederick, Prince of Wales. whose death made his son heir to the throne. The mother of George III. had plans of her own. and was aided by the Earl of Bute. There were political parties in church and state; scheming bishops and intriguing politicians. each striving for his own

The glasses were filled, and the health of the king drunk.

"Our king is a right royal sovereign," said Mr. Newville.

"Yes, royal, but stupid now and then," Mr. Dapper responded, to the amazement of the company, and especially Mrs. Newville. "The fact is, my dear madam, our king, unfortunately, has the reputation of being the dullest sovereign in Europe. Perhaps you know there was not much of him to begin with, as he was only a little pinch of a baby when he was born, so puny and weak the nurses said he wouldn't stay here long. He sat in their laps, and was coddled till six years old, when he was put under that scheming, narrow-minded bigot, Reverend Doctor Ayscough. And what do you suppose the reverend donkey set him to doing? Why, learning hymns, written by another reverend gentleman, Doctor Philip Doddridge. Very good religious hymns, no doubt, but not quite so attractive as Mother Goose would have been to the little fellow. After learning a few hymns and a few words in Latin, he was set to making verses in that language, when he could not read a story book without spelling half the words."

"How preposterous!" exclaimed Miss Milford.

"Somewhat absurd, I will admit," said Mr. Dapper, bowing. "One reverend doctor was not sufficient," he continued, "to look after the education of the prince, and so my Lord Bishop Hayter of Norwich

advancement, or the advancement of his party. George III. during his early years had frequent changes of governors and tutors, several of whom were intense Jacobites. holding reactionary opinions. Being dull of intellect. his education tended to make him a bigot.

was associated with Doctor Ayscough. Then the Old Harry was let loose. My Lord Bishop of Norwich was scheming to be made Archbishop of Canterbury, and Ayscough wanted to become Bishop of Bristol. Both were striving to rival little Jack Horner in putting their thumbs into the pie."

The ladies were amused — excepting Mrs. Newville, who laid down her knife and fork, folded her hands, and looked earnestly at Mr. Dapper.

" Do you mean to say there is scheming among the reverend prelates of our most holy church ? " she asked.

" Why, madam, human nature is pretty much the same in the church as out of it, and there is quite as much intrigue among the prelates of the church as among the politicians at court. His majesty, talking about his early years not long since, said there was nothing but disagreement and intrigue among those who had charge of him during his early years. Mr. Scott, his tutor, did what he could for the little fellow, but it was n't much. His father, Fred, Prince of Wales, delighted in private theatricals. He had several plays performed at Leicester House by children, employing Jimmy Quin[1] to teach them their parts. Now, my dear madam, you will see that with three bishops disputing as to how the boy should be instructed in theology; whether politically he should be a Jacobite or Whig ; when each was trying to get the biggest piece of pie and the most plums, — the

---

[1] The celebrated actor, James Quin, was employed by the Prince of Wales to direct the plays performed in Leicester House by the children of the nobility.

boy, the while, muddling his brains in trying to make Latin verses and learning tragedies, there was n't much chance for Master Scott to get him on in other things, especially when my lord the Bishop of Norwich was intriguing to get the master kicked downstairs, that he might put one of his favorites in the position of tutor to the prince."

" Why, Mr. Dapper ! " exclaimed Mrs. Newville.

" Then the prince had a change of governors about as often as the moon fulled," said Mr. Dapper. " Each, of course, had some directions to give in regard to his education. When Lord Harcourt was governor his chief concern was to have the prince turn out his toes when walking."

The ladies laughed at Mr. Dapper's droll way of narrating the manner of the king's education.

" I do not wonder you smile, ladies ; it is enough to make a horse laugh," he said. " Perhaps you would like to know how the prince was put through his paces from the time he opened his eyes in the morning till he was tucked in bed at

George III.

night. Lord North at one time was governor to the prince ; he gave me the programme of the daily routine. The boy was to be out of bed' at seven o'clock, eat breakfast and be ready for Mr. Scott from

eight o'clock to nine, or till the Reverend Doctor John
Thomas came, who had him in charge till eleven, when
he was to be turned over to Mr. Fung, for what purpose
Lord North did not know. At noon, Mr. Ruperti
had him for half an hour. From half past twelve till
three the prince could play ; that is, he could walk
through the grounds around Leicester House, trussed
up in fine clothes like a turkey for the spit, but he
couldn't kick up his heels or turn somersaults on the
grass ; he must be a nice little gentleman in lace and
ruffles. At three o'clock he had dinner. At half
past four the dancing-master, Mr. Deneyer, taught him
the minuet. At five o'clock he had another half hour
with Mr. Fung. From half past six to eight Mr.
Scott put him through his curriculum. At eight
o'clock he had supper, but must be in bed at ten. On
Sunday from half past nine till eleven Reverend
Doctor Ayscough lectured him on religion. To state
it plainly, our royal sovereign's real instructors were
the servants and chambermaids of Leicester House.
They told him nursery tales about hobgoblins, giant-
killers, and witches. Doctor Ayscough and the bishop
gave him lectures on theology. The Jacobite bishop
exalted the prerogatives of princes and kings. Lord
Waldegrave told me that, when he was appointed governor to Prince George, he found him to be a good,
narrow-minded little bigot, with his head full of nursery tales and not much else."

"Why, Mr. Dapper!" exclaimed Mrs. Newville,
laying down her knife and fork again, and holding
up her hands.

"I see that you are astonished, madam. Now I

would not for the world say anything disrespectful of
our gracious sovereign; he is not to be blamed for
the errors of those who had charge of him during his
minority, — he is to be commiserated rather; but you
will observe that it was not a course of education
calculated to enlighten a dull intellect. That he is
good at heart every one knows, but his ministers also
know that he is narrow-minded and obstinate."

"We must not forget that our most gracious
majesty, King George, is one of the Lord's chosen
instruments to carry out the plan of the divine
mind," said the rector.

"Oh, certainly, my dear sir; just as much of an
instrument as ever Samson was, flourishing the jaw-
bone of an ass, smiting the Philistines hip and
thigh," Mr. Dapper replied.

The ladies smiled, but the rector did not altogether
relish the reply.

"I never have quite understood how Earl Bute obtained his ascendency with the king," said Mr. Adams.

"It was through his influence with the mother of
the king," Mr. Dapper replied. "He had a great deal
to say about the king's education. It was Bute who
induced George II. to appoint Andrew Stone to have
charge of the young prince. Then the fat was in
the fire. The Bishop of Norwich accused Stone of
being a Jacobite, and the quarrel became hot — so
sharp that the bishop entered the schoolroom to have
it out with Master Stone. Now I suppose, my dear
rector, you would have staked your money on the
bishop, on the theory that the church militant should
also be the church triumphant."

" Possibly, if I were in the habit of laying wagers," the rector replied.

" I certainly should have done so, reverend sir, but I should have lost my money," continued Mr. Dapper ; " for Mr. Stone was plucky, used his fists beautifully, and gave it to my lord the bishop right between the eyes. The bishop was quite gamey, though, and aimed a blow at Stone's nose, but finally got shoved out of the room, greatly to his mortification. He could n't let the matter drop, and so accused Stone of being drunk. The matter finally got into Parliament where there was quite a row about it. Such were the auspices under which our good sovereign was educated to administer the affairs of the realm. His mother wanted to make him pious. She would not allow him to associate with other boys because they would corrupt his morals. Lord Bute advised the princess dowager to keep the prince tied to her apron strings, and succeeded."

" Lord Bute," Mr. Adams responded, " is very much disliked in the Colonies. When he was at the head of the ministry, he was hung in effigy on the Liberty Tree."

" So he was in London," Mr. Dapper replied. " Your detestation of him cannot be greater than it is in England. No one can quite understand how John Stuart made his way up to power. He was a poor Scotsman from the Frith of Clyde. He went to school at Eton and also at Cambridge, then came to London, hired a piece of land out a little way from the city, and raised peppermint, camomile, and other simples for medicine. He had a love for private theatricals,

had shapely legs and liked to show them. One evening the Prince of Wales saw his legs, and, taking a
fancy to the owner, told him to make himself at home
in Leicester House. That was enough for John
Stuart. Having got a foothold, he made himself use-
ful to Fred, and especially to the princess dowager.
George II. was getting on in years and irritable. The
old king took it upon himself to pick out a wife for
the prince, selecting the daughter of Charles, Duke of
Brunswick-Wolfenbüttel ; but the prince said he
wasn't going to be Wolfenbuttled by his grandsire.
Just what he meant by it no one knows, as the word is
not to be found in Doctor Johnson's big dictionary."

"Shall I help you to a bit of canvasback, my
lord ?" Mrs. Newville asked, interrupting the narrative.

"Canvasback! What may it be? Really, you
have most astonishing things to eat over here," Lord
Upperton replied.

Mrs. Newville explained that it was a duck, and
that it was regarded as a delicacy.

"I never ate anything so delicious," said Upperton.

Mr. Dapper also praised it.

"Was the marriage of our king and queen a love-
match?" Miss Chanson inquired.

"Well, hardly, at the beginning," said Mr. Dapper.
"When the prince was eighteen, he fell in love with
Lady Sarah Lennox, daughter of the Duke of Rich-
mond. She was seventeen, beautiful, and attractive.
She knew how to display her charms to the best
advantage, by going out with the haymakers on fine

summer mornings to wander in the meadows among
the daisies, wearing a fancy costume. No wonder the
prince, looking from the windows of Holland House,
thought it a delightful exhibition of Arcadian simplicity and made haste to chat with her. But love-making between the future king and a subject was not in
accordance with the princess dowager's ideas, and so
Earl Bute found it convenient to appear upon the
scene, — a gentle hint that there was to be no more
love-making. Their flirtations would make a long
story though, for Lord Newbottle was in love with
Lady Sarah and jealous of the prince, which made it
all the more interesting. Bute and the princess dowager put their heads together, and sent Colonel Graham on a prospecting tour among the German prin-
cipalities. He sent back word that the daughter of
the Duke of Mecklenburg-Strelitz would make a good
wife for his royal highness, and he judged well, for I
am sure you all love our Sophia Charlotte."

"Most certainly, and we would emulate her vir-
tues," said Mrs. Adams.

Mr. Newville proposed the health of the queen.

Their glasses drained, Mr. Dapper went on : —

"Lord Harcourt was sent as ambassador to negotiate a marriage, not with Sophia Charlotte, but with
her brother, the duke.

"Was not our queen consulted in regard to the
matter?" Ruth asked.

"Not at all. She knew very little about the world;
never had been a dozen miles from home, never
even had sat at the duke's table. She was a simple-
minded little girl who gave the chickens their dough

QUEEN SOPHIA CHARLOTTE

and gathered nosegays from her flower-garden. You can imagine, ladies, that she hardly knew what to make of it when told that an ambassador from England had arrived and wanted to see her. The duke told her to put on her best gown, mind what Harcourt said, and not be a baby. Suddenly the folding-doors leading to the ducal chamber opened, and there stood the ambassador. ' You are to be married to him by proxy, and be queen of England,' said the duke, which so surprised the poor girl that she nearly fainted. The ceremony over, Harcourt presented her with a necklace of diamonds. You see, ladies, it is almost the story of Cinderella over again ! "

" It is really romantic," responded Miss Milford.

" I would not be married to one whom I never had seen," exclaimed Ruth.

" A princess, Miss Newville, cannot always do as she would. She may be compelled to marry against her will," said Lord Upperton.

" I would not," Ruth replied.

" Not if the country required it ? " Lord Upperton asked.

" No, my lord ; and I am glad I am not a princess."

" Bravely spoken. Ladies and gentlemen, let us drink to the maiden who, though not of the blood royal, is yet a princess," said Mr. Dapper.

" Hear ! hear ! " exclaimed the admiral, thumping the table.

The company gazed admiringly at Ruth, peerless in her beauty, the warm blood suffusing her cheeks.

" I understand that our queen assumed the position of royalty with much grace," Mrs. Adams remarked.

" With charming simplicity, madam," responded Mr. Dapper. " She landed at Harwich, and had an ovation all the way to London. People hurrahed, bells rang, and cannon thundered. The poor girl was terribly frightened. The thought of meeting a husband whom she had never seen unstrung her nerves. The Duchess of Hamilton laughed at her, but it was a hot shot the queen let fly ; she said : ' You have been married twice to husbands of your own choosing, but poor me must marry a man whom I never have seen.' "

" Bravo ! that raked the quarter-deck," exclaimed the admiral.

" How did the king receive her ? " Ruth inquired.

When she stepped from the coach she knelt at his feet ; he gave her a kiss, and led her into the palace."

" Very gallant on the part of the king ; fitting and humble the action of the queen," said the rector.

" I would not have got down on my knees to him," said Ruth.

" May I ask why Miss Newville would not have knelt to her future husband and sovereign, had she been Princess Sophia ? " the rector asked.

" Because it was an acknowledgment at the outset that she was not his equal. She abased herself by taking an inferior position. In the days of chivalry, men knelt to women. The princess did not leave her happy home to be a subject of King George ; but to be his wife to stand by his side, and not crouch at his feet."

" Hurrah ! That 's a whole broadside. She 's sweeping your quarter-deck," shouted the admiral.

The rector grew red in the face.

"It is recorded in the Holy Scriptures, Miss Newville, that wives must be obedient to their husbands," he replied.

"Does the Bible say a wife must kneel at her husband's feet?" she asked.

"Perhaps not in so many words, but she is commanded to obey. Our holy church teaches the doctrine. When the princess knelt at the feet of his majesty, it signified she would obey him. Perhaps it is my duty, Miss Newville, to say that your sentiments would be regarded as heretical by the authorities of the church."

"Hold on, rector," said Mr. Adams. "Don't set the canons of the church to thundering."

"It is the gossip at court," said Mr. Dapper, "that the king wanted to retire soon after sundown, but the queen said she was n't going to bed with the hens. It is said he told her she must wear a particular dress, but she informed him he could dress as he pleased, and she should do the same."

"You will have to go to court, rector, and lecture the queen on heresy," said Mr. Adams.

The company laughed, and Ruth's eyes sparkled over the rector's discomfiture.

The meats had been removed and Pompey was serving the pastry and comfits.

"What delicious cheese you have. It is as toothsome as the finest Cheshire," said Lord Upperton.

"We think it of excellent flavor, and I am sure you will relish it all the more when I inform you, my lord, that it was made by a girl not older than myself," replied Ruth.

"Indeed! is it possible? How very clever she must be."

"She is a New Hampshire lady."

"Are dairymaids ladies?"

"Indeed they are, my lord. The young lady who made the cheese you are eating, I dare say, would adorn the court of our queen," responded Mr. Adams.

"Bless me! oysters, cranberries, succotash, canvas-back ducks, wild turkeys, pumpkin pie, dairymaids ladies, wives the equals of their husbands! Rector, will there be anything beyond these in the New Jerusalem?" exclaimed Lord Upperton.

Dinner over, the ladies passed into the parlor while the gentlemen smoked their pipes and finished their wine.

"I suppose, my lord," said Mr. Adams, "you have not been here sufficiently long to form an opinion in regard to the Colonies."

"Everything is so new and strange," Lord Upperton replied, "I hardly know what to make of it. I had an idea that I should find your people quite rude and uncultivated. I understand you have n't any theatre or anything of that sort; but, really, your ladies charm me by their conversation. Mrs. Adams informs me she has studied Latin and Greek."

"I am happy to say my wife can read Cicero and Homer in the originals," Mr. Adams replied.

"You astonish me," his lordship exclaimed.

"We are somewhat primitive, but the Colonies in time will make amends for whatever they may be lacking now." Mr. Adams responded, sipping his wine.

"The people who came to this Western world did so

mainly for conscience sake, and the time will come when this country will be the seat of empire. Society here is established on enduring foundations. One hundred years hence the chances are the people in the Colonies will outnumber those of England. We are loyal to the king, but we are a liberty-loving people and jealous of our rights. In time we shall be so strong that the united force of Europe will not be able to subdue us." [1]

" You have a great extent of country, but as a people you are widely scattered. You have only a little fringe of settlements along the seacoast. It will be an easy matter to divide you. England is rich, and has a great navy; she controls the sea. Her armies have been victors on many fields; she has wrested Canada from France," said his lordship.

"With the aid of the Colonies," interrupted Mr. Adams.

" Perhaps we had better give politics the go-by and join the ladies," said his lordship, rising and moving towards the parlor.

Pompey brought in the tea-urn, cups and saucers, sugar and cream.

"Shall I pass you a cup, Miss Newville?" Lord Upperton asked.

" Thank you, my lord, but I do not drink tea."

" Ha, ha! Miss Newville, so you have joined the other conspirators to outwit Lord North!"

"No, your lordship, I have not joined them, but I must say I admire their resolution in giving up a luxury to maintain a great principle."

---

[1] The paragraph is in substance the prophecy of John Adams, written to Nathan Webb, a school-teacher in Worcester, in 1755.

" As for myself," said Mr. Dapper, " I rather like the spirit of the Puritan mothers and daughters here in the Colonies; they are worthy descendants of the men who had it out with Charles I. It is all nonsense, this plea of Lord North, that the people in the Colonies ought to pay a portion of the debt incurred by England in the late war with France; it is the extravagance and corruption of Parliament and of those in power that grinds us, — the giving of grants, pensions, and gratuities to favorites, parasites, and hangers-on. During Bute's and Grenville's administrations the public money was sown broadcast. If votes were wanted, they were purchased. It was not unusual for a member of the Commons to find four hundred pounds in his napkin at dinner, or in a billet-doux left by the postman. Of course he understood the meaning of it. The ministers helped themselves to sugar-plums worth five thousand pounds. When the Duke of Grafton was at the head of the ministry, that parasite, Tom Bradshaw, who had done some nasty work for the Premier, received an annuity of fifteen hundred pounds and a suite of thirty rooms in Hampton Palace. He is there now, and has had the suite increased to seventy apartments. Not long ago the ministry put out one hundred thousand pounds to carry a measure through the Commons."

" You astonish me! Do you mean to intimate that our king has corrupt men around him?" Mrs. Newville inquired.

" My dear madam, the king is hardly responsible for this state of things. It is part of the political system. Politics is a game. Men can cheat in

government as well as in anything else, and there
are quite as many cheats in and around St. James's
as at Almack's or any of the other gambling resorts.
Other things are done in and around Westminster,
by those whom you are accustomed to revere, which
would astonish you could I but speak of them," said
Mr. Dapper.

The evening being beautiful, the air genial, the
company strolled in the garden, and ate the ripening
plums and pears. Lord Upperton, finding pleasure
in the society of Miss Newville, asked what recreation the young people in the Colonies enjoyed. She
told of the launching of the ship Berinthia Brandon,
the pung-ride and dance at the Greyhound Tavern,
the quiltings, huskings, and tea-parties.

" I hope, Miss Newville, this will not be the last
time I shall have the pleasure of seeing you. I shall
not soon forget the succotash and cranberries, and
shall improve an early opportunity to pay my respects to you," he said, as he bade her good-evening.

" By Jove, Dapper, she's as fine a piece of chintz
as can be picked up at St. James's or anywhere else,"
he said, as they returned to the Admiral Vernon.

XI.

SOCIETY LIFE IN LONDON.

On a pleasant afternoon Lord Upperton was once more ushered into the Newville mansion. Mrs. Newville being absent, he was graciously received by Ruth.

"I had such a delightful time in your hospitable home, Miss Newville, the other evening, that I could no longer refrain from paying my respects."

"It is certainly very kind of you, my lord."

"I cannot tell you how delighted I was when you told me about your recreations. How charming it must be to go riding in a pung, with a lot of ladies and gentlemen. I was wondering if I could not get up a pung-ride."

"We only do that in winter, when snow is on the ground, my lord," Ruth replied, hardly able to repress a smile.

"Oh, dear me! how stupid I am! Of course not," and his lordship laughed heartily at his blunder.

"Do you not have snow in London, my lord?"

"Yes, sometimes; but then we have n't any pungs. I don't know what they are. Maybe they are a sort of hackney or chariot?"

"We have no hackney coaches here, as yet, my lord, but Mr. Hancock and the governor and a few of our citizens have coaches. A pung is not at all like a coach. It is, instead, a sort of box on runners."

" Oh, indeed, how interesting ! "

" May I ask, my lord, what recreations you have in London ? "

" We have quite a variety, I assure you, Miss Newville. We have card parties, where we play high or low, just as we feel. We have assemblies, where we tittle-tattle and gossip. We gentlemen lay bets on the winning horse at the next Derby. We go to Drury Lane or Covent Garden, and clap our hands at the acting of Davy Garrick or Jimmy Quin. At the opera we go wild when Mademoiselle Truffi soars like a nightingale up to high C. We dance at balls, array ourselves as harlequins and imps at masquerades, and see who can carry off the most bottles of port or sherry at dinner," said his lordship, again laughing.

" Are you not jesting, my lord ? "

" Oh no, Miss Newville ; I am telling you sober truth. It is not exaggeration at all. For instance, the masquerade which the Duke and Duchess of Richmond gave on the king's last birthday was so gay that I can hardly hope to picture it. The duke's villa is on the banks of the Thames. The willows, elms, and oaks in the park were hung with lanterns, the house was all ablaze — lights in every room. Dukes, duchesses, earls, barons, lords, and ladies — more than six hundred — assembled in masquerade dress. The Duchess of Hamilton and Argyle was hostess. She appeared as Night, with a black trailing robe illuminated with silver stars, while her father was dressed as a footman, with the portrait of his other daughter dangling from a ribbon tied to a button of his jacket."

" Was it not rather out of character for a man old enough to be grave and dignified to take such a part?" Miss Newville asked.

" Perhaps so, but then we are expected to do absurd things in masquerade. Her grace the Duchess of Richmond, for instance, appeared as the Sultana of Persia, in a costume purchased in the bazaar of Bagdad. The Duchess of Grafton displayed her charms as Cleopatra. Now when we remember that Egypt and the Orient have a climate in which a person can get along without any great amount of clothing, it really does seem somewhat absurd for a lady, in a country with a climate like that of England, to attempt to imitate in dress, or undress, that celebrated queen of the East."

Lord Upperton laughed again. " Miss Fitzroy," he continued, " undertook to represent the Sultana of Turkey. If I remember rightly, she appeared in baggy silk trousers, high-heeled pink slippers, crimson jacket, embroidered with gold, and a white turban. Her bewitching eyes peeped through two holes in a muslin yashmak spangled with silver stars. Among the gentlemen I recall Lord Augustus Hervey, who disguised himself so completely as a jester that no one could make out who he was. He said saucy things as a court fool. He even guyed his own wife, and she never mistrusted she was flirting with her own husband. but then, as she was ready to flirt with anybody, it made no difference."

Miss Newville hardly knew what reply to make as his lordship laughed again, and so remained silent.

"May I ask what character Lord Upperton assumed," she asked.

"Oh, certainly. I appeared as a young devil, with hoofs, horns, and a forked tail. His satanic majesty, you know, is supposed to whisper things in people's ears, and you may be sure I acted out the character I assumed. I did it so well that Lady Lucy Hastings said I was a perfect imp of darkness."

"Have you any other recreations?" Miss Newville inquired.

"Oh, yes, a great many. One diversion I am sure would charm you, — the club at Almack's, in which the ladies nominate gentlemen to membership and gentlemen the ladies. Only a few days before leaving London I attended a grand masquerade ball at Almack's, where my Lady Archer appeared as a boy wearing a postman's blue coat. Lord Edgecombe assumed the character of an old washerwoman. Sir Watkins Wynne rode into the hall on a goat, assuming the character of holy Saint David. The goat, more accustomed to browse in the pastures than take part in such high jinks, frightened by the blare of trumpets, the scraping of fiddles, and the whisking of the ladies' skirts as they went round in the dance, capered like mad, butted my Lady Winchester so that she fell flat upon the floor, upset holy Saint David, and kept the room in an uproar until a waiter seized the animal by the horns and another by the tail and led him from the hall."

Lord Upperton roared with laughter, and Miss Newville could but join him in the merriment.

"It was a picturesque scene, I assure you, with peddlers, haymakers, shepherdesses, gypsies, chimney-sweeps, and nymphs," his lordship said.

"May I ask, my lord, what a masquerade is supposed to represent?" Miss Newville inquired.

"Well, really now, I never thought of it. I suppose it means something, but just what, upon my soul, I cannot tell you, except to have a jolly good time and appear to be what we are not."

"Are such masquerade balls usually attended by noble lords and ladies?"

"Oh, yes. They are almost the exclusive patrons. I attended one a little while ago at Carlisle House. It was intended the king and queen should be patrons. Tickets were sent to his most gracious majesty, and, of course, there was a great crush. The king and queen returned the tickets, but everybody else was there. I remember that the Duke of Cleveland appeared as Henry VIII.; the Duke of Gloucester as a fine old English gentleman; the Duchess of Buccleugh as the Witch of Endor; Lady Edgecombe as a nun; the Duchess of Bolton as the goddess Diana; Lady Stanhope as Melopomene; the Countess of Waldegrave as Jane Shore; Lord Galway's daughter, Mrs. Monckton, as an Indian princess, in a golden robe, embroidered with diamonds, opals, and pearls worth thirty thousand pounds. One of the gentlemen came as a Swiss ballad-singer with a hurdy-gurdy, leading a tame bear with a muzzle on his nose. He had been stopped by the gate-keeper, because he had only a ticket and a half — the half ticket for the bear; but it being a she-bear and ladies being admitted at half price, the hurdy-gurdy man won the day. Everybody laughed and said it was the best joke of the season.

Lord Upperton saw a troubled look upon Miss Newville's face, as if she had heard quite enough about masquerades.

" The recreations of court life, I would not have you think, Miss Newville, are masquerades and balls, and nothing else. We have suppers which are quite different affairs, where we do not try to be what we are not. After the theatres are out we go to the banquet halls, where wine and wit flow together. We gossip, sing songs, and flirt with the Macaroni ladies. The opera girls sing to us if they are not too tipsy, and we have gay larks till the wagons begin to rumble around Covent Garden Market, and the green-grocers are displaying their onions and cabbages for the early morning sale."

" Who are the Macaroni ladies? " Miss Newville asked.

Lord Upperton laughed.

" I don't wonder that you inquire. We call them Macaronies, ladies and gentlemen alike, who have traveled on the Continent, flirted at Versailles, in Paris, or in the Palace Barberini in Rome ; who have eaten macaroni in Naples, and who have come home with all the follies, to say nothing of some of the vices of the nobility of other countries, in addition to what they had before they started on their travels. The gentlemen wear their hair in long curls; the ladies patch and paint their faces. If they have n't a pimple or a wart they make one. They wear gorgeous dresses. The gentlemen twiddle canes ornamented with dogs' heads or eagles' beaks, with gold tassels; carry attar of rose bottles in their gloved hands, and squirt rosewater on their handkerchiefs. They ogle the ladies through their quizzing glasses, wear high-heeled slippers, and diddle along on their toes like a French dancing-master teaching his pupils the minuet. The ladies simper and giggle and wink at the gentlemen from behind their fans, and leave you to imagine something they don't say."

Again Lord Upperton saw a troubled look upon Miss Newville's face.

"We have convivial parties," he continued. "If you like cards, you can try your hand at winning or losing. We play for fifty-pound rouleaux. There is always a great crowd, and not infrequently you may see ten thousand pounds on the table. Some play small; others plunge in regardless of consequences. My young friend, Lord Stravendale, before he was of age, one night lost eleven thousand pounds, but nothing daunted he played again, and as luck would have it got it all back at one hazard. He lamented he had not made the stakes larger, and said if he had been playing deep he might have made a million. It was really very clever in Stravendale."

Again his lordship laughed, but Miss Newville could not see anything in the narrative to cause her to smile.

"There is Charley Fox," Lord Upperton continued, "who goes in rather strong. He makes grand speeches in the Commons; but almost always gets

fleeced at Almack's. The Jews, who are usually on
hand in one of the outside rooms with their shekels,
waiting to lend money, charge exorbitant interest.
Charley calls it the Jerusalem Chamber. Sometimes
he gets completely cleaned out, and has to borrow a
guinea to pay the waiter who brings him his brandy.
One night at the beginning he won eight thousand
pounds, but before morning lost the last sixpence."

"Do ladies play?" Miss Newville asked.

"Certainly; they love gaming as well as the men.
Her royal highness the Duchess of Cumberland not
long ago set up card playing and gaming in her drawing-rooms. Her sister, Lady Elizabeth Lutterell, is
one of the best gamesters in London. It is whispered,
though, that she cheats on the sly. Lady Essex gives
grand card parties, where there is high gaming. One
lady, whom I know, lost three thousand guineas at
loo. It is whispered that two ladies, not long since,
had high words at one of Lady Essex's parties; that
they rode out to St. Pancras and fought a duel with
pistols, and that one was wounded; which shows that
our noble women have real grit."

"Is what you are saying a fair picture of life
among the nobility?" Ruth asked.

"I would not have you think, Miss Newville, that
everybody of noble birth or high position is a gambler,
but every one who plays, of course, wants a stake of
some kind."

"Pardon me, my lord, but I do not see any fun in
losing money in the way you speak of."

"Well, perhaps there isn't any fun in losing, but it
is real jolly when you win. It is like drinking wine;
it warms you up."

" Do you have any other recreations equally attractive and delightful ? " Miss Newville inquired.

" We have gay times at the Derby during the races.
Of course you have felt the excitement of a horse-race,
Miss Newville ? "

" No, for we do not have horse-racing here ; but I
believe they do in Virginia."

" No racing ! I am astonished.   Are not your people rather slow ? "

" We have few diversions, my lord ; we do not win
money by racing."

" You can have no conception of what a grand sight
it is.   Everybody goes to the Derby — dukes, lords,
bishops, rectors, ladies, and gentlemen.   Before the
race begins, we have our lunch parties.   All are
eating, talking, laughing, or laying bets.   The horses
come out from their stalls with the jockey boys in red,
green, blue. and yellow, in their saddles.   They draw
lots to see which shall have the inside, then go down
the track a little distance.   The horses understand
what they are to do just as well as we who stake our
money.   They sniff the air, step lightly, then break
into a run, and everybody is on tiptoe.   In a moment
they are down to the first turn, and come in full view.
There are four, perhaps, neck and neck.   You have
staked, say. on yellow.   He loses half a length, and
your heart goes down : but he gains a little, is up even
once more — half a length ahead. and you yell and
double your stakes.   They are round the second turn,
going like a whirlwind : yellow and blue are ahead of
the others. neck and neck.

" ' Two to one on yellow ! ' you shout.

" ' I 'll take it ! ' roars Lord Pilkington.

- " ' Two to one on blue ! ' he shouts back.

" ' Put me down for it ! ' you answer.

" They are on the home run. There is a great hub-bub, like the roaring of a tornado, as they sweep under the line, yellow ahead. You swing your hat, and yell as loud as you can. You are ten thousand in. Oh, it is just the jolliest excitement a man can have ! "

" If you win, my lord, does not somebody else lose ? "

" Of course, Miss Newville."

" Do they feel equally jolly ? "

" Possibly not. Sometimes we are out of pocket, and do not feel quite so hilarious, but we swallow a stiff nipper of brandy and draw our checks like men. I won five thousand from Lord Pilkington, three thousand from Lady Merryfield, and quite a number of one hundred pounders from the ladies of my set, who bet on the blue, while I planked mine on the yellow. You see, Miss Newville, that ladies are sometimes influenced by fancy. Lady Somers, for instance, allowed fancy to get the better of judgment. She likes blue as a color, above yellow. She is quite horsey, and thinks she can drive a tandem. I had examined blue, felt of his muscles, and made up my mind that by and by he would have ringbone on his left fore leg. I believed that yellow had the best wind and bottom ; but the ladies followed the lead of Lady Somers, and so I raked in their shekels. They all ponied up promptly, though, and paid their outs, like true-born English ladies."

" I do not think," said Miss Newville, " that I should like to lose or win money in that way."

" Why, Miss Newville, once get into it, and you would say it is the most delightful sport in the world. If you think, however, that you would not like to participate in such pleasures, we have the fox hunt, which is the most charming and innocent diversion imaginable. You don't bet any money in that, but have a rollicking good time riding over the country, ladies and gentlemen — leaping hedges and ditches, following the hounds, running Reynard to cover, and having a lunch at the close of the hunt."

" Foxes are plentiful in this country, but we do not run them down with horses," Miss Newville replied.

" Do ladies ride horseback in the Colonies?"

" Oh, yes. Were you to attend meeting in the country on the Sabbath, you would see many ladies riding up to the horse-block, wives on pillions behind their husbands. Do the ladies who hunt foxes attend meeting on the Sabbath, my lord?"

" Ha, ha! I suspect what you call going to meeting, with us is going to church. Oh, we are very devout. On Sunday we all go to church, kneel on our hassocks, and confess we are miserable sinners, recite the creed, pray for the king, queen, Prince of Wales, the army and navy. We do our full duty as Christians, and are loyal to the church, as well as to his majesty. My rector, at Halford, is a very good man. To be sure the living is n't much, but he reads the prayers well, preaches a nice little sermon of ten minutes or so, for he knows I don't care to be bored by the hour. He enjoys a fox hunt, says grace at dinner, and makes a point of having a little game of cards with me Saturday evening. He does n't know much about cards, so I usually let him win a few shillings, knowing the poor fellow will feel better Sunday morning while reading the service if he knows he has a half-crown in his pocket, instead of being out that much. I know how it is, Miss Newville. I can be more devout and comfortable on Sunday after winning instead of losing five or ten thousand at Almack's."

" Perhaps, my lord, you feel you are not quite such a miserable sinner as you might be after all."

" You have stated it correctly, Miss Newville," his lordship replied, not discerning the quiet sarcasm. " Of course I am not, for if I lose, I curse my luck, and am ready to punch somebody's head, and rip out some swear words, but if I win, I am ready to bless the other fellow for playing a king when he should have laid down an ace."

His lordship apologized for having tarried so long, and took his departure.

" She 's a Puritan, through and through. As lovely and pure as an angel in heaven," he said to himself as he walked down the street.

While the months were going by, Roger Stanley, student of Harvard College, was learning about life in Rumford, as a surveyor of land, spending his evenings in the house of Joshua Walden, with Robert and Rachel to keep him company, especially Rachel. He found pleasure in telling her the story of Ulysses and Penelope. Most of the young men of Rumford who came to the Walden home could only talk about oxen, which pair of steers could pull the heaviest load, or whose horse could out-trot all others. When the surveying was done, Roger accepted the invitation of the committeemen to keep the winter school. Never before had there been a master who could keep the big boys in order without using the ferule, but somehow the great strapping fellows, who might have put the master on his back in a twinkling, could not find it in their hearts to do anything that would trouble him. Other masters were content if they went through the regular daily stint of reading, writing. spelling, and ciphering, but he told them about men who made the most of themselves, and who had done great things, — Cæsar, Augustus, Charlemagne, Alfred the Great.

It was the schoolmaster who suggested that the people should meet once a week in the schoolhouse to discuss the great questions affecting the welfare of the Colonies. and who wrote out the questions to be considered : —

" What are the inalienable rights of the people ? "

" Has Parliament any right to tax the people of America without their consent ? "

" Is it right ever to resist the authority of the king ? "

" Ought the Colonies to unite for self-defense ? "

" Ought the Colonies, in any event, to separate from England ? "

People from the back roads came to hear what Esquire Walden. Deacon Kent. Shoemaker Noyes, Blacksmith Temple, and Schoolmaster Stanley had to say upon these questions before the parliament of the people, in the schoolhouse, lighted by two tallow candles and the fire blazing on the hearth. King George and Frederick North might have learned some fundamental principles of government, had they been present.

Like sitting in heavenly places were the mornings and evenings to Roger Stanley in the Walden home, where he passed the first and the last two weeks of the term. The food upon the table was appetizing; deft hands had prepared the bannock — Rachel's hands. The plates, knives, and forks had been laid by her. It was she who glided like a fairy around the room. How could his eyes help following her? And when seated at the table, how radiant her face, beaming with health! In the early morning, long before breakfast-time, he heard her feet tripping down the stairs. While about her work, he could hear her humming a song which he had sung to her. Very pleasant the "good-morning" that came from her lips when he appeared. In the evening it was a pleasure to hold a skein of yarn for her to wind. He was sorry when the last thread dropped from his wrists, and wished she had another for him to hold.

It was the old, old story; the growth of mutual respect, honor, and love, becoming daily more tender and true; the love that needed no pledge, because it was so deep and abiding.

XII.

A NEW ENGLAND GIRL.

LORD UPPERTON was prolonging his stay in America. He visited New York and Philadelphia, and was once more in Boston. He called upon Thomas Hutchinson, governor; upon Thomas Flucker, secretary; and upon the officials of the custom house. He accepted many invitations to dinner from gentlemen and ladies, and took excursions into the country on horseback. Lady Frankland hospitably entertained him in her country house, where he enjoyed himself shooting squirrels and partridges. Returning to Boston, he frequently called to pay his respects to Mr. and Mrs. Newville, never failing to ask for Miss Newville, prolonging his calls till past the ringing of the nine o'clock bell. He was very courteous, and had many entertaining stories to tell of life in England, of his ancestral home at Halford. The old castle was gray with age; the ivy, ever green upon its towers, hanging in graceful festoons from the battlements. Herds of deer roamed the surrounding park; pheasants crooned and cackled beneath the stalwart oaks; hares burrowed in the forest; nightingales made the midnight melodious with their dulcet singing. Old tapestries adorned the walls of the spacious apartments. In the banqueting halls were the portraits of ances-

tors, — lords, dukes, and earls reaching down to the
first Earl Upperton created by William of Normandy,
for valor on the field of Hastings. On the maternal
side were portraits of beautiful ladies who had been
maids of honor and train-bearers at the coronations
of Margaret and Elizabeth. The brain of Ruth could
not keep track of all the branches of the ancestral tree;
she could only conclude it was stalwart and strong.

Lord Upperton was heartily welcomed by Mrs.
Newville, who esteemed it one of heaven's blessings
to be thus honored. On an evening, after a visit
from his lordship, Mrs. Newville, with radiant face,
drew Ruth to her bosom. "My dear," she said, "I
have joyful information for you. Lord Upperton has
done us the distinguished honor to say to your father
and me that he has become so much interested in our
daughter that he presumes to ask the privilege of paying his addresses to her. It is not, Ruth, altogether
a surprise to me, for I have seen his growing fondness
for you."

"Fondness for me, mother?"

"Yes, dear; he has not been able to keep his eyes
off you of late. I have noticed that if you had occasion to leave the room, he fidgeted till you returned.
We have given our consent, and he will call to-morrow
evening to make a formal proposal to you."

"But I do not desire he should make a proposal to
me, mother!"

"Don't want him to make an offer of marriage,
child! Why, Ruth, what are you thinking of? Not
wish to receive the attentions of a noble lord! I am
astonished. Do you forget that he can trace his line-

age down to the time of William the Conqueror, and
I don't know how much farther?   You surprise me!"

" I doubt not Lord Upperton may have a noble ancestry, but I don't see how that concerns me.   I am
not going to marry his ancestors, am I?"

" Why, daughter, he has a crest, — an escutcheon of
azure, sable, and sanguine, a lion rampant, a unicorn
passant, and an eagle volent."

" What would a crest do for me?"

The question puzzled Mrs. Newville.   " I really do
not know, daughter, just what it would do, but it
would be painted on your coach; it would be embroidered on the banners hanging in Lord Upperton's
baronial hall.   Just think of it!   The lion, the emblem of strength, the unicorn of energy, the eagle of
swiftness and far-sightedness, — it would represent
all those qualities!"

" But what if one has not the qualities?"

" I am not so sure, daughter, but that you have
those very characteristics in a remarkable degree.   I
know you have strength of will and energy.   What
you undertake you carry through; and you are far-
sighted, you see what others of your age do not see.
I do not say it to flatter you, daughter, but I am sure
Lord Upperton's coat-of-arms is emblematic of the
character of the lady whom he wishes to see mistress
of Halford Castle," said Mrs. Newville, with radiant
face.

It seemed to her that the fond hope of years was
about to be realized; that the time was at hand when
the Newville family was to be ennobled; when she,
herself, could bid farewell to America, and be admitted

to the charmed society of dukes, barons, princes, kings, and queens.

" Lord Upperton will call to-morrow evening, dear, and I will have Madame Riggoletti come in the afternoon to do your hair. You had better wear your corn-colored satin brocade, which is so becoming to you."

" No, mother, I do not wish to wear it. I prefer to dress plainly. I want Lord Upperton to see me just as I am, a simple girl, who has had few advantages to fit her for the life in which he moves. I cannot appear to be what I am not."

Ruth paused a moment as if considering whether she should speak the words upon her lips.

" Lord Upperton, you say, desires to pay his addresses to me and you have given consent. It is an honor for any lady to receive attentions from a gentleman of superior station, but I cannot promise you, mother, that I shall look with favor upon his suit, honorable though it may be."

It was said calmly but with resolution.

" I dare say, daughter, you may think so now. It is quite natural. It is just what I said when my mother informed me that Theodore, your father, had asked permission to pay his addresses to me. I said I would not see him ; but I did, and have been very glad ever since. After a little while, I used to listen for his footsteps. There were none like his. He always called Thursday evening after the lecture,[1] and

---

[1] The lecture on Thursday of each week was instituted by the Puritans soon after the settlement of Boston. There was a moral if not a legal obligation upon every person to attend it. Consequently in

I used to sit by the window an hour before it was time for him to put in an appearance, looking for him. So it will be with you, child. Now go to bed, dear, and think of the great honor which Lord Upperton is conferring upon us in asking for your hand! "

"Shall I give him my hand, if I cannot at the same time give him my heart?" Ruth asked, her earnest eyes scanning her mother's face.

" Oh, but you will do both, dear. Many a girl has asked the same question at first, but soon found that the heart and hand went together."

" I think," Ruth replied, " if one may judge from outward appearances, there are some women who have given their hands to their husbands, but never their hearts. I see faces, now and then, which make me think of what I have read descriptive of deserts where there is no water to quench the thirst, no oasis with its green palms giving grateful shade from the summer heat. —faces that tell of hunger and thirst for the bread and water of love and sympathy."

" You fancy it is so. and possibly here and there you may find a mismated couple. but. daughter, you will see things in a different light when once you get acquainted with Lord Upperton. I believe there is not another girl in Boston who would not jump at such a catch. You may not fancy him this moment, but in a short time you will say there is not another like him in all the world. You feel just as I did towards

the earlier years of the Colony all business ceased. shops were closed, usual occupations suspended. and the entire community flocked to the meetinghouse of the parish to listen to the discourse of the minister. At the time this story begins. the obligation was not quite so binding as in former years.

Theodore. At first, I almost hated him, because he presumed to ask permission to visit me, but now he is the best man that ever lived. Just think of the offer that has come to you in contrast with what your father had to offer me. Lord Upperton brings you his high station in life, his nobility, his long line of ancestors, a barony, a castle with its ivied walls, a retinue of servants, his armorial bearings inscribed on banners borne by Crusaders. He will offer you rank, wealth, privilege, honor at his majesty's court. Theodore had only himself to offer me. He was not much then, but he is more now. I have done what I could to make him what he is, and now our daughter has the prospect of wearing laces such as are worn by duchesses; to be received at court; to be spoken of as Her Grace. Now to bed, dear, and be happy in thinking it over."

"But I do not love Lord Upperton, nor shall I ever care for him."

"Don't talk in that way, Ruth. You think so now, but when you are once married and begin to enjoy what will be yours, — a coach, waiting-maids to do your bidding, and are invited to the court of his majesty the king, and preside over your own table in the great baronial hall, with the high-born gentlemen and ladies doing you honor, it stands to reason that you will love him who brings these things to you."

"You speak, mother, of the society in which I shall move, but I have no taste for such associations."

"Tush, child; you know nothing about it."

"Lord Upperton has given me a description of the employment and pleasures of the society in which he moves, and I have no desire to enter it. I shall not find happiness in its circles. I want to be just what I am, your daughter, in our happy home."

"But, Ruth, you cannot always be with us. Your father and I earnestly desire your future welfare and happiness. I am sure he will be surprised and pained to hear that you do not wish to receive the attentions of Lord Upperton."

Mr. Newville entered the room. He saw the trouble on the face of his daughter.

"What is it?" he asked.

"Ruth thinks she never can love Lord Upperton and does not desire to receive his attentions, but I have told her it is only a present whim, just as mine was towards you."

"Of course, daughter," said Mr. Newville, with fatherly dignity, "it could hardly be expected you would feel any very strong attachment for Lord Upperton on so short an acquaintance. Conjugal love is a plant of slow growth, but I think you would, ere long, appreciate the great honors and the high privileges which he would confer upon you, and that your heart would go out to him."

The troubled look upon the face of the daughter became more intense. Her father as well as her mother would have her receive the attentions of a man between whom and herself there was no possible sympathy. What should she say? A tear trickled down her cheek: she made no movement to wipe it away, but lifted her loving eyes and gazed steadily into her father's.

"Since you both so earnestly desire, it I will meet

Lord Upperton to-morrow evening and hear what he has to say," she replied.

"You could hardly do otherwise. I think the more you see of him the better you will like him," said Mr. Newville.

"Of course you will, my child; and now, dear, think it over in your chamber. I am sure you will see that a great opportunity has come to you," said Mrs. Newville, giving her a kiss.

It was a summer night. The air was fragrant with the perfume of lilacs and apple-blooms. The young moon was going down in the west, throwing its departing beams upon the unfinished tower of King's Chapel. Ruth, looking out from her white-curtained window, beheld a handful of cloud drift across the crescent orb and dissolve in thin air. She could hear the footsteps of passers along the street growing fainter as they receded. The bell on the Old Brick Meetinghouse struck the hour, and then, in the distance, she heard the watchman's voice, " Ten o'clock, and all is well." With perturbed spirit, she laid her head upon the white linen pillow which her own deft hands had made. So Lord Upperton was to solicit her heart and hand, and she had consented to meet him. What should she say to him? Why should he, having an acquaintance with the noble families of England, come across the sea and offer his attentions to an obscure New England girl, and desire to make her mistress at Halford Castle? Ought she not to feel flattered in having a noble lord for a lover? The thought did not stir her blood. Why was she averse to receiving his attentions? What was there about him that made the thought repellent? Was he not a gentleman? Was he not polite? Did he not show proper respect not only to herself but to everybody? Why not make an effort to overcome her repugnance to him? Would any other girl in Boston or anywhere else hesitate a moment over such an opportunity as had come to her to be called My Lady, — to be mistress of a ducal castle, — a position of power and influence among the lords and ladies of the kingdom? To have diamonds and pearls? To have precedence over others of lower station in social life? Questions came in troops before her; vain her attempts to answer them.

Again the deep tones of the bell rang upon the still night air, and once more she heard the watchman's voice announce the hour. For a moment it interrupted her reverie, but again the questioning went on. Her father and mother not only had given their consent for Lord Upperton to make proposal, but they earnestly desired she should become his wife. She could understand the motives that animated them. She was her father's idol, her mother's joy — very dear to them. Were they not ever doing what they could for her? Would not her marriage to Lord Upperton contribute to their happiness? Might not her father, through Lord Upperton's influence at court, attain a more exalted position? Would not her marriage fill her mother's life with happiness? Would it be an exhibition of filial duty were she to disappoint them? And yet, what right had they to make a decision for her when her own life's happiness was concerned? Was she not her own? Had she not a right to do as she pleased? Ought she to sacrifice herself to their

selfish interests? She did not like to think it was
wholly selfishness on their part, but rather an earnest
desire to provide for her future welfare. Ought she
not to abide their judgment as to what was best for
her? Could she ever be happy with Lord Upperton?
Could she find pleasure in fine dressing, card playing,
and masquerading as he had described them? What
would such a life be worth? Were position in society, pleasure, gratification of self, to be the end and
aim of life? There seemed to be another somebody
beside herself propounding the questions; as if an
unseen visitor were standing by her bedside in the
silent night. Was she awake or dreaming? She
had heard the great lawyer, James Otis, put questions
to a witness in a court where her father in his judicial
robe sat as magistrate. It seemed as if she herself
had been summoned to a tribunal, and one more
searching than the great lawyer was putting questions
which she must answer. Should she give her hand to
Lord Upperton and keep back her heart? Ought
she to allow prospective pleasure or position to influence her choice? Could she in any way barter her
future welfare for the present life and for the larger
life beyond? Was Lord Upperton of such lofty
character that she could render him honor and respect, even if she could not give to him a loving
heart?

In the half-dreaming hour another face looked down
upon her — the face of him, who, in a time of agony,
had been as an angel of God, rescuing her from the
hands of ruffians. Oh, if it were he who solicited
permission to pay his addresses, how would she lean

her head upon his bosom and rest contentedly clasped forever by those strong and loving arms! Through the intervening months his face had been ever present. She lived again the hour of their first meeting, that of the afternoon tea-party, the launching of the Berinthia Brandon, the ride in the pung. She had received several letters from him, which were laid carefully away in her writing-desk. Many times had they been read and with increasing pleasure. He had not declared his undying love for her; the declaration was unwritten, but it was between the lines. He wanted to be more than he was, and she could help him. He wanted to do something for justice, truth, and liberty; to stand resolutely with those who were ready to make sacrifices for their fellow-men. What a sentence was this: " I want to be better than I am; I want to do something to make the world better than it is; and you are pointing the way."

Ever as she read the words her eyes had filled with tears. She pointing the way! Those words in one end of the scale, and Halford Castle and everything connected with it in the other, and the writing tipped the beam.

The night was sultry; her pulses bounding; her brow hot with fever. She sat by the window to breathe the pure air. The stars were shining in their ethereal brightness; the dipper was wheeling around the polar star; the great white river, the milky way, was illumining the arch of heaven. She thought of Him who created the gleaming worlds. Beneath her window the fireflies were lighting their lamps, and living their little lives. She could hear the swallows crooning in their nests beneath the eaves.

" He made them ; He cares for them ; He will
care for me," she said to herself. The night air
cooled her brow, a holy peace and calm came to her
troubled heart. Kneeling, she repeated as her prayer
the psalm which the rector had read on Sunday.

> "He that dwelleth in the secret place of the Most High
> Shall abide under the shadow of the Almighty.
> I will say of the Lord, He is my refuge, and my strength.
> My God, in Him will I trust."

In white garments, without adornment, Ruth Newville courtesied to Lord Upperton the following evening as he entered the parlor. Never before had she
seemed to him, or to her father and mother, so beautiful, so sweet, and pure.

" Miss Newville," he said, " I take it for granted
that you have been duly informed of the purpose of
my visit this evening."

" I have, my lord."

" I come to offer you my hand and heart. I have
been charmed by your qualities of character and
your beauty, and I fain would make you mistress of
Halford Castle. I am soon to return to England,
and I desire to take you with me as my bride. I
have received the gracious permission of your honored parents to begin my suit, and I fondly hope that
I may receive an affirmative answer from your lips."

" My lord, I am not insensible of the honor you
confer upon me, but I am not worthy of it. I am
an obscure girl. I am not fitted to fill the exalted
station in which you desire to place me."

" Pardon me, Miss Newville, I have met many a

fair maiden, but none so charming as the flower which I desire to transplant from the Colonies to old England. My best judgment has selected you from them all."

" My lord, I appreciate your kind words, and what you would give me — your honor, respect, and love, and an exalted social position. I have heard from your lips somewhat concerning the life you would expect me to lead, — the society in which you would have me move. I trust you will pardon my frankness, but it does not attract me."

" I can quite understand you, dear Miss Newville ; it is natural that you should shrink from such a change, but I am sure you would adorn the position."

" More than what I have said, my lord, I do not think I should be happy in such a position."

" Oh, I think you would. Certainly, it would be my desire to place before you every advantage that could contribute to your welfare and happiness. The nobility of the realm would follow in your train. You would captivate them with your grace and beauty. No party, rout. or ball would be complete without you. I am sure that her most gracious majesty the queen would desire your presence at court to grace her receptions."

" You flatter me. my lord. but I do not think that fine dressing. the adornment of pearls and diamonds, promenading. dancing. card playing. and masquerading would give me the highest happiness. I think that life has a nobler meaning. I should despise myself if I made them the end and aim of my existence."

Lord Upperton could not quite comprehend her.

He was aware that across the sea many a mamma was laying her plans to make her daughter mistress of Halford, and the daughters had looked at him with languishing eyes, but here was a girl, guileless and pure, who was putting aside the great boon he would gladly bestow upon her. He must set before her the greatness of the gift. He described his estate — its parks, meadows, groves of oak, the herds of deer, flocks of pheasants; the rooms of the castle, the baronial hall, with antlers nailed upon the beams and rafters, banners that had been carried by ancestors at Crécy and Agincourt. He pictured life in London, scenes in Parliament, the queen's drawing-rooms, the pageantry and etiquette at St. James's. Miss Newville heard him in silence.

" Whatever there is to be had, whatever will contribute to your happiness, I shall lay at your feet, dear Miss Newville."

What should she say to him? How inform him that all the pageantry of King George's court, all the wealth inherited from his ancestors, was of little account in her esteem when set against eternal verities, and one of those verities was fidelity to the conviction that she must be true to herself.

" My lord," she said, " you may think me unappreciative; you may regard me as strange, but I must be true to myself. I cannot do violence to my better nature. I cannot barter my convictions. I could honor and respect you, but something more would be your due; that I could not give you. I could not make you happy, and I should forever despise myself."

It was spoken clearly, distinctly, but with a tremor

of voice and a flush upon her cheek that heightened her beauty. Lord Upperton sat in silence, pondering her words. It was dawning upon him that a girl of the Colonies had rejected his suit. He had come to her with his castle, his ancestry, his title, his position as a peer of the realm, but she had put them all aside. Not with them could he win his suit. Instead of accepting what he had to give, she stood calm, serene, beautiful, radiant, and pure, upon a height so far above him that he never could stand by her side. The silence was embarrassing.

"Miss Newville," he said, rising and standing before her, "your answer is painful to me. I had anticipated the winning of your hand and heart. It had not occurred to me that I should fail. I appreciate what you have said. A loftier ideal of the nobleness of true womanhood has come to me. My honor, respect, and love for you are deeper than ever, but I see that what I desired cannot be. I bid you farewell."

She courtesied to his bow, and extended her hand. He touched it to his lips, and passed from the room.

Her head was pressing her pillow once more. The bell struck the midnight hour. Once more she heard the watchman's voice.

"Twelve o'clock, and all is well."

"Yes, all is well." she said, — and her sleep for the night was calm and peaceful.

XIII.

On the evening of October 29, 1773, the Sons of Liberty again assembled at the Green Dragon. A ship had dropped anchor during the day off Castle William, bringing the news that Parliament had passed a law taxing tea. Ever watchful for the welfare of the people, they came together to hear what the London newspapers and their friends in England had to say about it, in letters which Samuel Adams had received. The night being cool, the landlord lighted a fire to warm the room, and enable those who might like a mug of flip to heat the loggerhead in the glowing coals. Upon the table, as usual, were the punch-bowl, crackers, cheese, tobacco, and pipes. Mr. Adams seated himself by the table and opened a letter.

"It is from Mr. Benjamin Franklin," he said, "who writes that Parliament has passed a law levying three pence per pound on tea. It is not to be collected here, as on other articles, but the merchant who ships it is to pay the duty. It is a very adroit attempt to collect revenue. The consignees in the Colonies, of course, will add the amount in their sales, and so the revenue will be collected without any agency on the part of the custom houses."

"I suppose," said Doctor Warren, "Lord North

and the whole British nation think we are such simpletons, we shall not see the cat in the meal."

" It is an insidious act," Mr. Adams resumed, " intended to undermine the political virtue of the people. Two years ago our wives and daughters exhibited their allegiance to lofty principles by signing an agreement not to drink tea until the obnoxious laws then existing were repealed. Lord North laughed at the time, but he has discovered that the people of the Colonies can be loyal to a great principle. The East India Company's receipts have fallen off at the rate of five hundred thousand pounds value per annum. The company has seventeen million pounds of tea stored in London, intended for the Colonies, and for which there is no market. It owes the government a vast sum. The merchants who have grown rich out of their profits in the past are not receiving any dividends. The shares of the company, which a few months ago were quoted at high rates, have become unsalable. Parliament has repealed the obnoxious laws for taxing the Colonies, and passed this act, doubtless thinking that, so long as we do not pay it directly into the custom house, we shall acquiesce and go to drinking tea again. And there is where the danger lies. We have been so true to our convictions the revenue received from its sale last year in all the Colonies was only fifteen hundred pounds. It is very humiliating to the king and ministry to turn to the other side of the ledger and find that it has cost several hundred thousand pounds to maintain the troops sent to the Colonies to aid in enforcing the revenue laws upon a reluctant people. This new act, by having all the customs machinery in England, will have a tendency to seduce the people from their allegiance to a great principle. How to thwart the plans of the ministry is the all-important question for us to consider. Mr. Franklin writes that several vessels are soon to leave London for different colonial ports — three of them for Boston."

"There is an old song," said Doctor Warren, "about a crafty old spider inviting a silly little fly into his parlor. I don't believe the fly will accept the invitation this time."

"The consignees," said Mr. Adams, "are Elisha and Thomas Hutchinson, the governor's two sons; Richard Clark and sons, Benjamin Faneuil, Junior, and Joshua Winslow, — all honorable merchants; but their sympathies, as we know, are not with the people. If we allow the tea to be landed, I fear the consequences. We must not permit the levying of a tax, without our consent, in any form."

"I move," said John Rowe, "that we do not permit the landing of any tea."

The meeting voted to adopt the motion. The formal business ended, they refilled their pipes, helped themselves to crackers and cheese, punch and flip.

Berinthia Brandon, the following week, could not understand why Tom wanted Dinah to make him a pot of paste; nor why he was out so late at night, — not getting home till three o'clock in the morning. None of the watchmen, going their rounds, saw anybody pasting handbills on the walls of the houses, but everybody saw the bills in the morning.

TO THE FREEMEN OF THIS AND NEIGHBORING TOWNS.

GENTLEMEN, — You are desired to meet at Liberty Tree, this day at twelve o'clock noon, then and there to hear the persons to whom the tea shipped by the East India Company is consigned make a public resignation of their office on oath as consignees; and also swear that they will reship any tea that may be consigned to them by said company, by the first vessel sailing for London.   O. C.

Secretary.

BOSTON, Nov. 3, 1773.

Show us the man that dare take this down ! ! ! ! !

Early in the morning the town crier was jingling his bell and calling upon the people to be at the Liberty Tree at the appointed hour. Samuel Adams, John Hancock, Doctor Warren, and William Molineux were there, and a great crowd. The consignees were assembled in Richard Clark's store. The people voted to choose a committee to inform them that, if they did not resign or pledge themselves not to land the tea, they would be regarded as the enemies of their country. William Molineux, Doctor Warren, and six others were chosen.

A great crowd accompanied the committee. Governor Hutchinson, looking out upon them from the window of the council chamber, saw that they were the foremost men of Boston. The consignees were in Richard Clark's store, and the door was locked.

"From whom are you a committee," asked Clark, opening a window.

" From the whole people."

" I shall have nothing to do with you."

" Then you will be regarded as an enemy of your country," replied Molineux.

" Out with them ! " cried somebody.

" Hold on. Don't let us make fools of ourselves," said Tom Brandon.

There was a murmuring in the crowd.

" In the king's name, I command you to disperse," said the sheriff, stepping forward.

It was not he, however, but Doctor Warren, who, by a wave of his hand, stilled the people, and persuaded them to depart.

On Sunday morning, November 29, Tom Brandon, looking with the telescope, saw a ship at Nantasket, and knew by the signals that it was the Dartmouth, Captain Hall. When meeting was over at noon, he called upon Doctor Warren and found him writing a circular to be sent to the surrounding towns, asking the people to assemble on Monday morning in Faneuil Hall. Tom took the writing to the printing office of Edes & Gill in Queen Street, and a printer quickly put it in type. On Monday morning the people of Boston, Charlestown, Cambridge, and all surrounding towns were reading it.

FRIENDS! COUNTRYMEN! BROTHERS!

The worst of plagues, the detested tea, shipped for this port by the East India Company, has arrived. The hour of destruction or manly opposition to the machinations of tyranny stares you in the face. Every friend to his country, to himself, and posterity

is now called upon to meet at Faneuil Hall at nine
o'clock this day, at which time the bells will ring, to
make a united resistance to this last, worst, and most
destructive measure of administration!

BOSTON, Nov. 30, 1773.

The bells rang. The people surged into Faneuil
Hall. There was a crowd in the square around the
building, — so many people that they adjourned to the
Old South Meetinghouse, where they voted that the
tea must go back to England, and that twenty-five men
should keep watch day and night, to prevent its being
landed. The meeting adjourned till Tuesday morning
to hear what the consignees would do.

Through the night Abraham Duncan and the other
watchmen patrolled the wharves. The Dartmouth had
sailed up the harbor and was riding at anchor.

A great crowd filled the meetinghouse at nine
o'clock Tuesday. The moderator read a letter from
Richard Clark and the other consignees, who said
they could not send the tea back, but would put it in
their stores till they could hear from the East India
Company.

"No! no! no!" shouted the people, who were more
than ever determined that it should not be landed.

Tom saw the sheriff, with his sword by his side, as
the emblem of authority, enter the meetinghouse, with
a paper in his hand.

"It is from his excellency, the governor," said the
sheriff, bowing to the moderator.

"We don't want to hear it," shouted the people.

"We are assembled in orderly town meeting. I

think we had better hear what the governor has to communicate," said Samuel Adams, and the great audience became silent. Tom's blood began to boil as the sheriff read : —

"You are openly violating, defying, and setting at nought the good and wholesome laws of the Province under which you live. I warn you, exhort, and require each of you, thus unlawfully assembled, forthwith to disperse, and to surcease all further unlawful proceedings at your utmost peril."

Tom, and all around him hissed.

"We won't disperse till we 've done our business," shouted a man in the centre of the house.

"We will attend to our affairs, and Tommy Hutchinson may mind his own business," cried another.

"Let us hear from Mr. Rotch," the shout.

Mr. Rotch, a young merchant, wearing a broad-brimmed hat, and who owned the Dartmouth, rose.

"I am willing the tea should go back without being landed," he said.

The people clapped their hands.

"Hall! Hall! Let us hear from Captain Hall," they cried.

The captain of the Dartmouth, sunburned by exposure, said it made no difference to him. He would just as soon carry the tea back as anything else. Once more the people decided the tea should not be brought on shore. To prevent its being landed it was voted that the watch should be maintained; that if the attempt was made by day, the meetinghouse bells would ring, if by night, they were to toll.

A few days later, the Beaver, commanded by Cap-

tain Coffin, and the Elenor, commanded by Captain
Bruce, arrived.   Tom, once more looking down the
harbor, saw the warship Kingfisher drop down below
the Castle and anchor in the channel; also the Active.
He understood the meaning of the movement — that
• the governor did not intend the ships should depart
with the tea on board.   He knew things would soon
come to a head, for under the law, unless a vessel discharged its cargo within twenty days after arriving
in port, the ship and cargo would be confiscated.
Once more the people assembled, electing Thomas
Savage moderator, and passing a vote directing Mr.
Rotch to ask the collector to clear the Dartmouth for
London.

Rain was falling, and the wind east, rolling the
waves into the harbor, on the morning of December
16.   Unmindful of the storm, people from Boston
and all the surrounding towns were gathering in
the Old South Meetinghouse.   Little did the farthest
sighted among them comprehend that the fullness
of time had come for the opening of a mighty
drama ; that the bell up in the tower was heralding
the beginning of a new era in human government.

Tom and Abraham found seats in the gallery.
After prayer, Samuel Adams said the committee
appointed at a previous meeting had called upon the
collector, with Mr. Rotch, asking him to clear the
Dartmouth, but the request was not granted.

" We all know," he continued, " that the twenty
days will expire at twelve o'clock to-night.   After
that hour the Dartmouth will be moored under the
guns of Admiral Montague's warships, and will be

taken possession of by a party of marines. I therefore move that Mr. Rotch be directed to enter his
protest at the Custom House, and that he be further
directed by this meeting to apply to Governor Hutchinson for a permit that shall allow the Dartmouth to
pass the Castle and sail for London."

"All in favor of that motion will say aye," said the
moderator.

"Aye!" thundered the floor, galleries, aisles, and
pulpit stairs.

"All opposed will say no."

The silence was so profound that Tom could hear
his heart beat.

"This meeting stands adjourned to three o'clock,"
said the moderator, and the great crowd thereupon
surged into the streets. Some went to the Cromwell's
Head; others to the Bunch of Grapes, White Lamb,
Tun and Bacchus, drank mugs of flip, and warmed
themselves by the bright wood-fires blazing on the
hearths. The meeting had adjourned to give Mr. Rotch
time to jump into his chaise and ride out to Milton
to see Governor Hutchinson.

Tom and Abraham walked towards the Cromwell's
Head. They were surprised and delighted to meet
Roger Stanley.

"I didn't hear of the meeting till last evening,"
said Roger, "and I have come in to see what is
going on."

The rain had drenched his clothes.

"See here, Roger, you are wet to the skin; you
must have some toddy. Come along, I'll stand
treat," said Tom.

They entered the Cromwell's Head, and each took a glass of flip, then made their way to the Long Room in Queen Street. Climbing the stairs, Tom rapped on a door. A moment later a panel opened, and a nose, mouth, and eyes appeared. Tom gave another rap which the nose, mouth, and eyes seemed to understand, for the door opened, and they passed in and it closed behind them.

Several of the Sons of Liberty were already there. Some were smoking pipes, others sipping mugs of hot punch. Edward Preston was sitting at a table writing.

" The sachem has just finished his proclamation, and is going to read it," said Henry Purkett.

The room became still, and Preston read what he had written.

Abrant Kan-ak-ar-a-toph-qua, Chief Sachem of the Mohawks, King of the Six Nations and Lord of all their Castles, etc., etc., to all Liege Subjects. Health.

Whereas, tea is an Indian Plant and of right belongs to the Indians of every land and tribe ; and whereas, our good allies, the English, have in lieu of it given us that pernicious liquor, Rum, which they have poured down our throats to steal away our brains; and whereas, the English have learned the most expeditious way or method of drawing an infusion of said *Tea*, without the expense of wood or trouble of fire, to the benefit and emolument of the East India trade, and, as vastly greater quantities may be used by that method than by that heretofore practiced in this country, and therefore help to support the East India Company under the present melancholy circumstances:

THEREFORE, we of our certain knowledge, special grace, and mere motion will permit, or allow any of our liege subjects to barter, buy, or procure of any of our English allies, *Teas* of any kind: *provided* always each man can purchase not less than ten nor more than one hundred and fourteen boxes at a time and those the property of the East India Company; and *provided* also that they pour the same into the lakes, rivers, and ponds, that, while our subjects in their hunting, instead of slaking their thirst with cold water, they may do it with tea.

Of all which our subjects will take notice and govern themselves accordingly. By command,

To-NE-TER-A-QUE.

"Attention, braves," said the sachem. "Each subject will provide himself with a tomahawk and be at the wigwam one hour after candle-lighting to-night, prepared to carry out the proclamation. The tribe will remember that the Mohawks do not talk much, but do in silence what they have to do."

They heard the proclamation in silence, and one by one took their departure. Roger said he would be in the Old South Meetinghouse at three o'clock to hear the result of the visit of Mr. Rotch to Governor Hutchinson.

"I doubt if I shall be there; I may have an engagement early in the evening," said Tom.

Abraham Duncan said the same.

" I went down to the shipyard this morning and got two tomahawks. They are in my chamber, together with the feathers and war-paint and the other things. Come round early, Abe," said Tom as they parted.

Again at three o'clock a great crowd filled the meetinghouse. The clouds had rolled away, and the setting sun was throwing its beams upon the gilded weather-vane when Roger Stanley entered the building. It was so full that he could only stand in one of the aisles. The moderator was reading letters from the selectmen of the surrounding towns, saying that they would stand by Boston in whatever might be done to prevent the landing of the tea.

" Their letters," said William Molineux, rising in one of the front pews, " are all very well; they show the determined spirit of our fellow-citizens; but we must have a committee whose duty it shall be to prevent the landing of the tea. I move the appointment of such a committee."

The meeting voted that a committee should be appointed.

The evening shades were falling and the housewives lighting their candles. In the Brandon house Tom and Abraham were putting on Indian uniforms which Mr. Brandon years before brought home from the tribes along the shores of the St. Lawrence — buckskin breeches and coats, fur caps trimmed with eagle's feathers. Tom tripped upstairs to the garret, and returned with a bunch of garget berries, with which they stained their faces and hands.

" You look just like Indians," said Berinthia.

"Say nothing to nobody as to what you have seen, 'Rinth," said Tom, as he closed the door and walked with Abraham rapidly along the street.

In the Old South Meetinghouse Josiah Quincy was speaking. The sexton brought in two tallow candles and placed them on the table before the moderator. There was a stir at the door — a commotion — a turning of necks in the pews, as the young merchant, Mr. Rotch, entered the building. Many in the audience thought he had been lukewarm in his desire to have the tea sent back to London, and were ready to hiss at him.

"Let us be just," said Doctor Young. "Let no one utter a word against our fellow-citizen. He is doing all it is possible for him to do to have the detested tea sent back."

The murmuring ceased as Samuel Adams addressed him : —

"Will you, Mr. Rotch, send the Dartmouth back to London with the tea on board?"

"Were I to make the attempt in compliance with the request of the people it would be my ruin."

Roger and all around him saw what they had not seen before, that were he to make the effort his ship would be seized and himself arrested, and in all probability sent to England to be tried for treason.

"Who knows how tea will mix with salt water?" shouted John Rowe.

"Let us treat the fishes to a cup of tea," shouted another, and the windows rattled with their stamping.

"Whoop! Whoop! Whoop!"

It was a yell from the street.

" Let the meeting be in order. It is a trick of our enemies to distract us," shouted some one.

" Order, gentlemen ! " cried the moderator.

" Whoop ! Whoop ! Whoop ! "

Longer and louder the yell.

" The Mohawks! the Mohawks ! " the cry at the door.

Those in the galleries left their seats and hastened down the stairs. People were rising in the pews and crowding the aisles.

" This meeting can do no more," said Mr. Adams, and he declared it adjourned.

The people saw forty or fifty Indians who had suddenly appeared upon the street. Where they came from no one knew, but they were rapidly making their way to Griffin's Wharf where the ships were lying. Roger Stanley and a great number of citizens followed them. The sentinels with muskets on their shoulders, keeping watch over the ships, made no effort to stop the Mohawks. Roger saw the ship Dartmouth alongside the wharf and the Elenor and Beaver a little distance from it. The chief leaped on board the Dartmouth. The captain was on the quarter-deck ; the crew huddled at the bow were astonished to see Indians with tomahawks climbing over the sides of the vessel.

" The Mohawks will unload your tea. Please direct your men to open the hatches and then order them below into the forecastle." said the chief, addressing the captain. " You will retire to your cabin. The Mohawks will not injure your ship or do you any harm."

It was spoken resolutely and in such good English that the captain understood every word. The sailors lifted the hatches, provided hoisting tackle, and disappeared down the forward hatchway, and the captain retired to his cabin. Roger saw an Indian run up the shrouds by the mainmast and hitch a tackle. He thought the savage had some resemblance to Tom Brandon. He also saw by the light of the moon, near its first quarter, that while one party of savages were at work upon the Dartmouth, others were warping the Elenor and the Beaver to the dock. It was nearly low tide, and the waves were swashing the timbers beneath the wharf. Not far away lay the Romney with her cannon peeping from the portholes. Very quietly the Mohawks began their work, hoisting chests from the hold, cutting them with hatchets, pouring the contents over the sides of the vessels. Roger felt a desire to take part in the work. Running to a blacksmith's shop, he smeared his face and hands with charcoal, took off his coat, turned it inside out, put it on, leaped on board the ship, seized a hatchet, smashed the chests, and tumbled them overboard. The Indians worked in silence. The clock was striking ten when the last chest was thrown into the dock. Their work finished, the chief rapped upon the cabin door, and the captain opened it.

" We have discharged your tea, captain, but we have disturbed nothing else. If we have we will cheerfully pay the damage."

The captain thanked him for being so considerate.

Tom, Abraham, and Roger, and the other Indians, walked up the street past the house of Nathaniel

Coffin, his majesty's receiver-general.   His eldest son, Isaac, one of Tom's schoolmates, had just sailed for England, Admiral Montague having obtained a commission for him in the king's navy, but John, the younger brother, was at home.

Admiral Montague was there standing by an open window.

"Well, boys, you have had a fine, pleasant evening for your Indian caper; but don't forget, you will have to pay the fiddler by and by."

" Oh, never mind, admiral, we are ready to pay him now," Tom replied.

The other Indians laughed as the admiral closed the window and turned away.

Very quietly the Mohawks separated.   Abraham went to his own house, Roger went with Tom.   They were soon in their chamber washing the garget stains and charcoal from their faces and hands.

" Rat-a-tat-tat ! " went the knocker on the door.

They heard feet tripping over the stairs and then Berinthia's voice.   " Oh, Tom, the officers are at the door.   Put out your light.   Let me have your Indian clothes.   Get to bed, quick."

Tom raised the window, emptied the water from the bowl into the alley behind the house, handed his Indian suit to Berinthia, put out the light, and jumped into bed.   Captain Brandon was not at home, having gone to Maine to obtain timber for the building of a ship.   Berinthia returned to her room, lifted the sheets and blankets, tucked Tom's suit safely away between the feather bed and the straw mattress beneath it.

" Rat-a-tat-tat! Rat-a-tat-tat! " went the knocker, louder than before. Tom heard Berinthia's window open.

" Who 's there, and what is wanted ? " It was Berinthia speaking. ·

" Is Captain Brandon at home ? " asked one of the men at the door.

" He is not. He is in Maine."

" We want to search your house."

" Why do you wish to search it ? "

" An outrage has been committed, and we believe that his son had a hand in it!"

" My brother is in bed, and a friend is spending the night with him; but I will go and tell him."

Several minutes passed before Tom could strike a light with the tinder-box, put on his clothes, and get to the door. Before descending the stairs he looked in the glass to see that the stains had been wholly removed from his face, and examined the floor to ascertain that no tea-leaves had been dropped from their clothing. He then descended the stairs and opened the door.

" Good-evening. What is it you wish ? " he said.

" You are Tom Brandon, are you not ? " asked one of the officers.

" That is my name."

" It is believed, Mr. Brandon, that you were one of the party who poured the tea into the harbor this evening, and we have come to search for evidence."

" Come right in, gentlemen."

The officers stepped into the hall.

" This is the parlor, here is the sitting-room, and

beyond it is the pantry. I don't think you will find much tea, for we quit drinking it three years ago, and have n't had any since," said Tom.

"Shall we see your chamber, Mr. Brandon?"

"Certainly; you will find my old schoolmate, Roger Stanley of Concord, in bed, but he won't mind."

They climbed the stairs, entered the chamber, asked Mr. Stanley's pardon for intruding, took a look at the washbowl, opened a clothespress, got down on their knees and looked at the floor, to see if they could find any tea.

"Here is another chamber, my sister's; she spoke to you from the window. You will hardly think of entering the room till she has had time to put on her dress."

"Oh, no; we would not be so rude as to enter her chamber. We do not suppose she had anything to do with it," said the officers.

"Will you not take a look at the garret?" Tom asked.

"No. You have covered your tracks so well, I do not suppose we should find anything."

"Thank you. If, as you say, I had a hand in it, I regard it quite a compliment that I have covered my tracks so well," Tom replied, as the officers took their departure. He went upstairs and opened the door to Berinthia's chamber a little.

"'Rinth, you are the best girl that ever lived," he said.

"Oh. Tom, you did that splendidly," she replied.

There was merry laughter from her lips as he closed the door and returned to his chamber.

XIV.

THE summer of 1774 was waning. Once more Robert, Walden was on his way to Boston. The wagon which Jenny and Paul were dragging was loaded with bags filled with corn and rye, not to be sold in the market, but a gift from Joshua Walden and his fellow-citizens of Rumford to the people of Boston. Parliament, in retaliation for the destruction of the tea, had passed an act closing the port to commerce.[1] After the first day of June, no vessels other than those of the navy could enter or depart from the harbor. Fishermen could no longer catch cod or mackerel for the market. Farmers on the banks of the Mystic could not dig potatoes from their fields and transport them down the river on the ebbing tide to the town dock. The people of Charlestown could not gather cabbages from their gardens, take them

---

[1] It is known in history as the Boston Port Bill. It was passed as a retaliatory measure. No possible advantage could accrue to government by its passage and enforcement. It was designed not only to awe the people into submission, but to overturn the government of the people and establish kingly prerogative. Parliament could not have committed a greater blunder. Instead of humbling the people of Boston, it aroused the sympathies of the entire country, and became a potent influence in bringing about the union of the Colonies. Contributions of food, wheat, corn, rye, peas, beans, flocks of sheep, and herds of cattle came from all of the Colonies.

across the ferry, and peddle them in Boston. Only by the road leading to Roxbury could the suffering people be supplied with food. Besides closing the port, Parliament had abolished the charter of Massachusetts. The people no longer could elect thirty-six councilors; they were to be appointed by the king, instead. No more could they lawfully assemble in town meeting to elect representatives to the legislature. All rights and privileges were swept away.

It was near sunset when Robert turned into the highway leading from Roxbury to Boston. He was surprised to find fortifications — a ditch and embankment and cannon mounted upon it — at the narrowest part of the Neck. The sentinels glared at him, but did not offer any insult.[1] He knew several regiments of troops had already arrived, and it was reported that others would soon be sent from England to enforce the laws. He drove slowly along the street, past the Liberty Tree. A half dozen citizens were sitting on the benches beneath it smoking their pipes. There were few people but many soldiers in the streets. He watered the horses at the pump, then drove to the Green Dragon.

It was a hearty welcome which he received in the Brandon home.

" You find us under the harrow." said Mr. Brandon. " The king and ministry are determined to crush the life out of us. All business has stopped. Grass is growing in the streets. Ship-carpenters,

---

[1] Several regiments of troops had already arrived in Boston, and fortifications were being constructed on Roxbury Neck, making it a garrisoned town.

joiners, blacksmiths, ropemakers, are idle; no one has any work for them. Thousands have already left town, and others are going. Nobody can earn a penny, and we are all growing poorer. We should starve in a short time were it not for the kindness and benevolence of the people. We are receiving contributions of food from everywhere. Doctor Warren, John Hancock, and a large number of our public-spirited citizens are distributing the gifts."

Tom said he was aiding the committee, looking after the poor. Not only were kind-hearted people sending grain, but flocks and herds.

"Only yesterday," he said, "Colonel Israel Putnam, who served in the French and Indian war, arrived with a flock of sheep from Connecticut. Day before yesterday a sloop dropped anchor in Salem harbor, loaded with corn contributed by the people of North Carolina. It will be teamed into Boston. The Marblehead fishermen have just sent between two and three hundred quintals of codfish. The committee has received a letter from Mr. Gadsden of South Carolina, expressing the hope that we never will pay a cent for the blasted tea. As evidence that South Carolina is with us, he sent one hundred casks of rice, contributed by his fellow-citizens, shipping it to Providence, to be hauled the rest of the way by teams. The people of Baltimore loaded a vessel with three thousand bushels of corn, twenty barrels of rye flour, and as many of shipbread. Herds of cattle and flocks of sheep are driven in every day. The town of Lebanon, Connecticut, sent three hundred and seventy sheep; Norwich, two hundred and ninety; Groton, one hun-

dred sheep and twenty-six fat cattle. Two schooners
have arrived at Salem, bringing three thousand bushels of corn from Maryland. Another vessel brought
one thousand bushels from Virginia."

"These contributions," said Mr. Brandon, "show
that the people of the Colonies, or at least a large
portion of them, sympathize with us in our resistance
to tyranny."

"You have not told me about Rachel; is she well?"
Berinthia asked.

Robert informed her she was quite well, and hard
at work as usual.

"I suppose she is spinning for herself, these days?"
said Berinthia, smiling.

"Yes. I dare say; she has been making sheets and
pillow-cases since Roger Stanley was in Rumford."

"She has written me about him, and thinks there
is nobody else in the world so good as he. I'm glad
they are engaged. She is just the one for him and
he for her."

There was one person whom Robert wished to
know about, who had been in his thoughts through
every step of his journey. How should he ask about
Miss Newville without revealing his interest in her?
How ascertain if she were well; if her heart was still
her own?

"I suppose the arbitrary acts of Parliament may
have brought about estrangements between old-time
friends," he said.

"Yes, former friendships are being broken. Many
of my old acquaintances do not speak to me."

"Is it so bad as that?"

"Yes, families are being divided. Fathers and mothers taking sides with the king, sons and daughters standing resolutely for the rights of the people. You remember that sweet girl, Lucy Flucker, whom you met at Miss Newville's garden party?"

"Yes, a lovely lady."

"Her father is secretary of the Colony, and of course sides with the king, but she is soon to be married to the bookseller, Mr. Knox, greatly against the wishes of the family; not because he is not worthy of her, but because he opposes the king and his ministers," said Berinthia.

"Are you and Miss Newville still friends?"

"Yes, just as good friends as ever. Her father, of course, is a Tory, and her mother is a red-hot one, but Ruth keeps her own counsel. You can have no idea what a noble girl she is, gracious to everybody, but true to herself. She had an offer of marriage from Lord Upperton, a little while ago, and refused him, to the astonishment of all her friends, and especially her mother. Just why she rejected his suit no one knows. Intimate as we are, she never has let me into the secret."

"From what little I have seen of Miss Newville, she seems to be a lady of sterling character," Robert replied.

"She has many admirers, especially among his majesty's officers. She receives them with charming courtesy, listens to their flattering words, but is very chary of her favors. I do not wonder that half a dozen colonels, majors, and captains are dead in love with her. I hope you will see her while here. She often inquires about you and Rachel, and wishes she could have another ride in a pung. I'll tell you what I'll do, — invite her to take supper with us, and then you'll see what a glorious girl she is."

" I can believe all you say of her."

Once more, the following morning, Robert had the pleasure of shaking hands with Doctor Warren and Samuel Adams, and receiving the thanks of the committee of supply for the contribution from Rumford.

Mr. Adams said the Colonies must prepare to enter upon a struggle to maintain their liberties. Governor Gage was carrying things with a high hand. A few nights before, a body of troops had seized the powder in the magazines out towards Medford, and taken it to the Castle.[1] General Gage was seizing muskets. He had purchased cannon and cohorn mortars, and chain-shot of Mr. Scott, and had paid him five hun-

---

[1] The powder belonging to the Province was stored in a magazine on Quarry Hill, in Charlestown. During the month of August, 1774, several of the towns removed their proportion of the ammunition. At half past four o'clock, on the morning of September 1, Lieutenant-Colonel Madison, with 260 men, embarked in thirteen large boats at Long Wharf, rowed up Mystic River, and landed at Mr. Temple's farm, seized 250 half barrels of powder and landed it in the Castle, also two cannon from the gun-houses in Cambridge. The news spread, and before evening nearly 5,000 people had assembled in Cambridge with their muskets. They compelled Mr. Danforth, member of the governor's council, to resign. The high-sheriff promised to serve no warrant under the new act of parliament. Lieutenant-Governor Oliver hastened to Boston, and informed General Gage that if he were to send a body of troops into the country the people would rise in their anger. Upon his return to Cambridge the people surrounded his house and compelled him to resign his commission. General Gage wrote to London that he must have more troops to enable him to strike a decisive blow. He expected the people would march into Boston. In order to prevent surprise, the guards were doubled, and the troops ordered to lay on their arms through the night.

dred pounds for them. He hoped the people of Rumford would put themselves in a condition to be ready at a minute's warning to resist any aggressions on the part of the troops. It was evident that the king was determined to carry out his plans by force of arms.

Having delivered the donation to the committee, Robert strolled through the town, finding many houses, shops, and stores tenantless. There was a strange silence, — no hurrying of feet, no rumbling of teams, no piles of merchandise. The stores were closed, the shutters fastened. Grass was growing in the streets and tufts of oats were springing up where the horses, a few weeks before, had munched their provender. Here and there he met men and boys, wandering listlessly, with sadness in their faces, but yet behind the sorrow there was a determination to endure to the bitter end.

Robert visited his old acquaintance, Henry Knox, no longer in the bookstore at the corner of King Street, opposite the Town House, but in a store of his own on Cornhill. He passed a tailor's shop and a harness-maker's before he came to Mr. Knox's bookstore, where he was heartily welcomed.

"I remember the book which you purchased the first time we met; I hope you liked it."

"It is very entertaining, and has been read by nearly everybody in Rumford, and is pretty much worn out," Robert replied.

While talking with Mr. Knox, he saw a white-haired gentleman pass the store. The next moment he heard a bell jingling in the shop of the harness-maker, then in the shoemaker's, and lastly in the tailor's. Mr. Knox laughed as the gentleman quickened his pace.

" Possibly, Mr. Walden, you do not understand the ringing of the bells in succession. The gentleman is one of the Tory councilors recently appointed by Governor Gage. He has accepted the appointment and the citizens are worrying the life out of him. Each shopman has a bell which he jingles the moment he spies a councilor, giving notice to the other shopmen." Mr. Knox looked up at the clock. " It is about time for the council to assemble in the Town House; quite likely you will hear the bells tinkle again. More than half of those appointed by General Gage have already resigned, and I do not doubt others will ere long throw up their commissions. Not much honor is to be gained by holding an office against public opinion."

" It is not a pleasing sight — the presence of so many troops," Robert remarked.

" Nominally, we are under civil law; but in reality our civil rights are gone, and we are under military government," Mr. Knox replied.

Two officers entered the store and were courteously received by the bookseller, who showed them the latest books received from London. He informed Robert, in a whisper, that they were Major John Small and Ensign De Berniere. Another gentleman entered, a citizen, whose coat was covered with dust, as if he had been long on the road. He was heartily welcomed by Mr. Knox, who introduced him to Robert as Colonel Israel Putnam of Connecticut.

"I think I have heard my father speak of you; he was a lieutenant under Captain Stark at Ticonderoga. Perhaps you remember him," Robert said.

"Indeed I do remember Joshua Walden, and a braver man never wore a uniform in the Rifle Rangers than he."

The major of the king's troops laid down his book and approached with outstretched hand.

"Well, I declare! If here is n't my old friend Putnam," he said.

There was mutual hand-shaking between Major Small and Colonel Putnam, who had fought side by side under the walls of Ticonderoga and at Fort Edward.

"And so you are here to enforce the Regulation Act," said Putnam.

"It is because you are rebellious," Small replied.

"You are attempting to subvert our liberties by enforcing unrighteous laws. The Colonies exhibited their loyalty to the king when we stood side by side to drive out the French. We taxed ourselves to the utmost. England has repaid but a very small proportion of the cost. We were loyal then, and we are loyal now; but we never will submit to tyranny," continued Putnam.

"The people of this town threw the tea into the dock, and now they must pay for it. Those that dance must settle with the fiddler," Small replied.

"Not one penny will we ever pay. Parliament and the king have closed the port, bringing distress upon the community; but it has awakened the sympathies of the country from Passamaquoddy to Savannah.

Now, Small, you are an old soldier, and so am I; we have smelled gunpowder, and can afford to talk plainly. You are here, five thousand or more, with several thousand additional troops just ready to sail from England. You have come to overawe us by force of arms. You have changed the charter of this Province; if this, why not all the others? Why do you do it? I say you, for you represent the king; you do it because you are determined to make the Colonies subservient to the crown. You cannot bear to have us manufacture anything this side of the sea, and are determined to make us your milch cow. Let me tell you that you won't succeed. You do not know the spirit of the people. Let one drop of blood be shed by the troops, and a mighty host of armed men will close around you. I know you can fight, and so can we; if you don't think so, try it."

" Ha, ha! Put, you are the same old flint, ever ready to strike fire. We won't quarrel now. Come, let us step down to the Bunch of Grapes, have a glass of wine, and talk over old times."

Arm in arm they walked down King Street to the tavern.

Early the following afternoon Miss Newville was welcomed to the Brandon home.

" It is a long time since we have met," she said, reaching out her hand to Robert. " I am pleased to see you once more. I hope you are well. And how is Rachel?"

Many times he had thought of her as he last beheld her, standing beneath the portico of her home in the radiant light of the moon. Her parting words had been an abiding memory — "Good-by, till we meet again." Once more her hand was resting in his. She was no longer a girl, but entering upon womanhood. He told the reason of his being there, to bring the gift of Rumford to the suffering poor. She had many questions to ask about Rachel. Was she still making cheese? Had she many flowers?

"I suppose Rachel's brother prepares the flower-beds as in former years," she said, laughing.

"Yes, I spaded them for her."

"Berinthia informs me that she has found her true love."

"So it appears."

"I doubt not she is very happy."

"She seems to be ; she is singing from morning till night."

"I am so glad. I only saw Mr. Stanley at the time of the launching of the ship, you remember, but thought him worthy of any woman's love. Do you still have delightful times at quiltings and huskings?"

"In the country, customs rarely change. The young ladies still have their quilting parties. Rachel will soon be getting her fixings, and we doubtless shall have jolly times."

"I should like to be able to help her. With so many things to care for, I do not suppose she finds much time for reading?"

"Very little. Besides, we do not have many books to read. 'The New Hampshire Gazette' comes once a week, giving us a little glimpse of what is going on in the world."

"I forgot you have no bookstore with all the new

volumes printed in London, — history, travel, poetry, and novels, as we have here."

She said that Mr. Knox, the bookseller, had been very kind to her, supplying her with the new books arriving from London, and had just handed her the poems of Oliver Goldsmith.

The afternoon waned.

" Shall we go up on the housetop and see the sun set ? " Berinthia asked.

The harbor, the fleet of warships at anchor, the distant ocean, the distant woodlands, made a beautiful panorama.

" When I see such beauty," said Miss Newville, " I want to be an artist or a poet to give expression to my feelings.   See the purple and gold on the Milton Hills, the light on the water, the russet and crimson of the forests !   How beautiful ! " she cried, with a rich bloom upon her cheek as she gazed upon the landscape. The tap of a drum and the tramping of a regiment along the street attracted her attention.   " I am weary of seeing scarlet uniforms," she said.

" Will you not make an exception of those who call upon Miss Newville ? " Berinthia asked.

" No.   I do not even care to see General Gage or Earl Percy in their gold-laced coats.   They are delightful gentlemen, and frequent visitors in our home.   I find much pleasure in listening to Earl Percy's description of things in London ; but I should be better pleased were he to visit us as a citizen, laying aside his military trappings, the emblems of arbitrary power."

The sun was sinking behind the western hills.   As

LORD PERCY

the last beams faded from the gilded vane of Christ Church, they heard the beating of drums and the shrill piping of boatswain's whistles on the decks of the warships. A cannon flashed on the bastion of the Castle, and the boom of the gun rolled far away as the Cross of St. George descended from flagstaff and topmast to be furled for the night.

"It is the sunset gun; the signal for taking down the flags," said Berinthia.

"I often watch from my chamber window for the flashing of the cannon," Miss Newville remarked.

"It is a beautiful sight; but would be more exhilarating if the flag was what it ought to be," said Robert.

The twilight had not faded from the sky when Robert accompanied Miss Newville to her home. Officers of the king's regiments lifted their hats to her upon the way; their attentions were recognized with dignified grace. Robert saw scowls on their faces as they glared at him, as if to challenge his right to be her escort.

"The night is hot and the air sultry, and if you please, Mr. Walden, we will sit in the garden rather than in the house," she said.

They strolled beneath the trees bending with the weight of ripening fruit, and seated themselves in a rustic arbor. The early grapes were purpling above them.

"I do not know, Mr. Walden, that I quite comprehended your meaning when you said the flag would be more beautiful if it were what it ought to be. I think it very beautiful as it is."

" I did not have reference, Miss Newville, to the texture or quality of the cloth, or the arrangement of colors, neither to the devices, — the crosses of St. George and St. Andrew, — but thought of it as a symbol of power. My father fought under it, and it has waved in triumph on many battlefields ; but just now it is being used to deprive us of our rights."

" Have you ever read the legend of St. George?" she asked.

" I have not, and I hardly know what the Cross of St. George stands for."

" It is a beautiful story. I read it not long ago in a book which I found in Mr. Knox's store. Would you like to hear it?"

" Please tell me about it."

" The story runs that ever so many years ago there was a terrible dragon — a monster, part snake, part crocodile, with sharp teeth, a forked tongue, claws, and wings. It could crawl upon the land or swim in the water. Every day it came from its lair and ate the sheep in the pastures around the old city of Berytus. When the sheep were gone it ate little children. The king of the city could think of nothing better than to issue an edict requiring the selection of two children under fifteen years old by lot, to be given to the dragon. One day the lot fell upon the king's daughter, the Princess Cleodolinda, a beautiful girl, and as good as she was beautiful. It was a terrible blow to the king. He offered all his gold, precious stones, glittering diamonds, and emeralds, and half his kingdom, if the people would consent to her exemption, which they wouldn't do. He had made the edict; they had given their children; he must give his daughter. Being king, he thought he could take somebody's else daughter. That made the people angry, and they threatened to kill him. Then the princess showed how good and noble and true she was. She said she would die rather than there should be any trouble. It was a sad morning when she bade her father and mother and all her friends good-by, and went out from the city, all the people weeping to see her in her youth and beauty, so calm, peaceful, and resigned, walking in the green field, waiting for the dragon. They saw the monster crawl towards her. Just then they beheld a young man with a shining shield and waving plume, on horseback, with sword and lance, approaching. It was George of Cappadocia, a brave Christian youth. 'Fly! fly!' shouted the princess. 'Why should I fly?' he asked. 'Do you not see the dragon? He will eat you as he will me.' 'I am not afraid of him, and I will deliver you,' said he, rushing upon the dragon with his lance. It was a terrible fight. The monster hissing, running out his tongue, snapping his jaws, striking with his tail and sharp claws; but the brave George kept up the fight, striking his lance through the thick hide and shiny scales, and pinning the writhing creature to the earth. 'It is not by my own might, but God, through Jesus Christ, who has given me the power to subdue this Apollyon,' he said. At that, the whole city accepted the Christian religion. In recognition of the victory he put the sign of the letter X, representing the cross, upon his flag. The king was so pleased that, besides becoming a Christian, he offered

George all his gold and silver and diamonds and precious stones; but the prince would not keep them; he gave them to the poor."

"It is indeed a beautiful story," said Robert, charmed by the narration.

"I suppose the legend represents the conflict between wickedness and righteousness," added Miss Newville.

"Did George become the son-in-law of the king?" Robert asked.

Miss Newville laughed heartily.

"If it were a story in a novel," she said, "of course that would be the outcome of the romance. No; he went on his travels converting people to Christianity. The Greek Christians kept him in remembrance by adopting the letter X as the sign of the cross. When Richard the Lion-Hearted started on his crusade to rescue the holy sepulchre from the Moslems, he selected St. George as his protector. He is the patron saint of England. He stands for courage in defense of the truth."

"That is what the Cross of St. George should stand for, Miss Newville, but just now it represents tyranny and oppression. It is a beautiful flag, the crosses of St. George and St. Andrew combined, in red, white, and blue. No other banner symbolizes so much that is precious of what men have done, but the king and his ministers are perverting it. St. George and St. Andrew were representatives of justice and righteousness. They died for principles which in their nature are eternal, which will remain, when we are gone. I have taken pride in being an Englishman. The flag thrills me. I like to think of the brave deeds that have been done under it. No other banner means so much. It stirs me to think of it as waving not only in England, but here, in Canada, in South America, and on the banks of the Ganges. Of course, the flag, the crosses upon it, signify suffering, devotion, heroism, bravery. It is these things that warm my blood."

"Go on, please, Mr. Walden. I want to hear more," said Miss Newville as he paused.

"I have delighted in being an Englishman because the flag stands for all I hold most dear, but I am conscious that my love for it is not what it was. The king and his ministers by their arbitrary acts, Parliament by passing laws taking away chartered rights, are alienating the affections of the Colonies. We are not so meek that we are ready to kiss the hand that smites us. The time may come, Miss Newville, when the people this side the Atlantic will have a flag of their own. If we do it will be a symbol of a larger liberty than we now have. The world does not stand still. I do not know what Almighty God has been reserving this Western world for through all the ages; but it must be for some grand purpose. It is a great land and it will be peopled some day. We have made our laws in the past, and we shall not surrender our right to do so. The king and his ministers are not using the crosses of St. George and St. Andrew for the good of all. The crosses should represent brotherhood, but they do not. I think the time may come, though, when there will be such a flag."

Again he paused, and again Miss Newville begged him to go on.

" I cannot tell when it will be, but I know what I would like to see."

" Please tell me," she said earnestly.

" I would like to see the time when men will recognize their fellow-men as brothers, and when the flag will stand for equality, unity, liberty, and brotherhood."

" Do you think such a time will ever come ? "

" I do not doubt it. The prophets in the Bible have predicted it, and it seems to me that the human race is advancing in that direction. Have you not noticed that almost everything we prize has come through sacrifice and suffering? I came here with food because the people of this town are suffering. The bags of corn which I have brought are an expression of brotherhood, of unity, love, and good will. The people all the way from the Penobscot to the Savannah are acting from such motives. It is curious that Parliament by passing a wicked law is uniting the Colonies as nothing else could have done. What the king designed for a punishment, in the end may be a great blessing."

" I see it, and I want to thank you, Mr. Walden, for your words. You have made clear what hitherto I have not been able to understand. Of course, you must be aware that I hear many conversations upon affairs in the Colonies. General Gage and Earl Percy are frequent guests in our home, as are many gentlemen who sympathize with the king and the ministry rather than with Mr. Adams and Doctor Warren. I do not see how the king, who they say is kind-hearted, could assent to a law which would bring suffering and starvation to so many people."

She sat in silence a moment, and then went on.

"I like to hear you, Mr. Walden, speak of that good time that is to come. I should like to do something to hasten it. I feel that I am stronger for what you have said. Shall we take a stroll through the grounds?"

Through the day he had been looking forward to a possible hour when he could be with her alone, to feel the charm of her presence. And now that it had come, what should he say, how let her know she had been an inspiration to him; how since their first meeting his last thought at night and the first of the morning had been of her? Were he to say the thought of her had filled the days with happiness, would she not think him presumptuous? They were widely separated by the circumstances of life, — he of the country, a farmer, swinging the scythe, holding the plow, driving oxen, feeding pigs; she, on the contrary, was a star in cultured society, entertaining high-born ladies and gentlemen, lords, earls, and governors; chance, only, had made them acquainted. She had been very kind. No, he must not presume upon her graciousness and tell her that his heart had gone out to her in a wonderful way. Many men had proffered their love, but had been rejected. It was blessedness unspeakable to be permitted to walk by her side, to hear her voice, to enjoy her esteem, friendship, and confidence.

The song-birds of summer had gone, but the crickets were merrily chirping around them; flowers were fading, but fruits were ripening. Slowly they walked the winding paths, stopping at times to gaze upon the clouds, silver-lined, in the bright light of the full-orbed moon.

"I shall not soon forget this quiet evening with you, Mr. Walden, nor the words you have spoken. I have thought it was my foreboding, but now I can see that there may be trying times before us, — times which will test friendships."

"I trust, Miss Newville, that I may ever be worthy to be numbered among your friends."

"I know you will." After a moment's hesitation she added, "The time may come when I shall need your friendship."

Her voice was tremulous. The nine o'clock bell was ringing. They were by the gate leading to the street.

"You go home to-morrow. Will it be long before we shall see you again? I may want such strength as you can give," she said.

"I trust that in God's good time we may meet again. How soon I may be here or what may bring me I do not foresee; but be assured, Miss Newville, I shall ever be your friend."

"I do not doubt it. Good-by," she said.

She heard his retreating footsteps growing fainter.

"Oh, if he had only said, 'I love you,'" the whisper on her lips.

"I could die for her; no, I'll live for her," he said to himself, as he walked towards the Brandon home.

XV

THE MIDNIGHT RIDE.

ABEL SHRIMPTON, loyal to the king, hated Samuel Adams and John Hancock and the Sons of Liberty, holding them responsible for the troubles that had come to the people. In Mr. Shrimpton's attractive home, made beautiful by the presence of his daughter, Tom Brandon had been a welcome visitor, but the relations between Mr. Shrimpton and Tom were changing.

"The Regulation Act," said Tom, "which in fact makes the king the government, deprives the people of their liberties."

"People who abuse their liberties ought to be deprived of them," Mr. Shrimpton replied.

"We are not allowed to select jurors. The law takes away our right to assemble in town meeting, except by permission, and then we can only elect selectmen to look after town affairs," said Tom.

"The people have shown they are not fit to govern themselves," said Mr. Shrimpton. "They allow the mob to run riot. It was a mob that smashed Chief Justice Hutchinson's windows. Your gatherings under the Liberty Tree are in reality nothing but mobs; you have no legal authority for assembling. It was a mob that assaulted the king's troops on the 5th of

March; a mob threw the tea into the harbor, and I strongly suspect that Tom Brandon had a hand in that iniquity. The king stands for law and order. The troops are here in the interest of good government, by constituted authority, to enforce the law and put down riots."

"Just who had a hand in throwing the tea overboard no one can find out, but I am glad it was done," said Tom.

"So you uphold lawlessness, Mr. Brandon?"

"I stand against the unrighteous acts of Parliament. We will not be slaves; we will not be deprived of our liberties. If King George and Lord North think they can starve the people of this town into submission. they will find themselves mistaken," said Tom.

"I hope he will compel every one of you to obey the laws, and that whoever had a hand in destroying the tea will suffer for it," Mr. Shrimpton replied.

Tom saw the smile fade from the countenance of Mary as she listened to the conversation. Her quick insight. and acquaintance with her father's surly temper, enabled her to see what was withholden from Tom's slower perception.

"Mary," said Mr. Shrimpton, after Tom took his departure. "I want you to stop having anything to do with Tom."

"Why. father?"

"Because I don't like him."

"But I do like him."

"No matter. He's an enemy to the king. I have good reason to believe he had a hand in throwing the tea overboard. If he did, he is no better than a thief. He willfully, wantonly, and with malice aforethought stole the property of others from the holds of the ships, and destroyed it. It was burglary — breaking and entering. It was a malicious destruction of property of the East India Company. It was a heinous affair — not mere larceny to be punished by standing in the pillory, or sitting in the stocks, or tied up to the whipping-post and flogged, but an offense which, if it could be proved, would send every one of the marauders to jail for ten or twenty years. Now I don't want the name of Shrimpton mixed up with that of Brandon. So you can cut Tom adrift."

" But, father " —

" I don't want any buts. You will do as I tell you if you know what is good for yourself."

" Have you not, father, said in the past that he was an estimable young man ? "

" But he is not estimable now. He meets others in secret to plot mischief. I have had spies on his track. He is a lawbreaker, a mischief-maker, and sooner or later will be in jail, and possibly may be brought to the gallows. Now, once for all, I tell you I will not have him coming here."

Mr. Shrimpton said it with a flushed face, setting his teeth firmly together as he rose from his chair.

" Very well, father," said Mary, wiping the tears from her eyes.

She knew how irascible he was at times, — how he allowed his anger to master reason, and hoped it might pass away. Through the night the words were repeating themselves. What course should she pursue? Give up Tom? What if he did help destroy the tea; was it not a righteous protest against the tyranny of the king and Parliament? He did not do it as an individual, but as a member of the community; it was the only course for them to pursue. Tom was not therefore a thief at heart. Was he not kind-hearted? Was he not giving his time and strength to relieve suffering? Had he not just as much right to stand resolutely for the liberties of the people as her father for the prerogatives of the king? Must she stop seeing him to please her father? It would not be pleasant to have Tom call upon her, and have her father shut the door in his face; that would be an indignity. Should she withdraw her engagement? Should she plunge a knife into her own heart to please her father? Never. Come what would, she would be true to Tom. She would not anger her father by inviting Tom to continue his visits, but there were the elms of Long Acre, Beacon Hill, the market, and other places, where from time to time they might meet for a few moments. True love could wait for better days.

There came a morning when the people saw a handbill posted upon the walls which said that the men who were misleading the people were bankrupt in purse and character. Tom Brandon's blood was at fever heat as he read the closing words : —

" Ask pardon of God, submit to our king and Parliament. whom we have wickedly and grievously offended. Let us seize our seducers, make peace with our mother country, and save ourselves and children."

He knew that the sentiments of the handbill were those of Mr. Shrimpton, and suspected that his hand had penned it. The rumor was abroad that the king had sent word to General Gage to seize the two arch leaders of the rebels, Adams and Hancock. The following evening Tom and other Sons gathered at the Green Dragon, laid their hands upon the Bible, and made a solemn oath to watch constantly the movements of the Tories and soldiers, and give information to Samuel Adams, John Hancock, Doctor Warren, and Benjamin Church, and to no others.

There came a day when a great multitude assembled in town meeting, in the Old South Meetinghouse, to listen to Doctor Warren's oration commemorative of the massacre of the people by the troops. Citizens from all the surrounding towns were there to let General Gage know they had not forgotten it; besides, they knew they would hear burning words from the lips of the fearless patriot.

Tom Brandon and Abraham Duncan, looking down from the gallery upon the great throng, saw Samuel Adams elected moderator. He invited the officers of the regiments to take seats upon the platform. Tom wondered if they were present to make mischief. The pulpit was draped in black. Every part of the house was filled, — aisles, windows, seats, — and there was a great crowd in the porches. Tom was wondering if it would be possible for Doctor Warren to edge his way through the solid body of men, when he saw the window behind the pulpit opened by one of the selectmen and the doctor, wearing a student's black gown, enter through the window. The audience welcomed him with applause. For more than an hour they listened spellbound to his patriotic and fearless words. At times the people made the building shake with their applause. Some of the king's officers grew red in the face when he alluded to their presence in Boston to suppress the liberties of the people. One of the officers of the Welsh Fusileers sitting on the stairs was very insulting. Tom saw him take some bullets from his pocket and hold them in the palm of his hand to annoy Doctor Warren, but instead of being frightened, he very quietly rebuked the officer's insolence by letting his handkerchief drop upon the bullets. Bold and eloquent were his closing words.

" Fellow-citizens," he said, " you will maintain your rights or perish in the glorious struggle. However difficult the combat, you will never decline it when freedom is the prize. Independence of Great Britain is not our aim. Our wish is that Britain and the Colonies may, like the oak and the ivy, grow and increase in strength together. If pacific measures fail, and it appears that the only way to safety is through fields of blood, I know you will not turn your faces from your foes, but will press forward till tyranny is trodden under foot and you have placed your adored goddess Liberty on her American throne."

The building shook with applause when he sat down.

" It is moved that the thanks of the town be presented to Doctor Warren for his oration," said the moderator.

" No, no! fie, fie ! " shouted a captain of the Royal Irish Regiment, and the other officers around thumped the floor with their canes.

Tom's blood was hot, as was the blood of those around him. Some of the people under the galleries, who could not see what was going on, thought the officers were crying fire, to break up the meeting. Very quietly Samuel Adams raised his hand. The people became calm. The officers left the building, and the town went on with its business. The people were learning self-control.

When the meeting was over, Tom and Abraham walked along Cornhill, and turned down King Street on their way home. They saw a crowd around the British Coffee House tavern, — the officers who a little while before had left the Old South Meetinghouse, laughing, talking, and drinking their toddy. Tom soon discovered they were having a mock town meeting. One was acting as moderator, pounding with his cane and calling them to order. They chose seven select-men and a clerk. Then one went upstairs and soon appeared upon the balcony wearing a rusty and ragged old black gown, a gray wig with a fox's tail dangling down his back. He bowed to those below, and began a mock oration. He called Samuel Adams, Doctor Warren, and John Hancock scoundrels, blackguards, knaves, and other vile names. His language was so scurrilous, profane, and indecent that Tom could not repeat it to his mother and Berinthia. Those who listened clapped their hands. Tom and Abraham came to the conclusion that most of the officers of the newly arrived regiments were too vile to be worthy the society of decent people.

Tom was boiling hot two nights later, at the treatment given Thomas Ditson of Billerica, who had come to market. A soldier persuaded the guileless young farmer to buy an old worn-out gun. The next moment he was seized by a file of soldiers and thrust into the guardhouse for buying anything of a soldier against the law. He had only the bare floor to sleep on. In the morning, Lieutenant-Colonel Nesbit ordered the soldiers to strip off Ditson's clothes, and tar and feather him.

It was a pitiful spectacle which Ruth Newville saw, — Colonel Nesbit marching at the head of his regiment, the soldiers with their bayonets surrounding a man stripped to the waist, smeared with tar, covered with feathers, the fifes playing, and the drums beating the Rogue's March.

"It is disgraceful," she said, with flashing eyes, to her mother. "Colonel Nesbit ought to be ashamed of himself. If he ever calls here again, I'll not speak to him."

Fast Day came, and again the eyes of Miss Newville flashed when she saw the king's troops parading the streets; the drummers and fifers taking their stations by the doors of the meetinghouses to annoy the people, playing so loud they could scarcely hear a word of what the minister was saying.

" Do you think, father, that General Gage will win back the affections of the people, or even retain their respect by permitting such outrages?" Ruth asked.

" Perhaps it is not the wisest course to pursue. Quite likely the officers of the regiments did it of their own notion." Mr. Newville replied.

If Lord North and King George thought a show of military force would overawe the people of Boston town, they were mistaken. Possibly they did not reflect that military repression might beget resistance by arms; but when the regiments began to arrive, the Sons of Liberty resolved to prepare for whatever might happen. They appointed a committee of safety to protect the rights of the people.

Winter was over, and with their singing the birds were making the April mornings melodious. The Provincial Congress was in session at Cambridge, and Samuel Adams and John Hancock had left Boston and with Dorothy Quincy were with Reverend Mr. Clark in Lexington. Abraham Duncan discovered that General Gage had sent Captain Brown and Ensign De Berniere into the country to see the roads.[1] Sharp-eyed Sons of Liberty watched the movements of the soldiers. They saw Lord Percy march his brigade to Roxbury, and return as if for exercise, with no one opposing them.

"We can march from one end of the continent to the other, without opposition from the cowardly Yankees," said the boasting soldiers.

Paul Revere, Tom Brandon, Robert Newman, and a score of the Sons of Liberty were keeping watch of the movements of the redcoats. They saw the sailors of the warships, and of the vessels which had brought the new troops, launching their boats and putting them in order. They knew General Gage

[1] Captain Brown and Ensign De Berniere, March 20, visited Concord and Worcester and intermediate towns, dressed as citizens. The vigilant Sons of Liberty were cognizant of all their movements and notified the patriotic citizens, who had them under surveillance every moment. Ensign De Berniere has written a narrative of the journey.

wanted to seize Samuel Adams and John Hancock, and quite likely the military supplies which the committee of safety had collected at Concord. Paul Revere rode out to Lexington on Sunday to see Adams and Hancock, and let them know what was going on in Boston.

"The launching of the ship's boat means something," said Mr. Adams. "It looks as if the troops were going to make a short cut across Charles River instead of marching over Roxbury Neck."

"We will keep our eyes open and let you know the moment they make any movement," said Revere.

"Quite likely Gage will set a patrol so you can't leave Boston," said Hancock.

"I'll tell ye what we'll do. If the troops leave in the night by way of Roxbury, I'll get Robert Newman to hang a lantern in the steeple of Christ Church; if they take boats to make the short cut across Charles River, I'll have him hang out two lanterns. I'll tell Deacon Larkin and Colonel Conant, over in Charlestown, to keep their eyes on the steeple."

It was Tuesday morning, April 18. Abraham Duncan wondered how it happened that so many British officers with their overcoats on were mounting their horses and riding out towards Roxbury, not in a group, but singly, or two together, with pistols in their holsters.

"We will dine at Winship's tavern in Cambridge, and then go on," he heard one say.

He also noticed that the grenadiers and light infantry guards were not on duty as on other days.

He hastened to inform Doctor Warren, who sent a messenger with a letter to the committee of safety.

It was evening when Richard Devens and Abraham Watson, members of the committee of safety, shook hands with their fellow members, Elbridge Gerry, Asa Orne, and Colonel Lee at Wetherby's, bade them good-night, and stepped into their chaise to return to their homes in Charlestown. The others would spend the night at Wetherby's, and they would all meet in Woburn in the morning.

Satisfying to the appetite was the dinner which landlord Winship set before a dozen British officers, — roast beef, dish gravy, mealy potatoes, plum-pudding, mince pie, crackers and cheese, prime old port, and brandy distilled from the grapes of Bordeaux.

" We will jog on slowly; it won't do to get there too early," said one of the officers as they mounted their horses and rode up past the green, and along the wide and level highways, towards Menotomy, paying no attention to Solomon Brown, plodding homeward in his horse-cart from market. When the old mare lagged to a walk, they rode past him; when he stirred her up with his switch she made the old cart rattle past them. The twinkling eyes peeping out from under his shaggy brows saw that their pistols were in the holsters, and their swords were clanking at times.

" I passed nine of them," he said to Sergeant Munroe when he reached Lexington Common; and the sergeant, mistrusting they might be coming to nab Adams and Hancock, summoned eight of his company to guard the house of Mr. Clark.

Mr. Devens and Mr. Watson met the Britishers.

"They mean mischief. We must let Gerry, Orne, and Joe know," Mr. Devens said.

Quickly the chaise turned, and they rode back to Wetherby's. The moon was higher in the eastern sky, and the hands of the clock pointed to the figure nine when the officers rode past the house.

"We must put Adams and Hancock on their guard," said Mr. Gerry; and a little later a messenger on horseback was scurrying along a bypath towards Lexington.

In Boston, Abraham Duncan was keeping his eyes and ears open.

"What's the news, Billy?" was his question to Billy Baker, apprentice to Mr. Hall, who sold toddy to the redcoats.

"I guess something is going to happen," said Billy.

"What makes you think so?"

"'Cause a woman who belongs to one of the redcoats was in just now after a toddy; she said the lobsters were going somewhere."

"Is that so?"

"Yes; and they are packing their knapsacks."

Abraham whispered it to Doctor Warren, and a few minutes later William Dawes was mounting his old mare and riding toward Roxbury. She was thin in flesh, and showed her ribs; and the man on her back, who dressed calf-skins for a living, jogged along Cornhill as if in no hurry. The red-coated sentinels, keeping guard by the fortifications on the Neck, said to themselves he was an old farmer, but were surprised to see him, after passing them, going like the wind out towards Roxbury, to the Parting Stone, then turning towards Cambridge, making the gravel fly from her heels as she tore along the road.

Berinthia Brandon, sitting in her chamber, looking out into the starlit night, saw the faint light of the rising moon along the eastern horizon. Twilight was still lingering in the western sky. In the gloaming, she saw the sailors of the warships and transports were stepping into their boats and floating with the incoming tide up the Charles. What was the meaning of it? She ran downstairs and told her father and Tom what she had seen ; and Tom,

Paul Revere's House.

seizing his hat, tore along Salem Street and over the bridge across Mill Creek to Doctor Warren's. The clock on the Old Brick Meetinghouse was striking ten when he rattled the knocker.

" The boats are on their way up the river with the tide," he said, out of breath with his running.

Abraham Duncan came in, also out of breath.

" The lobsters are marching across the Common, toward Barton's Point," he said.

" All of which means, they are going to take the boats and cross Charles River, instead of marching by way of Roxbury," said the doctor, reflecting a moment.

He asked Tom.if he would please run down to North Square and ask Paul Revere to come and see him.

A few minutes later Revere was there.

" I 've already sent Dawes, but for fear Gage's spies may pick him up, I want you to take the short cut to Lexington and alarm people on your way; you 'll have to look sharp for Gage's officers. Tell Newman to hang out the two signals."

Revere hastened down Salem Street, whispered a word in the ear of Robert Newman, ran to his own home for his overcoat, told two young men to accompany him, then ran to the riverside and stepped into his boat. The great black hull of the frigate Somerset rose before him. By the light of the rising moon he could see a marine, with his gun on his shoulder, pacing the deck; but no challenge came, and the rowers quickly landed him in Charlestown.[1]

[1] In the *Tales of a Wayside Inn*, the poet Longfellow represents Paul Revere as impatiently waiting beside his horse, on the Charlestown shore. for the signal lights: —

> " On the opposite shore walked Paul Revere.
> Now he patted his horse's side,
> Now gazed at the landscape far and near,
> Then, impetuous, stamped the earth,
> And turned and tightened his saddle-girth ;
> But mostly watched with eager search
> The belfry tower of the Old North Church,
> As it rose above the graves on the hill,
> Lonely and spectral and sombre and still.
> And lo ! as he looks. on the belfry height
> A glimmer, and then a gleam of light !
> He springs to the saddle, the bridle he turns,
> But lingers and gazes, till full on his sight
> A second lamp in the belfry burns ! "

From the narrative of Paul Revere in the archives of the Massachu-

Robert Newman, sexton, had gone to bed. The officers of one of the king's regiments, occupying the front chamber, saw him retire, but did not see him a minute later crawl out of a window to the roof of a shed, drop lightly to the ground, make his way to the church, enter, turn the key, lock the door, climb the stairs to the tower, and hang the lanterns in the loft above the bell. It was but the work of a moment. Having done it, he hastened down the stairway, past the organ, to the floor of the church. The full moon was flooding the arches above him with its mellow light; but he did not tarry to behold the beauty of the scene; not that he feared ghosts would rise from the coffins in the crypt beneath the church, — he was not afraid of dead men, — but he would rather the redcoats should not know what he had been doing. He raised a window, dropped from it to the ground, ran down an alley, reached his house, climbed the shed, and was in bed when officers of one of the regiments came to make inquiry about the lanterns. Of course, Robert, being in bed, could not have hung them there. It must have been done by somebody else.[1]

setts Historical Society, we learn that the signals were seen before he reached the Charlestown shore : —

"When I got into town, I met Colonel Conant and several others ; they said they had seen our signals; I told them what was acting, and I went to get me a horse; I got a horse of Deacon Larkin. While the horse was preparing, Richard Devens, Esq., who was one of the Committee of Safety, came to me and told me that he came down the road from Lexington after sundown, that evening ; that he met ten British officers, all well mounted and armed, going up the road."

[1] Paul Revere in his narrative says "a friend" made the signals. It has been claimed that John Pulling, and not Robert Newman, hung the lanterns. The evidence favoring Newman and Pulling is

Paul Revere the while is flying up Main Street towards Charlestown Neck. It is a pleasant night. The grass in the fields is fresh and green; the trees above him are putting forth their young and tender leaves. He is thinking of what Richard Devens has said, and keeps his eyes open. He crosses the narrow neck of land between the Mystic and Charles rivers, and sees before him the tree where Mark was hung ten years before for poisoning his master. The bones of the negro no longer rattle in the wind; the eyeless sockets of the once ghostly skeleton no longer glare at people coming from Cambridge and Medford to Charlestown, and Paul Revere has no fear of seeing Mark's ghost hovering around the tree. It is for the living — Gage's spies — that he peers into the night. Bucephalus suddenly pricks up his ears. Ah! there they are! two men in uniform on horseback beneath the tree. He is abreast of them. They advance. Quickly he wheels, and rides back towards Charlestown. He reaches the road leading to Medford, reins Bucephalus into it. He sees one of them riding across the field to cut him off; the other is following him along the road. Suddenly the rider in the field disappears, — going head foremost into a clay pit. " Ha! ha ! " laughs Revere, as the fleet steed bears him on towards Medford town. He clatters

in each case circumstantial. Both were Sons of Liberty and intimate with Revere. Newman was sexton in possession of the keys of the church. It is said that Pulling obtained them ; that the suspicion was so strong against him he was obliged to leave the town secretly, not daring to apply for a pass. Newman was arrested, but General Gage could find no direct evidence against him. I have followed the generally accepted opinion, favoring Newman.

across Mystic bridge, halts long enough to awaken the captain of the minute-men, and then rattles on towards Menotomy.[1]

It is past eleven o'clock. The fires have been covered for the night in the farmhouses, and the people are asleep.

"Turn out! turn out! the redcoats are coming!"

Paul Revere is shouting it at every door, as Bucephalus bears him swiftly on. The farmers spring from their beds, peer through their window-panes into the darkness, — seeing a vanishing form, and flashing sparks struck from the stones by the hoofs of the flying horse. Once more across the Mystic on to Menotomy, past the meetinghouse and the houses of the slumbering people, up the hill, along the valley, to Lexington Green; past the meetinghouse, not halting at Buckman's tavern, but pushing on, leaping from his foaming steed and rapping upon Mr. Clark's door.

"Who are ye, and what d' ye want?" Sergeant Munroe asked the question.

"I want to see Mr. Hancock."

"Well, you can't. The minister and his family must n't be disturbed, so just keep still and don't make a racket."

---

[1] "After I passed Charlestown Neck, and got nearly opposite where Mark was hung in chains, I saw two men on horseback under the tree. When I got near them I discovered they were British officers. One tried to get ahead of me, and the other to take me. I turned my horse quick and galloped towards Charlestown Neck, and then pushed for the Medford road. The one who chased me, endeavoring to cut me off, got into a clay pond. I got clear of him and went through Medford over the bridge up to Menotomy. In Medford I awaked the captain of the minute-men, and after that I alarmed every house till I got to Lexington." — Revere's *Narrative.*

"There'll be a racket pretty soon, for the redcoats are coming," said Paul.

"Who are you and what do you wish?" asked Reverend Mr. Clark in his night-dress from the window.

"I want to see Adams and Hancock."

"It is Revere; let him in!" shouted Hancock down the stairway.

"The regulars are coming, several hundred of them, to seize you!"

"It is the supplies at Concord they are after," cried Mr. Adams.

A moment later other hoofs were striking fire from the stones, and another horseman, William Dawes, appeared, confirming what Revere had said.

REVEREND JONAS CLARK'S HOUSE

Where Samuel Adams, John Hancock, and Dorothy Quincy were staying

XVI.

THE MORNING DRUMBEAT.

"Ring the bell!"

Samuel Adams said it, and one of Sergeant Munroe's men ran to the green, seized the bell-rope, and set the meetinghouse bell to clanging, sending the alarm far and wide upon the still night air.

In the farmhouses candles were quickly lighted, and the minute-men, who had agreed to obey a summons at a moment's warning, came running with musket, bullet-pouch, and powder-horn, to the rendezvous. They formed in line, but, no redcoats appearing, broke ranks and went into Buckman's tavern.

Silently, without tap of drum, the grenadiers and light infantry under Colonel Francis Smith, at midnight, marched from their quarters to Barton's Point, together with the marines under Major Pitcairn.

"Where are we going?" Lieutenant Edward Gould of the King's Own put the question to Captain Lawrie.

"I suppose General Gage and the Lord, and perhaps Colonel Smith, know, but I don't," the captain replied, as he stepped into a boat with his company.

It was eleven o'clock when the last boat-load of troops reached Lechmere's Point, — not landing on solid ground, but amid the last year's reeds and marshes. The tide was flowing into the creek and eddies, and the mud beneath the feet of the king's troops was soft and slippery.

"May his satanic majesty take the man who ordered us into this bog," said a soldier whose feet suddenly went out from under him and sent him sprawling into the slimy oose.

" By holy Saint Patrick, is n't the water nice and warm !" said one of the marines as he waded into the flowing tide fresh from the sea.

"Gineral Gage intends to teach us how to swim," said another.

With jokes upon their lips, but inwardly cursing whoever had directed them to march across the marsh, the troops splashed through the water, reached the main road leading to Menotomy, and waited while the commissary distributed their rations. It was past two o'clock before Colonel Smith was ready to move on. Looking at his watch in the moonlight and seeing how late it was, he directed Major Pitcairn to take six companies of the light infantry and hasten on to Lexington.

From the house of Reverend Mr. Clark, Paul Revere, William Dawes, and young Doctor Prescott of Concord, who had been sparking his intended wife in Lexington village, started on their horses up the road towards Concord. From the deep shade of the alders a half dozen men suddenly confronted them.

"Surrender, or I will blow out your brains !" shouts one of the officers.

BUCKMAN'S TAVERN

Revere and Dawes are prisoners; but Doctor Prescott, quick of eye, ear, and motion, is leaping his horse over the stone wall, riding through fields and pastures, along bypaths, his saddle-bags flopping, his horse, young and fresh, bearing him swiftly on over the meadows to the slumbering village, with the news that the redcoats are coming.[1]

"Tell us where we can find those arch traitors to his majesty the king, or you are dead men," the threat of an officer.

Paul Revere sees the muzzle of the pistol within a foot of his breast, but it does not frighten him.

"Ah, gentlemen, you have missed your aim."

"What aim?"

"You won't get what you came for. I left Boston an hour before your troops were ready to cross Charles River. Messengers left before me, and the alarm will soon be fifty miles away. Had I not known it, I would have risked a shot from you before allowing myself to be captured."

From the belfry of the meetinghouse the bell was

---

[1] Longfellow in his poem has Revere riding on to Concord bridge.

> "It was two by the village clock,
> When he came to the bridge in Concord town."

Revere's account reads: —

"We had got nearly half way; Mr. Dawes and the Doctor stopped to alarm the people of a house. I was about one hundred rods ahead when I saw two men, in nearly the same situation as those officers were near Charlestown. I called for the Doctor and Dawes to come up; in an instant I was surrounded by four. . . . We tried to get out there; the Doctor jumped his horse over a low stone wall and got to Concord. I observed a wood at a small distance and made for that. When I got there. out rushed six officers on horseback and ordered me to dismount."

sending its peals far and wide over fields and woodlands.

" Do you not hear it ?   The town is alarmed," said
Revere.

" Rub-a-dub-dub ! rub-a-dub-dub ! rub-a-dub, rub-a-
dub, rub-a-dub-dub ! "   It was the drummer beating
the long roll.

" The minute-men are forming ; you are dead men ! "
said Dawes.

The drumbeat, with the clanging bell, was breaking
the stillness of the early morning.   The officers put
their heads together and whispered a moment.

" Get off your horses," ordered Captain Parsons of
the king's Tenth Regiment.

Revere and Dawes obeyed.

" We 'll keep this ; the other is only fit for the
crows to pick," said one of the officers, cutting the
saddle-girth of Dawes's horse, turning it loose, and
mounting Bucephalus.   Then all rode away, dashing
past the minute-men on Lexington Green.

" The minute-men are forming, — three hundred of
them," reported the officers to Colonel Smith, who was
marching up the road.[1]

The bell and the drumbeat, the lights in Buckman's
tavern and the other houses, the minute-men in line by
the meetinghouse, had quickened the imagination of
the excited Britishers.

" The country is alarmed.   It is reported there are

[1] " We heard there were some hundreds of people collected there,
intending to oppose us and stop our going out. At five o'clock we
arrived there, and a number of people, I believe between two and
three hundred, formed on a common in the middle of the town."
' Diary of a British Officer." *Atlantic Monthly*. April, 1877.

five hundred rebels gathered to oppose me. I shall need reinforcements." Such was the message of Colonel Smith to General Gage.

He directed Major Pitcairn to push on rapidly with six companies of light infantry.

"Jonathan! Jonathan! Get up quick! The redcoats are coming and something must be done!"[1]

Abigail Harrington shouted it, bursting into her son Jonathan's chamber. He had not heard the bell, nor the commotion in the street. Jonathan was only sixteen years old, but was fifer for the minute-men. In a twinkling he was dressed, and seizing his fife ran to join the company forming in line by the meeting-house; answering to their names, as clerk Daniel Harrington called the roll.

John Hancock and Samuel Adams hear the drumbeat; Hancock seizes his gun.

"This is no place for you; you must go to a place of safety," said Reverend Mr. Clark.

"Never will I turn my back to the redcoats," said Hancock.

"The country will need your counsels. Others must meet the enemy face to face," was the calm, wise reply of the patriotic minister.

Other friends expostulate; they cross the road and enter a thick wood crowning the hill.

"Stand your ground. If war is to come, let it begin here. Don't fire till you are fired upon," said Captain John Parker, walking along the lines of his company.

---

[1] There were two Jonathan Harringtons. The fifer to the Lexington minute-men was sixteen years old. He died March 27, 1854, the last survivor of the battle, and was buried with distinguished honors. See *Hist. Lexington.*

The sun is just rising. Its level beams glint from the brightly polished gun-barrels and bayonets of the light infantry of King George, as the battalion under Major Pitcairn marches towards Lexington meeting-house. The trees above them have put forth their tender leaves. The rising sun, the green foliage, the white cross-belts, the shining buckles, the scarlet coats of the soldiers, and the farmers standing in line, firmly grasping their muskets, make up the picture of the morning.

Major Pitcairn, sitting in his saddle, beholds the line of minute-men, rebels in arms against the sovereign, formed in line to dispute his way. What right have they to be standing there? King George is supreme!

"Disperse, you rebels! Lay down your arms and disperse!" he shouts.

Captain John Parker hears it. The men behind him, citizens in their everyday clothes, with powder-horns slung under their right arms, hear it, but stand firm and resolute in their places. They see the Britisher raise his arm; his pistol flashes. Instantly the front platoon of redcoats raise their muskets. A volley rends the air. Not a man has been injured. Another volley, and a half dozen are reeling to the ground. John Munroe, Jonas Parker, and their comrades bring their muskets to a level and pull the triggers. With the beams of the rising sun falling on their faces, they accept the conflict with arbitrary power.

"What a glorious morning is this!" the exclamation of Samuel Adams on yonder hill.

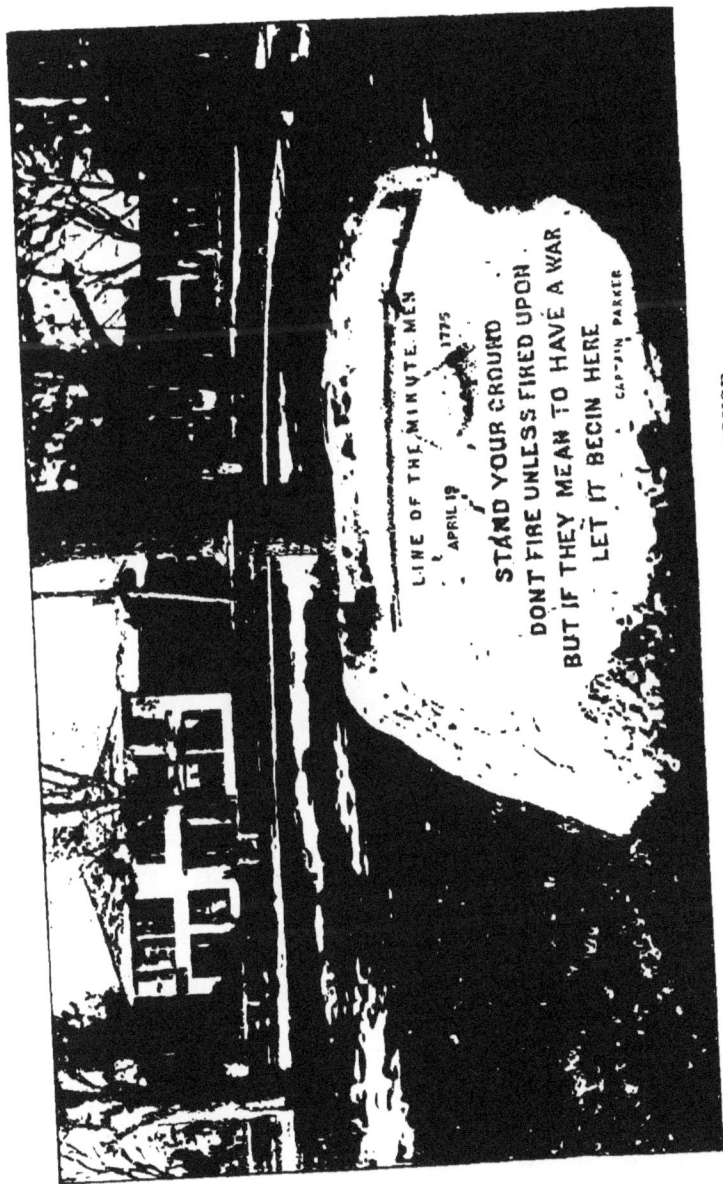

LINE OF THE MINUTE MEN

APRIL 19   1775

STAND YOUR GROUND
DONT FIRE UNLESS FIRED UPON .
BUT IF THEY MEAN TO HAVE A WAR
LET IT BEGIN HERE

CAPTAIN PARKER

JONATHAN HARRINGTON'S HOUSE.

Jonathan Harrington was wounded where the stone now stands, and fell dead at the doorstep of his house

Seven minute-men have been killed, nine wounded. Captain Parker sees that it is useless for his little handful of men to contend with a force ten times larger, and orders them to disperse.

The redcoats look down exultantly upon the dying and the dead, give a hurrah, and shoot at the fleeing rebels.[1]

Jonas Parker will not run.

"Others may do as they will, I never will turn my back to a redcoat," he said a few minutes ago. He is on his knees now, wounded, but reloading his gun. The charge is rammed home, the priming in the pan, but his strength is going; his arms are weary; his hands feeble. The redcoats rush upon him, and a bayonet pierces his breast. He dies where he fell.

With the blood spurting from his breast, Jonathan Harrington staggers towards his home. His loving wife is standing in the doorway. He reaches out his arms to her, and falls dead at her feet.

Caleb Harrington falls by the meetinghouse step. A ball plows through the arm of John Comee, by Mr. Munroe's doorway.

The Britishers are wild with excitement, and remorselessly take aim at the fleeing provincials. They have conquered and dispersed the rebels. Colonel Smith joins Major Pitcairn, and, glorying over the easy victory, they swing their hats, hurrah for King George, and march on towards Concord.

---

[1] "We then formed on the Common. but with some difficulty. The men were so wild they could hear no orders. We waited a considerable time, and at length proceeded on our way to Concord, which we then learned was our destination." "Diary of a British Officer," *Atlantic Monthly,* April, 1877.

XVII.

BEGINNING OF A NEW ERA.

ROGER STANLEY, asleep in the old farmhouse on the banks of Concord River, was aroused from slumber by his mother.

"Roger! Roger! the meetinghouse bell is ringing!" she shouted up the stairs to him.

With a bound he was on his feet, raised the window and heard the sweet-toned bell. He understood its meaning, that the redcoats were coming. Quickly putting on his clothes, he seized the powder-horn and bullet-pouch which his father carried at Louisburg.

"You must eat something, Roger, before you go," said his mother.

A moment later and his breakfast was on the table, bread and butter, a slice of cold beef, a mug of cider.

"There's no knowing when I shall be back, mother, for if the war has begun, as I fear it has, I shall be in the ranks till the last redcoat is driven from the country."

"I know it. Roger. Your father would have done just what you are doing. I know you'll do your duty. You won't show the white feather. Here's some lunch for you." she said, putting a package into his knapsack.

"Good-by."

Her arms were about his neck; tears were on her cheeks as she kissed his lips.

He ran across the meadow to the village. The minute-men and militia were gathering. In the stillness of the morning they could hear the report of guns far away, and knew that they of Sudbury and Acton were hearing the alarm. People were hurrying to and fro in the village, loading barrels of flour into carts, removing the supplies purchased by the committee of safety. Reverend Mr. Emerson was there with his gun and powder - horn. Many times

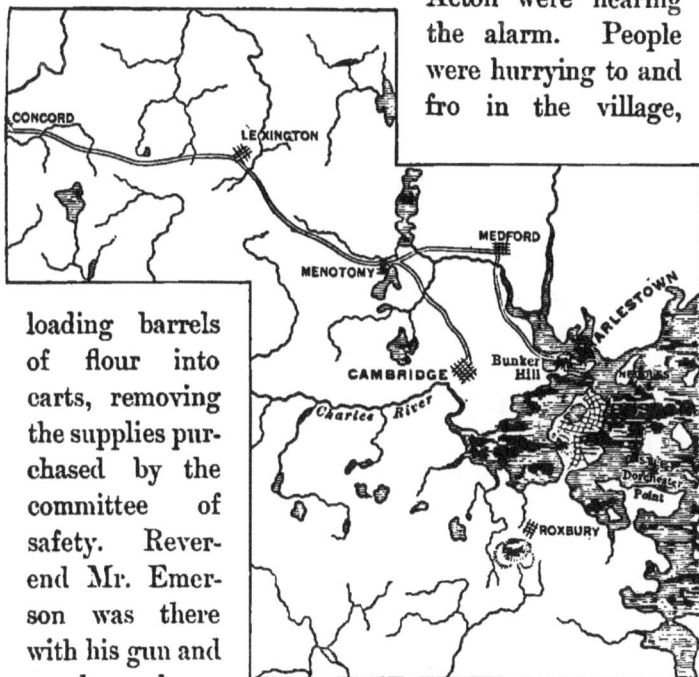

Route of the British to Concord.

Roger had listened to his preaching. It was gratifying to see him ready to stand in the ranks with his parishioners. He told the women not to be frightened, and smiled upon the boys who took off their hats, and the girls who courtesied to him.

They heard, far away, the drumbeat of the advancing British.

No messengers had arrived to inform the minutemen of Concord what had happened at Lexington; for Doctor Prescott did not know that British muskets had fired a fatal volley.

From the burial ground Roger could look far down the road and see the sunlight glinting from the bayonets of the grenadiers, as the red-coated platoons emerged from the woodland into the open highway.

Major Buttrick with the minute-men and Colonel Barrett with the militia formed in line by the liberty pole.

" Prime and load ! " his order.

Roger poured the powder into the palm of his hand, emptied it into the gun, and rammed it home with a ball. Never had he experienced such a sensation as at the moment. He was not doing it to take aim at a deer or fox, but to send it through the heart of a fellow-being if need be ; to maintain justice and liberty. He could die in their defense ; why should it trouble him, then, to think of shooting those who were assailing what he held so dear?

" I am doing right. Liberty shall live, cost what it may," he said to himself as he poured the priming into the pan.

On in serried ranks came the British.

" We are too few, they are three to our one. We must cross the river and wait till we are stronger," said Colonel Barrett.

They were only two hundred. They filed into the road, marched past the Reverend Mr. Emerson's house

REVEREND WILLIAM EMERSON'S HOUSE—THE OLD MANSE

The conflict at the Bridge was in plain view from this house

to the north bridge, crossed the river, and came to a halt on a hill overlooking the meadows, the village, and surrounding country. They could see the British dividing, — one party crossing the south bridge and going towards Colonel Barrett's house to destroy the supplies collected there; another party advancing to the north bridge. Roger saw groups of officers in the graveyard using their spy-glasses. A soldier was cutting down the liberty pole. Other soldiers were entering houses, helping themselves to what food was left on the breakfast-tables or in the pantries. Colonel Smith and Major Pitcairn rested themselves in Mr. Wright's tavern.

" I 'll stir the Yankee blood before night, just as I stir this brandy, " said Pitcairn, stirring the spirit in his tumbler with his finger.

A party of British crossed the south bridge, made their way to Colonel Barrett's house, and burned the cannon carriages stored in his barn.

Roger was glad to see Captain Isaac Davis and the minute-men of Acton march up the hill to join them. Captain Davis was thirty years old. He had kissed his young wife and four children good-by.

" Take good care of the children, Hannah," he said as he bade her farewell.

Twice a week he had drilled his company. He was brave, resolute, kind-hearted. His men loved him because he demanded strict obedience. They had stopped long enough at his home for his young wife to powder their hair, that they might appear neat and trim like gentlemen when meeting the British. They were thirty-five, all told. Keeping step to Luther Blan-

chard's fifing of the White Cockade, and Francis
Barker's drumming, they marched past the men from
Concord and formed on their left.

THE WHITE COCKADE.

WRIGHT'S TAVERN

" Order arms ! "   They rested their muskets on the
ground and wiped the perspiration from their fore-
heads.

Men from Westford, Lincoln, and Carlisle are arriving.   They are four hundred now.   The officers stand
apart, talking in low tones.   The redcoats had
crossed the bridge to the western bank.

" Let us drive the redcoats across the river," said
Captain Smith.

" I have n't a man that is afraid," said Captain
Davis.

He was heavy-hearted in the early morning when
he kissed the young wife and took the baby from the
cradle in his arms, but is resolute now.

" Attention, battalion !   Trail arms !   Left in front !
March ! "   Luther Blanchard pipes the tune, and the
battalion — the men of Acton leading — descends the
hill.

The redcoats had recrossed the river and were taking up the planks of the bridge.   A moment later
muskets flash beneath the elms and maples along the
farthest bank and there is a whistling of bullets in
the air.   Roger's heart is in his throat, but he gulps
it down.   Another volley, and Captain Davis, Abner
Hosmer, and Luther Blanchard reel to the ground.
Never again will Hannah receive a parting kiss, or the
father caress the baby crooning in the cradle.[1]

" Fire ! For God's sake, fire ! " shouts Major Buttrick. Roger cocks his gun, takes aim at the line of scar-

[1] " The fire soon began from a dropping shot on our side, when
they and the front company fired almost at the same instant."
" Diary of a British Officer," *Atlantic Monthly*, April, 1877.

let beneath the trees and pulls the trigger. Through the smoke he sees men throw up their arms and tumble to the ground. The scarlet line dissolves, the soldiers fleeing in confusion. No longer is Roger's heart in his throat. His nerves are iron and the hot blood is coursing through his veins. King George has begun the war; no longer is he his subject, but a rebel, never more to owe him allegiance.

The forenoon wore away. The British were returning from Colonel Barrett's, having destroyed the cannon carriages, thrown some bullets into a well, and broken open several barrels of flour. It was past noon when they formed in line once more to return to Boston.

"We will head them off at Merriam's Corner," said Colonel Barrett.

The planks which the British had removed from the bridge were quickly replaced. The minute-men crossed the stream, turned into a field to the left, and hastened over the meadow to the road leading to Bedford. It was past three o'clock when they reached Mr. Merriam's house. Roger saw the British marching down the road. Suddenly a platoon wheeled towards the minute-men and brought their guns to a level. There was a flash, a white cloud, and bullets whistled over their heads. Once more he took aim, as did others, and several redcoats fell. Before he could reload, the serried ranks disappeared, marching rapidly towards Lexington. The minute-men hastened on, and at the tavern of Mr. Brooks he sent another bullet into the ranks of the retreating foe.[1]

"We set out upon our return. Before the whole had quitted the

NORTH BRIDGE

The minute-men stood under the trees at the right; the British, the other side of the river

"Scatter now! Get upon their flank! Pepper 'em from behind walls and trees!" shouted Colonel Barrett, who saw that it would be useless to follow the retreating enemy in battalion order, but each man, acting for himself, could run through fields and pastures and keep up a tormenting fire.

Acting upon the order, Roger and James Heywood ran through a piece of woods towards Fiske Hill. They came upon a British soldier drinking at a well by a house.

"You are a dead man," shouted the redcoat, raising his gun.

"So are you," said Heywood. Their muskets flashed and both fell, the Britisher with a bullet through his heart, and Heywood mortally wounded.

From rock heap, tree, fence, and thicket the guns of the minute-men were flashing. The soldiers who had marched so proudly, keeping step to the drumbeat in the morning, were running now. No hurrah went up as at sunrise on Lexington Common. There was no halting at Buckman's tavern, where they had fired their first volley. Their ranks were in confusion. Officers were trying to rally them, threatening to cut them down with their swords if they did not show a bold front to the minute-men, but the Yankees seemed to be everywhere and yet nowhere. Bullets were coming from every direction, yet the British could see no men in line, no ranks at which they could take aim or charge with the bayonet. They were still twelve

town we were fired on from houses and behind trees. and before we had gone half a mile we were fired on from all sides. but mostly from the rear. where the people had hid themselves in houses till we passed." "Diary of a British Officer," *Atlantic Monthly*, April, 1877.

miles from Boston, and their ammunition failing. They were worn and weary with the all-night march, and were hungry and thirsty. The road was strewn with their fallen comrades. The wounded were increasing in number, impeding their retreat. Their ranks were broken. All was confusion. Every moment some one was falling.[1] Blessed the sight that greeted them, — the brigade of Earl Percy, drawn up in hollow square by Mr. Munroe's tavern, with two cannon upon the hillocks by the roadside. They rushed into the square and dropped upon the ground, panting and exhausted with their rapid retreat.

Roger halted a few minutes on **Lexington Green**, where the conflict began in the morning. He saw the ground stained with the blood of those who had fallen, — crossed the threshold where Jonathan Harrington had died in the arms of his wife. Across the Common the house and barn of Joseph Loring were in flames, set on fire by the British.

Earl Percy's troops were ransacking the houses a little farther down the road. In Mr. Munroe's tavern they were compelling old John Raymond to bring them food, and because he could not give them what they wanted, sent a bullet through his heart.[2]

---

[1] "They were so concealed there was hardly any seeing them. In this way we marched between nine and ten miles, their numbers increasing from all parts, while ours was reducing by deaths, wounds, and fatigue, and we were totally surrounded with such an incessant fire as it is impossible to conceive. Our ammunition was likewise near expended." "Diary of a British Officer," *Atlantic Monthly*, April, 1877.

[1] "We marched pretty quiet for about two miles, when they began to pepper us again. We were now obliged to force almost every house in the road, for the rebels had taken possession of them and galled us exceedingly; but they suffered for their temerity, *for all that were*

MERRIAM'S CORNER

Once more the British were on the march.

Roger, rested and invigorated, ran through a pasture, crouched behind a bowlder, rested his gun upon it, and sent a bullet into the ranks. He was delighted when Doctor Joseph Warren came galloping over the hill. The doctor said he left Boston in the morning, rode to Cambridge and Watertown, then hastened on to Lexington. He was glad the minutemen and militia had resisted the British. While talking with Roger and those around him, a bullet whizzed past the doctor's head, knocking a pin from his ear-lock.

The rattling fire of the minute-men was increasing once more, — answered by volleys from Percy's platoons. The British, smarting under the tormenting fusilade, angry over the thought that they were being assailed by a rabble of farmers and were on the defensive, became wanton and barbaric, pillaging houses, and murdering inoffensive old men.

Roger was delighted to hear from Jonathan Loring, one of the Lexington minute-men, how his sister Lydia, fearing that the British would steal the communion cups and platters belonging to the church of which her father was deacon, took them in her apron, ran out into the orchard, and hid them under a pile of brush.

found in the houses were put to death." "Diary of a British Officer," Atlantic Monthly, April, 1877.

Earl Percy made the tavern of Mr. Munroe his headquarters.

"A party entered the tavern and, helping themselves, or rather compelling the inmates of the house to help them to whatever they wanted, they treacherously and with ruthlessness shot down John Raymond, an infirm old man, only because he, alarmed at this roughness and brutal conduct, was about leaving the house to seek a place of greater safety." Hudson's *Hist. of Lexington.*

Pitiful it was to see Widow Mulliken's house in flames, — wantonly set on fire by the red-coated ruffians.

Roger saw a soldier deliberately raise his gun, take aim, and send a bullet through the heart of Jason Russel, an old gray-haired man, standing in his own door. Again, at closer range, he took aim at the retreating column.

His indignation was aroused as he listened to the story told by Hannah Adams, a few minutes later. She was in bed in her chamber, with a new-born babe at her breast, when two redcoats entered the room. One pointed his musket at her.

" For the Lord's sake, do not kill me," she said.

" I am going to shoot you," the soldier replied, with an oath.

" No, you must n't shoot a woman," said the other, pushing aside the gun, " but we are going to set the house on fire, and you must get out."

With the babe in her arms, she crawled downstairs and into the yard.

The soldiers scattered the coals from the fireplace around the room, and left, but the older children ran in and put out the flames.

At Mr. Cooper's tavern was a ghastly sight; upon the floor lay the mangled bodies of Jason Wyman and Jesse Winship, two old men, who had come from their homes to learn the news. They were drinking toddy, when the head of Earl Percy's retreating troops arrived, and fired a volley into the house. The landlord and his wife fled to the cellar. The British swarmed into the tavern, mangled the bodies of the

MUNROE TAVERN

Lord Percy's headquarters

two old men with bayonet thrusts, and scattered their brains around the room.

In the morning Roger had felt some qualms of conscience as he took aim at the scarlet line of men by Concord River, but now to him the redcoats were fiends in human form. It gave him fresh courage to see Samuel Whittemore, eighty years old, come running with his musket, taking deliberate aim, firing three times, and bringing down a redcoat every time he pulled the trigger. But a soldier leaped from the ranks, ran upon and shot the old man, stabbed him with his bayonet, beat him with the butt of his musket, leaving him for dead.[1]

Roger swung his hat to welcome Captain Gideon Foster of Danvers, and his company, who had marched sixteen miles in four hours, coming upon the British at Menotomy meetinghouse. A moment later they were in the thick of the fight.

It was a thrilling story which Timothy Monroe had to tell, how he and Daniel Townsend fired, and each brought down a redcoat, and then ran into a house; how the British surrounded it, and killed Townsend; how he leaped through a window and ran, with a whole platoon firing at him, riddling his clothes with bullets, yet escaping without a scratch.

Again Roger rejoiced when he learned that before Earl Percy reached Menotomy a company of men had captured his baggage wagons, killing and wounding several British soldiers, and that the attacking party were led by Reverend Philip Payson, the minister of Chelsea.

---

[1] He was not dead, however, but lived many years.

It was almost sunset when Roger held his horn up
to the light once more, and saw there was little more
than enough powder for one charge, and that there
were only two bullets in the pouch. He decided to
put in all the powder and both bullets for his parting
shot. Another half hour and they would be under the
protection of the guns of the frigate Somerset. The
minute-men were getting so near and were so determined that Earl Percy ordered the cannon to unlim-
ber and open fire, while the soldiers, almost upon the
run, hastened towards Charlestown.

Roger, having reloaded his gun, made haste to
overtake them. Looking along the road, he saw a
crowd of panic-stricken people — men, women, and
children — fleeing from their houses. The picture of
the scene of Menotomy had stamped itself into his
memory. This last shot should be his best. Not
now would he crouch behind a fence, a tree, or
bowlder. He would confront the murderers like a
man. He walked deliberately forward. He was by
a farmhouse, so near the last file of soldiers which
had halted to ward off the minute-men a moment,
that he could see the whites of their eyes. He aimed
at the cross-belt of a man in the middle of the file,
and pulled the trigger. He caught a glimpse of a
man falling, but found himself reeling to the ground.
A bullet had pierced his breast. The British passed
on. A woman came from the house, and looked
down into his face.

"A drink of water, please marm," he said.

She ran to the well, sank the bucket into it,
brought a gourd full, and came and crouched by his
head while he drank.

" Thank you, marm."

He looked up into her face a moment.

" I think I am going," he whispered.

She pillowed his head upon her arm, laid back the hair from his manly brow, and fanned him with her apron.

" Please tell her," he whispered.

" Tell who ? "

She bowed her head to catch the word.

" Tell — Rachel."

The mild blue eyes were looking far away. A smile like the light of the morning came upon his face. One more breath, and he was one of the forty-nine who, during the day, gave their lives that they might inaugurate a new era in the republic of God.

XVIII.

Thomas Gage, governor, commanding his majesty's forces in America, was sitting in the Province House, greatly disturbed in mind. The expedition to Concord had not resulted as he expected. The troops had marched out bravely, destroyed a few barrels of flour, disabled half a dozen old cannon, burned some carriage wheels, but had returned to Boston on the run like a flock of sheep worried by dogs. The Tories had informed him that a couple of regiments could march from one end of the continent to the other, but the events of the preceding day were opening his eyes to a far different state of affairs. Till within a few hours the country had been at peace: farmers following the plow; blacksmiths hammering iron; carpenters pushing the plane. All had changed. · Thousands were under arms, gathering at Cambridge and Roxbury. The Colonies were aflame, — not only Massachusetts, but New Hampshire, Rhode Island, and Connecticut. The troops which marched to Concord so proudly were back in Boston, — not all: twenty-three had been killed, two hundred wounded and missing. Eighteen of the officers had been killed or wounded. Governor Gage could not gainsay the fact that the citizens were victors. They had followed

the troops to Charlestown till nightfall, like a swarm
of angry hornets. A great army was closing around
him, cutting off his supplies. No more fresh beef
or mutton would be for sale in the market; no teams
would bring potatoes and cabbages for the soldiers.

Province House.

What would King George say? What would the ministry think? What would they do? How would the
people of England regard his administration of affairs?
The unexpected had happened He had not dreamed
of such an uprising. What course should he pursue?

All Boston was in commotion.   People were packing their goods on carts, loading them on boats to flee from the town.   Women were wringing their hands, children crying, fathers walking the streets with care-worn faces, not knowing whither to go or what to do. Officers were gathering at the Province House await-ing orders and talking of what had happened, and smarting under the thought that the retreat had been a flight and almost a panic.   It was a humiliating reflection that disciplined soldiers had been put upon the run by a rabble of countrymen.   Earl Percy, after a sleepless night, weary and travel-worn, was gladly welcomed by Governor Gage.   He told the story of the retreat.

"If it had not been, your excellency, for my timely arrival, I fear few of Lieutenant-Colonel Smith's troops would have escaped, as they were completely exhausted, their ammunition gone, and the men upon the run.   I am free to say that I was completely astonished.   I formed my brigade in hollow square, and his men threw themselves on the ground with their tongues lolling from their mouths," he said.

"It is plain that you marched none too soon," the governor replied.

"I cannot account for such a sudden uprising.   I saw very few rebels.   There were no organized bodies of rebels to be seen, — not more than twenty or thirty in a group: but they were all around us, firing from fences, rocks, trees, ditches, houses.   If we charged and drove them, they were back again the moment we resumed our march.   I must admit they were brave and persistent.   They were like so many wasps," said the earl.

"I learn," said the governor, "that several thousand armed men have already gathered at Cambridge and Roxbury. A loyal citizen informs me they have been arriving through the night in great numbers. It seems probable that we are to be hemmed in by the provincials for the present, and must make preparations accordingly."

Fast and far the alarm had gone. Twenty-four hours and it was one hundred miles away, and Robert Walden of Rumford with bullet-pouch, powder-horn, and musket was on his way, as were Colonel John Stark, Captain Daniel Moore of Derryfield, and hundreds of others in New Hampshire, Israel Putnam, Thomas Knowlton of Connecticut, and their fellow-citizens, all animated by one thought, — to resist the armed aggressions of the myrmidons of the king. There was a brave heart behind Rachel's quivering lips when she pressed them to Robert's.

"Roger is sure to be there. Tell him I think of him every night before I go to sleep." Little did they know that he was being borne to his last resting-place on the banks of the winding river.

Robert was glad to learn when he reached Medford that John Stark was to be colonel of the New Hampshire troops.

Tom Brandon was working day and night to help people obtain passes from General Gage and leave the town. More than five thousand closed their houses and took their departure.[1] The governor would not

[1] For a week after the affair at Lexington and Concord, Governor Gage refused the request of the people to leave the town, but the growing scarcity of provisions compelled him to permit their departure.

allow any one to take their guns or swords, or anything which would in any way contribute to the success of the provincials.

The soldiers from Rumford, having unbounded confidence in Robert Walden, elected him lieutenant. When General Artemus Ward, commanding the troops at Cambridge, asked Colonel Stark if he had a trustworthy young man whom he could recommend to execute an important order, Lieutenant Walden was selected and directed to report at general headquarters. He was kindly received and informed he was to negotiate with the British for an exchange of prisoners.

Mounted upon his horse, Lieutenant Walden rode to Charlestown Neck, and from thence to the top of Bunker Hill to obtain a view of Boston and the harbor. He saw the warships were swinging at anchor in the stream. Across the river were the silent streets of the besieged town. He could distinguish the home of Captain Brandon, and the Green Dragon Tavern, — its doors closed. It was not these buildings, however, that most interested him, but a mansion on the slope of Beacon Hill, with its surrounding grounds, — the Newville home. The window of Miss Newville's chamber was open, the curtain drawn aside. His spyglass made it seem very near. How would she greet him were they to meet again? Would she be changed by the changing circumstances? Would she, daughter of a loyalist, deign to notice him, a rebel? Blessed vision! A figure in white appeared at the window. It was she for whom he could lay down his life, if need be. Oh, if he could but reach out his hand to her, hear once more the voice that had thrilled him

in the past! She stood by the window, looking upon
the flowers blooming in the garden. The vision was
but for a moment, for the window was soon closed
and the curtain drawn. He descended the hill, rode
through the village to the ferry landing, displaying a
white flag. It was answered by the waving of another on the deck of the Lively warship. Then a
boat brought a lieutenant of the fleet to the shore.

"Who are you and what do you want?" the curt
question of the Britisher.

"I am commissioned by the commander-in-chief of
the provincial army to ask if it will be agreeable to
General Gage to make an exchange of prisoners?"

"The rebel army, you mean."

"I said provincial, but if it suits you any better to
think of the Americans as rebels, I will not object.
We are rebels against tyranny and oppression, as I
trust we always shall be. We have several officers of
the king's troops in our hands, and you have some of
our men. If an exchange is desired by General Gage,
I am empowered to arrange the details," Robert said
with calm dignity.

The Britisher bowed, and the boat pulled back to
the ship, returning again after a time with an officer
commissioned to make arrangements for the transfer.

The sun was nearing the hour of noon. three days
later, when Lieutenant Walden, accompanied by General Putnam, Doctor Warren, and a detail of soldiers,
conducted the British officers and men to the ferry
landing, meeting Major Moncrief and other British
officers, with the provincial prisoners in their keeping.
The British soldiers, with tears upon their faces,

thanked Doctor Warren for the kind treatment they had received. The Americans had no thanks to give for what they had received on the strawless floor of the jail, the prison fare for food. Lieutenant Walden had engaged a dinner in the tavern. The landlord set forth his choicest wine. Putnam and Moncrief, being old acquaintances, chatted of the days at Ticonderoga while partaking of the viands and quaffing glasses of madeira.

"While the white flag is waving we will not let our differences mar the pleasure of the hour," said Doctor Warren, who delighted the company with his wit. Dinner over, there was a shaking of hands, expressions of personal good-will, and courteous salutes. With the furling of the white flag they were enemies once more.

Ships were arriving from England bringing General William Howe, General Henry Clinton, and General John Burgoyne, with several thousand troops to carry on the war. Every morning Miss Newville heard the drums beating the reveille and in the evening the tattoo. Many officers called at the hospitable home of Honorable Theodore Newville to enjoy the society of his charming daughter, who received them with grace and dignity.

With no fresh provisions in the market, the dinners given by Mr. Newville to the generals Howe, Clinton, and Burgoyne was not so elaborate as that to Lord Upperton, but more appetizing than those on shipboard while crossing the Atlantic. It was a pleasure to General Howe to escort Miss Newville to the dining-room, sit by her side, and listen to a voice that charmed him by its purity and sweetness. A lady so highly endowed, and with such grace of manner, would adorn any home, — even the drawing-room of her majesty the queen.

The home of Mrs. Martha Duncan, with its shrubbery and garden neatly kept, was selected by General Howe as a residence. He hoped it would not greatly inconvenience her; he would gladly remunerate her for any trouble he might make. It would be a pleasure to have her for a hostess. His own servant would attend to his personal wants.

"Of course, mother," said Abraham, "we cannot prevent him from taking possession of our home; we may as well make the best of it, accept the inevitable, and spoil the Egyptians if we can. He seems to be a gentleman, a man of honor, and will, doubtless, pay us well. Besides, possibly we may learn something that can be turned to good account, if we keep our eyes and ears open, and our wits about us."

"It will be only a plain table, my lord, I can provide. Since the provincials have closed around us, the market has been bare of provisions," said Mrs. Duncan.

"I am aware of it, madam, but I doubt not you will be able to furnish appetizing food, possibly a joint of roast mutton from the flocks of sheep accessible to us on the islands in the harbor, a fresh mackerel or cod. We are not yet shut in from the sea, and possibly we may soon have free access to the surrounding country, for I hear there is much discontent among the provincials, and their numbers are rapidly melting away, now that the first excitement is over," responded Lord Howe.

" Possibly I may be able to provide early vegetables, — lettuce, dandelions, greens, asparagus, and
water-cresses, my lord, if you will allow my negro servant, Cato, to pass the patrol to Charlestown," said
Mrs. Duncan.

" I will give him such permission," he replied, writing a pass, directing the sentinels along the wharves,
and the marine patrol in the harbor, to pass the
negro servant, Cato.

Not only Cato, but Mrs. Duncan and her son, Abraham, ship-carver and artist, were attentive to the wants
of General Howe, receiving shining guineas in return.
It was a pleasure to the British commander, just arrived from England, to talk with a young gentleman
so well informed and of such attainments as the son of
his hostess.

" I dare say, Mr. Duncan, you are quite well acquainted with the country around Boston ? " said his
lordship.

" I have been up the Charles and Mystic by boat
many times, my lord, and visited Cambridge to enjoy
the festivities of Class Day, and the orations of gradu-
ates at Commencement. I have rambled the Roxbury
fields and pastures for strawberries, and am pretty
well acquainted with the various localities."

General Howe spread out a map and asked many
questions in regard to the surrounding hills, valleys,
woods. and cleared lands. He was surprised to see
how well Mr. Duncan could sketch them in with his
pencil upon the map which Ensign De Berniere had
drawn. Lord Howe introduced him to Generals
Pigot and Clinton. who were pleased with the intelligent replies to their questions.

There came a day in June when Abraham heard General Howe say to the other commanders that the Charlestown Hills ought to be occupied at once, for fear the rebels might seize them. Were they to do so, Boston might be bombarded, and the ships driven from their anchorage.

" Doctor Warren and General Ward ought to know that," Abraham said to himself.

There were only a few words in the letter which Abraham Duncan tucked under the cuff of Cato's coat-sleeve the next morning, when he stepped into his boat to cross the river and gather young asparagus and water-cresses for General Howe's dinner. Cato was directed to hand the slip of paper to Deacon Larkin's negro, Jim, who would know what to do with it.

Faithful and true to their kind-hearted masters were Cato and Jim, passing the letter from hand to hand, till it reached Doctor Joseph Warren in consultation with General Artemus Ward and the committee of safety in Cambridge.

" Bunker's Hill is to be occupied at once." [1]

That was all, except an ink blot.

" It is authentic, — from a trustworthy Son of Liberty," said Doctor Warren.

" It has no signature," said General Ward.

" Therefore is not treasonable. Besides, it does not state who is to occupy Bunker's Hill, — the British or ourselves," the doctor replied.

---

[1] The two eminences in Charlestown were named Breed's and Bunker's Hill respectively, — that upon which the redoubt was constructed was Breed's Hill; the rail fence behind which the troops from New Hampshire fought was on the slope of Bunker's Hill.

"How do you know it is genuine — from the writing?"

"No; the hand is disguised. Nevertheless, I know the writer. He informs me that the British intend to take possession of Charlestown Heights."[1]

"Are you sure it is authentic information?"

"I have no doubt of it. The writer is in position to learn what they intend to do. He is a very quiet man, but has his eyes and ears open. It is not the first time he has shown his devotion to our cause. You say he has not signed it; true he has not written his name, not even the initials, yet his signature is upon the sheet, — the insignificant ink-blot. It would not be accepted as testimony in a court-martial, but it is sufficient for me," said Doctor Warren.

With the letter came a copy of a proclamation issued by General Gage. No longer were the selectmen of any towns in the Province of Massachusetts to have anything to say. Martial law was to supersede civil authority. The provincial soldiers were rebels and traitors who must lay down their arms at once and go home, if they would hope for pardon; but there was no pardon for Samuel Adams and John Hancock, who must pay the extreme penalty of the law for inciting the people to rebel against their kind and lenient king.

"We ask no favor of King George; he began the war, we will end it," said the soldiers as they read the proclamation.

[1] General Gage at the outset saw the value of Charlestown Heights from the military standpoint, but was not able to make any movement to take possession of the ground till the arrival of his reinforcements.

XIX.

BUNKER HILL.

IF the British regarded Charlestown Heights of such importance, why should not the provincials seize them? It must be done. Twilight was still lingering on the western horizon when the troops selected for the expedition paraded on Cambridge Common. Colonel William Prescott was to command them. He had fought at Louisburg, and was. cool and brave. With uncovered heads the regiments stood in front of the meetinghouse while Reverend Mr. Langdon, president of the college, offered prayer. Lieutenant Walden, having been upon Bunker Hill, led the way, followed by soldiers from Connecticut and Massachusetts, and two carts loaded with picks and shovels. They marched in silence. Lieutenant Walden conducted them across the Neck and up the slope of the Hill. It was nearly midnight before it was decided just where Colonel Gridley should mark out the contemplated fortifications.[1] Lieutenant Walden con-

---

[1] The orders to Prescott contained no definite instructions in regard to which of the hills should be fortified, and the veteran engineer, Gridley, doubted whether it would be best to begin the works on the highest eminence, or the lower one, nearer the shipping. It seems probable his intention was to construct works on both hills, but a lack of picks and shovels compelled him to confine his work to the single redoubt on Breed's Hill.

ducted Captain Nutting and ten sentinels to the ferry landing. They were but a little distance from the frigate Somerset at anchor in the stream. Farther up, towards Lechmere's Point, were the Glasgow, Cerberus, and Symetry. Down the river, off Moulton's Point, lay the Lively and Falcon.

Leaving the sentinels to guard the shore, he rode to the summit of the hill, where the men were hard at work, delving in silence with pick and spade. There were not sufficient implements for all, but when one was out of breath, another took his place, and before the first glimmer of dawn appeared, the trench had been made breast deep.

" Four o'clock and all's well! " came from the sentinel on the Somerset, but a moment later a sheet of flame and a white cloud burst from the side of the Lively, and the roar of a gun broke the stillness of the morning.

The thunder rolled far away, arousing the British army, the people of Boston, General Gage, and Lord Howe from their slumbers. Berinthia Brandon, from her chamber window, beheld the warship Lively shrouded in smoke. Upon the green hill, where, the day before, the farmers had been swinging their scythes, and where the partially cured hay was lying in windrows, she could see a bank of yellow earth. Again the thunder of the guns jarred her window, but at a signal from the Somerset the firing ceased.

Before sunrise all Boston was astir, moving towards Copp's Hill, gazing from windows and roofs upon the growing fortifications. Generals Gage and Howe ascended the steeple of Christ Church and looked at the embankment with their telescopes.[1] A little later officers were hurrying along the streets with orders to the several regiments to be ready to march at a moment's notice. Drums were beating; battalions moving towards Long Wharf, the selected rendezvous, from whence the troops were to be transported in boats to Moulton's Point, ascend the hill, and send the provincials flying from their chosen position.

Such was the information brought to the Brandon home by Abraham Duncan.

"You will have a splendid chance to see the battle from the housetop," he said to Captain Brandon.

Cannon carriages were rumbling through the street, passing the Brandon home, wheeling into the burial ground, and coming into position. The gunners loaded the pieces and lighted their port fires, waved their lint-stocks, and touched them to the priming. Flames and smoke belched from the muzzle of the guns with deafening roar, sending the missiles upon the fortification.

While the cannoneers were reloading the guns, Berinthia, upon the housetop with a telescope, saw a man leap up from the intrenchment and stand in full view upon the bank of earth, swinging his hat and shaking his fist.

"Oh father! mother! it is Tom! He's swinging his hat! Just see him!" she cried.

Again the cannon flamed, but with the flashing Tom leaped back into the trench and was safe from the shot.

---

[1] The headquarters of General Gage were in the house of Mr. Galloup, on Hull Street, a stone's-throw from Christ Church The house, a two-story wooden building with a gambrel roof, is still standing (1895).

" I 'm glad he 's there. He 's got the true stuff in him," said Mr. Brandon.

" I 'm afraid he 'll be killed! " exclaimed Mrs. Brandon, manifesting the mother's solicitude and love.

" I glory in his pluck," said Berinthia.

People came from other sections of the town to behold the impending battle.

" May we presume to trespass upon your hospitality, Captain Brandon," asked Mr. Newville, "and, if you have room, see this approaching contest from your housetop? "

" Certainly. We give you and your family hearty welcome. We doubtless shall see it from different political standpoints; you are truly loyal to the king; my sympathies, as you know, are with the provincials, but that shall not diminish our personal friendship or my hospitality," Captain Brandon replied, escorting Mr. and Mrs. Newville and Miss Newville to the top of the house and providing them seats.

The forenoon wore away; Mrs. Brandon was busy preparing a lunch, and Chloe soon had the table elaborately supplied with ham, tongue, the whitest bread, appetizing cheese, doughnuts, and crumpets. The company partook of the collation, drank each a glass of wine, and then ascended to the roof again.

Berinthia informed Ruth that Tom was in the redoubt. She had seen him through the telescope, standing on the embankment and waving his hat.

Lieutenant Robert Walden, at the moment, was five miles away, in Medford town, delivering a message to Colonel John Stark to hasten with his regiment to Bunker Hill.

The meetinghouse bell was ringing the hour of noon when the drummer beat the long roll for the parading of the regiment. The men filed past the quartermaster's tent and each received a gill of powder in his horn. And then with quickened step they crossed the Mystic and hastened along the road.

With the shot from the Symetry screeching around them, tossing the gravel in their faces, the men from New Hampshire crossed the neck of land, ascended the hill, and came into position by a low stone wall surmounted by rails. Lieutenant Walden's company was nearest the Mystic River. Captain Daniel Moore's came next in line. The regiment with Colonel Reed's New Hampshire regiment extended to the foot of the hill, in the direction of the redoubt.

" You will inform Colonel Prescott that I have arrived with my regiment and am in position," said Colonel Stark.

Riding towards the redoubt, Robert saluted General Putnam, who, mounted on a white horse, was going along the lines, telling the men to keep cool, save their powder, and aim at the cross-belts of the British.

It was a pleasure once more to meet Doctor Warren, who had been appointed general, but who had come as a volunteer to take part in the battle.

Colonel Prescott thanked Lieutenant Walden for the information sent by Colonel Stark. He did not doubt the men from New Hampshire would be as true as they were in the battles of Louisburg and Ticonderoga.[1]

---

[1] There is no evidence that Colonel Stark was directed to report to Colonel Prescott or any one else; neither is there any evidence to

Dismounting from his horse and giving it in charge of a soldier, Lieutenant Walden walked along the trench, looked over the embankment upon the British troops landing at Moulton's Point and forming in two columns, one of which, he concluded, was intending to march along the Mystic to gain the rear of the redoubt and cut off the retreat of those within it. If such were the contemplated movement it would be mainly against the regiments of Stark and Reed. The other body of troops seemed to be forming to advance directly upon the redoubt.

While he was thus gazing, a hand clasped his arm; turning, he beheld Tom Brandon.

"I've been wondering if you wouldn't be round here somewhere," said Tom.

"And I have been wondering where you would be," Robert replied.

"And so you are a lieutenant?" queried Tom, looking at the epaulet on his shoulder. "I congratulate you."

"The whole family are on the roof to see the battle," he continued.

"Perhaps you can bring them a little nearer with my telescope," said Robert, handing him the instrument.

Tom rested it on the embankment and looked towards the house.

show that Putnam was in command. We only know that Prescott was directed to occupy Charlestown Heights. Later in the war Putnam, by virtue of his rank, would have been in command, or possibly Warren, but Warren was there only as a volunteer, having been appointed general the day before the battle. It seems probable that no one exercised supreme command, but Prescott, Putnam, Stark, and Reed acted individually with their separate commands, as the exigencies of the moment demanded.

"There 's a crowd of 'em on the roof," he said, "father, mother, and Berinthia There 's a man with a white wig, — Mr. Newville, I guess; and there 's a girl talking with Berinthia — Ruth Newville."

With quickened pulse Robert adjusted the glass to his vision. Others than those mentioned by Tom were upon the roof, but one figure alone engaged his attention. Oh, if he could but know how she regarded the impending battle! Possibly since the events on Lexington Green and at Concord bridge her sympathies had been with the king. No, he could not think it. The instincts of one so noble, good, and large-hearted must ever be opposed to tyranny and oppression. Whether favoring or opposing the course of the Colonies, what matter to him? What probability of their ever meeting again? If meeting, would she ever be other than an old acquaintance? Never had he opened his heart to her; never by word or deed informed her that she was all the world to him. To her he would be only a friend of other days.

He could see a tall man in a general's uniform walking along the British lines. He halted, took off his cocked hat, stood erect, and said something to the soldiers. He concluded it was General Howe, telling them they were a noble body of men, and he did not doubt they would show themselves valiant soldiers. He should not ask them to go any farther than he himself was willing to go. Robert and Tom could hear the cheer which the soldiers gave him.

The columns began to march, — that commanded by General Howe along the bank of the Mystic; that by General Pigot straight up the hill towards the redoubt.

Robert ran to the spot where he had left his horse, but it was not there. He hastened down the slope, past the Connecticut troops under Colonel Knowlton, and reported to Colonel Stark, who was directing his soldiers to take up a rail fence in front of his line and reset it by the low stone wall, and fill the space between the fences with hay from the windrows.

" It will serve as a screen," he said.

Stepping in front a short distance, he drove a stake in the ground.

" Don't fire till the redcoats are up to it," was his order.

The sun was shining from a cloudless sky. They upon the roof of the Brandon home saw the scarlet columns of the British moving along the Mystic and towards the redoubt, the sunlight gleaming from their muskets and bayonets, the flags waving above them, the men keeping step to the drumbeat; the great guns of the fleet and those on Copp's Hill flaming and thundering; white powder-clouds floating away and dissolving in thin air. They saw puffs of smoke burst from the heads of the advancing columns and heard the rattle of muskets. Cannon-shot plowed the ground and tossed up the gravel around the redoubt. Only the six cannon of the provincials were replying. Nearer moved the scarlet line. Again a rattling volley, with no answering musket shot from fence or embankment. What the meaning of such silence? Suddenly a line of light streamed from the river to the foot of the hill, and like the lightning's

flash ran along the embankment and round the redoubt. A rattle and roar like the waves of the sea
upon a rocky shore came to their ears across the shining waters. Men were reeling to the ground, whole
ranks going down before the pitiless storm. The,
front ranks had melted away. For a few moments
there was a rattling like scattered raindrops, and
then another lightning flash, and the British were fleeing in confusion.

Mr. Newville clenched his hands.

" I fear the king's troops are discomfited," he said.

Mrs. Newville with a long-drawn sigh covered her
face with her handkerchief as if to shut out the un-
welcome spectacle.

" The redcoats are beaten ! " Berinthia exclaimed.

" It is too soon to say that, daughter. The battle
is not yet over; the king's troops would be cowardly
were they to give up with only one attempt."

Like a statue, her hands tightly grasping the balustrade, her bosom heaving with suppressed emotion,
Ruth gazed upon the spectacle, uttering no exclamation. Taking the telescope, she turned it upon the
scene, beholding the prostrate forms dotting the newly
mown fields. It was not difficult to distinguish Lord
Howe, the centre of a group of officers. He was evidently issuing orders to re-form the broken lines.
Colonels, majors, and captains were rallying the disheartened men. In the intervals of the cannonade
from the fleet a confused hum of voices could be
heard, officers shouting their orders. Beyond the
prostrate forms, behind the low stone wall and screen
of hay were the provincials, biding their time. Offi-

cers were walking to and fro, — one middle-aged, with a colonel's epaulets, evidently commanding the troops nearest the Mystic River. A subordinate officer of manly form was receiving orders and transmitting them to others. Where had she seen one like him? Long she gazed with unwonted bloom upon her cheeks.

Again the scarlet lines advanced, — the foremost platoons halting, firing, filing right and left, that those in the rear might reach the front. Unmindful of the bullets pattering around him, the young officer walked composedly along the provincial line, from which came no answering shot. Seemingly he was telling the men to wait. Suddenly, as before, the screen of hay became a sheet of flame, and the scarlet ranks again dissolved like a straw in a candle's flame, whole ranks reeling and falling, or fleeing to the place of landing.

Mr. Newville groaned aloud. Again Mrs. Newville covered her face. Captain Brandon, Mrs. Brandon, and Berinthia, out of respect to their guests, gave no sign of exultation; but from windows, roofs, doorways, and steeples, like the voice of many waters, came the joyful murmur of the multitude, revealing to General Gage, up in the tower of Christ Church, the sympathy of the people with the provincials.

No exclamation of satisfaction or disappointment fell from the lips of Ruth, still looking with the telescope towards the provincial line by the Mystic, and the manly figure of the officer receiving instructions from his superior.

There was a commotion among the troops in the burial ground before them.

" Fall in! Fall in! " General Clinton shouted. They hastily formed in column and marched down the steep descent to the ferry landing. From the tower of Christ Church, together with General Gage, Clinton had seen the discomfiture of Lord Howe and General Pigot, and, with three hundred men, was hastening to reinforce them, stepping into boats and crossing the river.

The people on the housetops needed no telescopes to see what was going on across the stream. Slowly the lines re-formed, the men reluctantly taking their places. They who had fought at Ticonderoga, who had won the victory on the Plains of Abraham at Quebec, never had faced so pitiless a storm.

" It is downright murder," said the men.

They upon the housetops could see the British officers flourishing their swords, gesticulating, and even striking the disheartened soldiers, compelling them to stand once more in the ranks. Twice they had advanced, encumbered with their knapsacks, in accordance with strict military rule; now they were laying them aside. There were fewer men in the ranks than at the beginning of the battle, but the honor of England was at stake. The rabble of undisciplined country bumpkins must be driven from their position, or the troops of England would be forever disgraced. General Howe had learned wisdom. He had thought to sweep aside the line of provincials behind the low stone wall, gain the rear, cut off the retreat of those in the redoubt, capture them, and win a notable victory. He had not expected such resistance, such a destructive fire as had greeted the light infantry along the

banks of the stream. In the two attempts, he had discovered the weak place in the provincial line, — the
space between the redoubt and the low stone wall. In
planning the third movement, he resolved to make
a feint of advancing once more towards the wall,
but would concentrate his attack upon the redoubt,
and especially upon that portion of the line least de-
fended.

The summer sun, shining from a cloudless sky, was
declining towards the western horizon. It was past
four o'clock before the lines were ready. Once more
the guns of the fleet hurled solid shot and shells upon
the redoubt. Captain Brandon, looking from his
housetop down upon the guns almost beneath him,
saw a gunner ramming an inflammable shell into the
cannon. The shell, with smoking torch, screamed
across the river, aimed not at the bank of yellow earth
on Bunker Hill, but at the houses in Charlestown.

"They intend to burn the village," he said.

Soon flames were bursting from window, doorway,
and roof. The wind, blowing from the south, carried
sparks and cinders to the adjoining houses, glowing in
the summer heat. A wail of horror from the people
rent the air.

"That is mean, cruel, wicked, dastardly!" exclaimed Ruth, with flashing eyes. "It's inhuman.
I shall hate the man who has ordered it."[1]

Through the previous stages of the conflict no
word of approval or disapproval had escaped her lips.

[1] The only defense of the British for the destruction of Charlestown is the assertion that the advancing troops were fired upon by
provincials secreted in one of the houses on the outskirts of the town.

" Ruth! Ruth! Don't say that!" Mr. Newville cried, astonished by such an outburst of indignation.

" If General Gage were here I would say it to his face. What have those people done that their homes should be destroyed? They are not fighting the battle. Does he think that by burning the town he will frighten those men in the redoubt into submission? Were I one of them, I would die before I would surrender."

Her eyes were flashing. In her earnestness she had removed her hat. The gentle breeze was fanning her heated brow. She stood erect, a queen in her dignity and beauty. Never had Mr. and Mrs. Newville dreamed that there was such pent-up fire in her soul, such energy, fearlessness, and instinctive comprehension of justice and right. Captain and Mrs. Brandon, Berinthia, and all around gazed upon her wonderingly and with admiration.

The fire was sweeping on, — leaping from building to building, licking up houses, stables, and workshop, reaching the meetinghouse, kindling the shingles on its roof, the clapboards upon its walls, bursting from doors and windows, climbing the spire to the gilded vane, burning till beams and timbers gave way; then came the crash, — a single stroke of the bell tolling as it were a requiem.

Under the cloud from the burning town the scarlet lines once more advanced, — not towards the screen of hay, but in the direction of the redoubt. With the glass Ruth saw the manly figure she had seen before, seemingly receiving instructions from his superior officer, and running towards the threatened point of attack. The scarlet lines were mounting the breastwork. Men were firing in each other's faces; thrusting with the bayonet. She could see a stalwart provincial in his shirt-sleeves beat out the brains of a Britisher with the butt of his musket, and the next moment go down with a bayonet through his heart. The manly figure was in the thick of the mêlée, — a half dozen redcoats rushing upon him. His sword was flashing in the sunlight as he parried their bayonets, keeping them at bay. Guns flashed, and the white powder-cloud shut out the scene. When it cleared, he had gone down, and the redcoats were swinging their hats. Their shout of victory came across the waters. Those around saw Ruth clasp her hand upon her heart.

"They are beaten, and he is shot!" she cried, sinking into Berinthia's arms.

"Who's shot?" her mother asked. There was no answer from the quivering lips.

"The excitement is too much for her," said Mrs. Newville, as they bore her to Berinthia's chamber.

XX.

TOM BRANDON, lying upon the green grass where the provincials had halted after the retreat, recalled the events of the day with his fellow soldiers, especially the last struggle. He had fired away his powder, as had many others. He had no bayonet, and could only defend himself with the butt of his gun. He remembered how bravely Doctor Warren behaved, telling the men to keep cool; how he took bandages from his pockets, and bound up the wounds of those disabled at the beginning; how a Britisher shot him down and stabbed him with a bayonet. As for himself, he hardly knew what he did, except to fight till almost the last of his comrades left the redoubt, when he leaped over the breastwork, and walked towards the British, approaching the western side as if to give himself up, then turned and ran as fast as he could, with the bullets whizzing past him.[1] He won-

---

[1] The experience of Tom Brandon was that of Eliakim Walker of Tewksbury, Mass., as narrated by him to the author:—

"I had fired away nearly all my powder before the last attack. I fired and was reloading my gun, when I heard a hurrah behind me. I looked round and saw the redcoats leaping over the breastwork. I saw a man beat out the brains of a Britisher with the butt of his gun; the next moment they stabbed him. Seeing I could n't get out that way, I jumped over the breastwork and ran towards Pigot's men, a rod or two, then turned and ran as fast as I could the other

dered if Lieutenant Walden had escaped unharmed. He walked a little way to Colonel Stark's regiment to inquire.

"I fear," said Captain Daniel Moore, "that Lieutenant Walden has been killed. During the day he took a conspicuous part. He was sent by General Ward to summon us from Medford. He carried several messages from Colonel Stark to Prescott and Putnam, and was with the men of his company at times. He was with us just before the last assault, and hastened towards the redoubt a moment before the redcoats swarmed over it. I fear the worst, for he was very brave."

The people of Boston never had beheld such a scene as that of the day following the battle. . The sun shone from a cloudless sky, but its rays fell upon the smouldering ruins of once happy homes; upon dying and dead soldiers; upon men groaning in agony as they were transported across the Charles to houses taken for hospitals. The wounded rebels— thirty-six in number — were laid upon the bare floor of the jail. They were to be treated as felons, and given prison fare.

Although the genial rays of the sun shone into the spacious apartments of the Province House, they gave no comfort to Thomas Gage, commander-in-chief of his majesty's forces in the Colonies. He was chagrined over the outcome of the battle, the losses sustained. His own officers were criticising the plan

way. The bullets whizzed past me, or struck the ground around me. I reached a rail fence, and pitched over it. A bullet struck a rail at the moment. I fell on the other side, laid still till I got my breath, then up and legged it again, and got away."

of attack. The soldiers said he had slaughtered their comrades. The people were condemning him for having burned Charlestown. He was conscious that he had gone down in the estimation of those who had given him loyal support. He knew that his military reputation had suffered an eclipse. Women were denouncing him as cruel and inhuman. The conviction came to General Gage that he was shut up in Boston, and that any attempt upon the position of the rebels at that point, or upon the hills beyond Charlestown, would result in disaster.

It was cheering news to Tom Brandon and all the soldiers of the provincial army, a few days later, to learn that Congress, sitting in Philadelphia, had selected George Washington of Virginia to command them. His coming was evidence that all the Colonies had united to resist the aggressions of the king. He fought bravely to drive the French from the valley of the Ohio, and saved the army in the battle near Fort Du Quesne. General Gage had been with him in that engagement, but now they would command opposing armies.

It was a beautiful summer morning, the 3d of July, when the regiments in Cambridge and some of the troops from Roxbury assembled on the Common at Cambridge to receive General Washington. Tom Brandon saw a tall, broad-shouldered man, sitting erect on a white horse, wearing a blue uniform trimmed with buff, accompanied by General Putnam, General Ward, and a large number of officers, ride out from General Ward's headquarters and take position under a great elm-tree.

" Attention, the army ! " shouted General Ward.

The officers repeated it, and every soldier stood erect.

" Salute your commander, Major-General George Washington ! "

The soldiers presented arms, the fifes began to play,

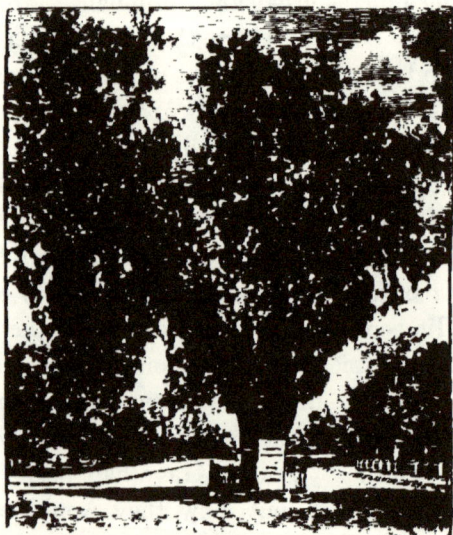

Where Washington assumed Command.

the drums to rattle. General Washington lifted his hat, bowed right and left, drew his sword from its scabbard, and rode along the line. The soldiers saw dignity, decision, and energy, yet calmness, in all his movements. They knew he had a great plantation on the bank of the Potomac River in Virginia ; that he could live at ease and enjoy life in hunting and fishing at his own pleasure, but he had left all at the call of Congress to take command of the army. His com-

ing gave them confidence and made them more than
ever determined to drive the redcoats out of Boston.
They kept such a strict guard that the British could
not obtain fresh provisions, neither could the inhabitants of the town. In the home of Captain Brandon,
the only meat to be had was the salt pork and beef in
the cellar, or the flounders caught by Mark Antony,
fishing from the wharves.

Even General Gage could have no great variety
of food. In contrast to this, Tom Brandon and his
fellow soldiers were living luxuriously, having fresh
beef three times a week, with flour, peas, beans, rice,
potatoes, onions, cabbages, turnips, beets, spruce beer,
and grog, and plenty of tobacco.

Tom took his turn standing guard, and found pleasure in chaffing the lobsters on picket, telling them
what he had for dinner. A thought came to him, —
to write a letter and hire a redcoat to take it to his
father. He wrote about the battle; how he saw the
family on the roof of the house, from the redoubt,
just before it began; how he escaped; how Robert
Walden went down in the thick of the fight and probably had been buried with the others somewhere on
Bunker Hill. The Britisher gladly agreed to take
the letter to Copp's Hill for the plug of tobacco which
Tom gave him.

Mark Antony, the following afternoon, wondered
what the soldier who was rattling the knocker on the
front door might want.

"Here's a letter for your master, Captain Brandon.
One of the rebs gave it to me. Maybe it's from his
son," said the soldier.

"A letter from Massa Tom," shouted the negro, dancing into the sitting-room.

Captain Brandon thanked the soldier, and told Mark Antony to mix a toddy for him.

It was gratifying to know that Tom was safe, but sad the information that Lieutenant Walden was numbered among the killed.

The fair brow of Ruth Newville through the summer months had been growing whiter day by day.

"I fear she is not well," said Mr. Newville.

"The battle, the burning of Charlestown, — the terrible spectacle was too much for her nerves," Mrs. Newville replied.

"Ought we not to call in the doctor?"

"No, she is not sick; you know how sympathetic she is. Don't you remember what she said when she saw the town in flames, — even speaking disrespectfully of General Gage, and swooning when the king's troops won the victory. The burning of so many houses has unstrung her nerves. I trust she will soon get over it. Since the battle she has spent most of her time in her chamber and has pleaded indisposition when gentlemen, especially officers, have called."

"Miss Ruth wants you to come up de stairs to her chamber," said Pompey, when Berinthia called at the Newville home to show her the letter Tom had written.

"So you have heard from Tom?"

"Yes, and he says that Robert Walden was killed at the very last of the battle."

"It is as I said. I saw him go down and their feet trample him in the dust!"

" Was it Robert you saw ? "

" Yes. With the telescope I had seen him all ·
through the battle, walking unharmed where the bullets were flying thickest."

" You did not tell us you saw him."

" No. I did not want to alarm you."

" And you saw him when he was killed ? "

" I saw his sword flashing in the sunlight as the
men in scarlet closed around him. A half dozen were
thrusting with their bayonets, and yet he kept them
at bay till they shot him."

Tears had wet her pillow, but none glistened on
her eyelids now. Through the sleepless hours she
had seen the stars go down beneath the western horizon ; in like manner something bright and shining
had gone out of her life. The stars would reappear ;
but that which had made it beautiful to live never
would return. The words " I love you " would never
be spoken by a voice forever silent.

Berinthia kissed the tremulous lips.

" I see it now, Ruth, dear; you loved him."

" Yes, I loved him. He was so noble and true,
how could I help it ? He never said he loved me, and
yet I think down deep in his heart he had a place for
me. I never have confessed it before, not even to
myself. I say it to you, because I should die if I
could not have some one to whom I could tell my sorrow. Let it be our secret, ours alone."

Through the sultry days of August the streets
were silent, except the beating of drums as other
regiments arrived, or as soldiers dying from wounds
or disease were borne to their burial. The distress of

the people could but increase. The provincials wounded in the battle were still held as felons in the jail. They were dying very fast. It was a spirited letter which the British commander received from General Washington, informing him that unless the prisoners were treated more humanely, British prisoners would be dealt with accordingly.[1]

Many times Abraham Duncan asked permission to see the prisoners confined in the jail, that he might minister to their needs and do something for their comfort and welfare, but as often had he been refused by the gruff red-coated sergeant in charge. Once more, after learning what General Washington had done, he asked permission, received a pass from the provost-marshal, and was admitted. He saw the floor was covered with prostrate forms, men with sunken eyes, emaciated hands, a few with old quilts beneath them, others upon the bare planks. There were festering wounds and cheeks hot with the flush of fever. Some of the sufferers gazed upon him wonderingly, others heeded not his coming. One, whose uniform was still soiled with the dust of the battlefield, lay with closed eyes, minding not his presence.

" His wound has about healed, but he is going with fever. He was fine-looking when brought here the day after the battle, but he is about done for. After to-morrow we shall have one less to exchange with Mr. Washington." said the sergeant.

---

[1] Reverend Andrew Eliot, minister of the New North Church, remained in Boston. The following is from a letter to Samuel Eliot under date of September 6, 1775: "I am at length allowed to visit the prisoners. They are only eleven out of thirty." *Proceedings Mass. Hist. Soc.* vol. xvi.

Abraham stooped and parted the matted beard from the fevered lips, and laid back the tangled hair from the brow. The eyes wearily opened, gazed languidly, then wonderingly.

" Do you know me ? "

The words were faintly spoken.

" Know you! What, Robert Walden! "

There was not strength in the arm sufficient to lift the weary hand. Abraham grasped it, looked one moment at the closing eyes, and hastened from the room. Breathless with running, he reached the Brandon home, telling the story.

" We must have him brought here instantly; he must not die there," said Mr. Brandon, who accompanied Abraham to the jail, only to find that the sergeant in charge could not permit the removal. Sadly they returned.

"I must tell Ruth about it," said Berinthia, putting on her bonnet and hastening from the house.

Ruth was sitting in her chamber. A strange, yet sweet peace had come into her soul. The heart that had struggled so sorely was at rest. She was repeating to herself the words spoken by the world's best friend, " My peace I leave you; not as the world giveth, give I unto you."

The summer birds were no longer singing; the swallows had gone. The melocotoons were no longer upon the trees, neither the early pears and ripening apples; the soldiers had plucked them. Her father's face was growing grave ; her mother's step less elastic. There was sorrow and desolation around her, and yet she was happy. She saw Berinthia walking up the path.

"Come right up," the cheerful invitation from the chamber window.

"Oh, Ruth, I've something to tell you. He's alive!"

"Who?"

"Robert — a prisoner in the jail."

She told the story; he was still breathing, but dying. Her father had been to get him, but no prisoner could be removed without an order from General Gage.

"We will go to the Province House," said Ruth quietly, rising and putting on her bonnet.

Her calmness, the manifest quiet, the business-like procedure of Ruth, amazed Berinthia. They hastened to the governor's home. General Gage received them courteously. He was pleased to welcome Miss Newville to the Province House, and recalled with pleasure the evening when he had the honor to escort her to her father's hospitable table.

"I have a favor to ask," said Ruth, "which I am sure your excellency will be pleased to grant. One of your prisoners, Lieutenant Robert Walden, in the jail, is a cousin of my friend Miss Brandon. I learn that he is far gone with fever and seemingly has not many hours to live, and I have come to ask if you will kindly permit his removal to her home?"

"Most certainly, my dear Miss Newville; it gives me pleasure to do this little office for you and your friend," he replied.

General Gage touched a bell and a sergeant entered the apartment.

"Sergeant, take two men of the guard, with a bier, and accompany these ladies to the jail to remove one of the sick prisoners, as they shall direct. See to it that the man is gently handled. Here is the order of delivery for the officer in charge."

" You are very kind, General, and I thank you not only for Miss Brandon, but for myself," said Ruth.

Never before had the people living along Hanover Street seen such a spectacle as that a few minutes later, — a sergeant in advance, two soldiers bearing a rebel officer, worn and wasted by disease, his life ebbing away, and two ladies looking anxiously to see if the flickering life would last a little longer.

In Tom's chamber the soiled uniform was removed, the matted hair laid back, the parched lips moistened, the unconscious invalid clothed in linen white and clean. A doctor came, bowed his ear to Robert's breast to catch the beating of the heart, and moistened the parched lips.

" Fever has burned him up. The tide is nearly out. It is only a question of a few hours," he said.

Through the night, Ruth, sitting by his bedside, in the calm and stillness, heard the clock strike the passing hours. At times she heard, through the open windows, the faint ripple of the surf rolling in from the restless sea. Soon for him the waves of life would break upon a shoreless ocean. It was her hand that fanned him; that wiped the death-damp from his forehead; dropped the refreshing cordial on his tongue; held the mirror to his nostrils to ascertain if still, perchance, he breathed. The tides of the ocean had reached their farthest ebb and were setting towards the flood once more, bringing sweet and refreshing odors from the ever-heaving sea. The night winds were drying the dampness from the marble brow. Day was dawning, its amber light flowing along the horizon. The fluttering heart was beating more strongly ; more deep the breathing.

"Oh, 'Rinthia! He is n't going ; he 's coming back. God has heard my prayer," said Ruth.

The sun was rising, and its rays streaming into the chamber. The closed eyes slowly opened and gazed wonderingly. Where was he ? What the meaning of this flood of light? No longer straggling beams through iron-grated windows, no longer the bare floor and earth-polluted garments, but linen white and clean. Was it an angel bending over him, — whose eyes of love and infinite tenderness looked into his own? Was it one of the seraphim that pressed her lips to his, that dropped tears upon his cheeks? Were there tears in Heaven ? Surely this must be Paradise ! The eyes closed, the vision faded, but the angel still was fanning the fevered cheeks.

As shone the face of Moses, the lawgiver of Israel, when he descended from the Mount of God, so the countenance of Ruth Newville was illuminated by a divine radiance when once more she entered her home. During the night she had been transfigured.

"What has happened, daughter ? " her father asked.

"Where have you been? what is it? " the exclamation of the mother, gazing with wonder and amazement upon the face of her child.

"Sit down, please, and I will tell you. I must go back to the beginning. Do you remember a day, six years ago, one September afternoon, when I came into the house greatly agitated? and when you asked, as you have now, what had happened, I would not make reply?"

"Yes, Ruth, and you have been a mystery to me ever since that afternoon," said Mrs. Newville.

. "I would not tell you then that I had been insulted by ruffian soldiers, that a stranger had rescued me from their clutches, for I knew it would trouble you. Who the gentleman was I did not know. I only saw he was noble and manly. I thanked him and hastened away. Right after that we had our last garden party, to which 'Rinthia brought her cousin, Mr. Walden, when I discovered it was he who rescued me."

"Mr. Walden!" Mrs. Newville exclaimed.

"A noble young man! I always liked his appearance," said Mr. Newville.

"Why didn't you tell us about it, Ruth, so we could have shown him some attention?" Mrs. Newville asked.

"It is not too late to do it now, mother."

She told the story, that he was a lieutenant, a prisoner, wounded, hovering between life and death; how she had brought about his removal from the jail to the Brandon home, watched over him during the night, wondering if the next moment would not be the last; that just before sunrise the tide had turned and he was going to live.

"You saving him! Wonderful!" Mrs. Newville exclaimed.

"It is just like you, daughter," said the father, clasping his arms around her and kissing her lips.

"I will go and help care for him, even if he is a rebel," said Mrs. Newville.

"Ruth, daughter," said the father, when they were alone, "did you keep that to yourself because you thought it would trouble us to hear that the soldiers of King George were vile ruffians?"

"Yes, father; I knew your loyalty to the king, and I would not disturb it. I did not want to pain you. And do you wonder I have hated the sight of a red-coat ever since? But, father dear, it was not the assault of the villains that led me to sympathize with the provincials, as you know I have done, but the conviction that they were in the right and the king and his ministers in the wrong. I can understand why you and mother do not see the conflict as I see it. Your high sense of honor, your oath of allegiance to the king, your position as an official, have made you loyal and true to King George, and you cannot see the side espoused by the people. This attempt of the ministry and king to subdue them by force of arms, by burning their houses, by treating them as felons, as they have Robert Walden, thrusting them into jail, allowing them to die uncared for, will fail; justice and right are on their side. I know it pains you, father dear, to have me say this, but I could not, even for the sake of pleasing you, be false to myself."

"I would not have you be false to yourself, my child, but always true to your convictions, no matter what may happen." He drew her to him and tenderly caressed her.

"I see it now, daughter. For a long while I have

not been able to comprehend you, but it is plain at last."

They sat in silence, her head pillowed on his breast, his arm around her.

" Ruth, daughter, I suspect you have not told me all; you need not unfold anything you may choose to keep to yourself, but I can understand that a very tender feeling may have sprung up between Mr. Walden and yourself."

" He never has said that he loved me. You would not have me ask him if he does, would you, father dear?" she said playfully, patting his lips with her fingers.

" I understand, daughter. Things of the heart are sacred and not to be talked about," he replied, kissing her once more and feeling as never before the greatness and richness of the treasure he had in her.

" Ah! I see," he said to himself as he paced the room. " It is all clear, now, why Lord Upperton and the rest of them have had no chance."

XXI.

THE ESCAPE.

THE October days were bright and clear, but the sun shone upon a home invaded by sickness. In the Brandon home, Lieutenant Walden was slowly recovering. Mrs. Brandon was an invalid, worn down with care and anxiety. Life upon the sea, hardship, and exposure had brought rheumatism to the joints of Captain Brandon, who was only able to hobble with his cane. One countenance in the home was always bright and cheerful; there was ever a smile upon 'Rinthia's face. Abraham Duncan was the ever helpful friend, not only ministering to their wants but giving information of what was going on, — that General Gage had been called to England, and General Howe was to succeed him as commander.

"The British soldiers," said Abraham, "are not sorry to have Gage go; they are ready to throw up their caps for General Howe, who showed his bravery at Bunker Hill, while Gage looked on with his spyglass from the steeple of Christ Church. The soldiers think Gage has been too kind-hearted in permitting you to have charge of Lieutenant Walden. Rebels are not entitled to mercy."

There came a night in October when the people were awakened by the thunder of cannon and the rattle of muskets. In the morning Abraham said that a party of Americans came down Charles River in flatboats and on rafts, and opened fire upon the troops encamped on the Common. Only one or two were injured, but it gave the British a great fright.

The sound of the strife stirred Robert's blood. He wanted to be there, — to take part in driving the red-coats into the sea. The thought nerved him; but when the uproar died away, he found himself weak, with his tongue parched and his blood at fever heat. Would strength ever come? Would he ever be able to take part again in the struggle for freedom?

Day after day there came one to see him, the sound of whose footsteps was more inspiring than the roll of the drums, the touch of whose hand gave him strength, whose presence was a benediction. She sat by his side and read to him from the poets; told him pleasant stories; laid her soft hand upon his brow. When he was a little stronger, she and 'Rinthia supported his faltering steps up the stairway to the roof of the mansion, where he could sit in the sunshine, gaze upon the beautiful panorama, inhale the life-giving air from the hills, and the odors wafted from the sea. Across the Charles was the line of yellow earth behind which he went down in the mêlée. Upon the higher hill were the new and stronger fortifications constructed by the British. The fields, where so many of the redcoats were cut down by the fire of the New Hampshire men, were dotted with white tents. At the base of the hill were the blackened ruins of Charlestown. On Prospect Hill were the earthworks of the provincials. He could not discover any fortifications on

Dorchester Heights, and wondered why either General Washington or the British commander had not taken possession of such a commanding position. The Americans ought to seize it; for, with cannon planted there, they could drive the warships from the harbor. He doubted if General Washington knew the value of the position. He was able now to go up and down the stairs without assistance; a few more days, and he would be strong and vigorous. Then what? He was a prisoner, and had not been paroled. If the British were to learn he was getting well, would they not be likely to send him on board one of the ships and pack him off to Halifax? Even if they did not take such a course, how could he remain there · doing nothing. Oh, if he could only be with the army again! But were he to go, he must say good-by to her who had saved his life. Why not remain and enjoy the blessedness of her presence? But would she not think him wanting in manliness? On the other hand, if he were to make his escape and go back to the army, would he not in a sense be lifting his hand against her father and mother in his efforts to drive the British from Boston? More than that, was it not becoming plain, that were the British to go, the Tories must also go? for the bitterness between those who stood for the king and those who supported Congress was deepening. Mr. Newville sided with the king; he was holding an office under the crown. If the British were driven out, he would be compelled to leave, and in all probability his estate would be confiscated. If he himself were to make his escape to the army, would he ever again behold the face of

Ruth Newville, ever again see the love beaming from her eyes, or feel the touch of her hand? How could he go and leave her with such uncertainty before him? And yet, would it not be ignoble to remain? If he could get away, was it not his duty to do so? Was not his country calling him?

Captain Brandon learned that General Howe had issued a proclamation threatening with death any one who might attempt to escape without a permit from himself. "More than this," said Mr. Brandon, "he has issued another proclamation for us to organize ourselves into companies to preserve order. He will furnish us with arms and supply us with provisions the same as the troops receive. We are commanded to report to Peter Oliver within four days. Being stiff in the joints, I shall not comply. Besides, I don't intend to leave such fare as you give me, Berinthia, for the salt junk and tainted pork doled out to the soldiers."

Once more there was a familiar step in the hall, and Ruth entered the room. The rich bloom of other days was once more on her cheeks, the old-time smile illumining her countenance. Her quick perception detected a mind disturbed. They sat down by the fire. She laid her hand in his, and leaned her head upon his shoulder.

"What is it?" she asked, smoothing the troubled brow.

"I have been thinking that I am still a prisoner, liable to be seized at any moment and sent far away or put in confinement. What ought I to do? Shall I attempt to escape, run the chance of being shot, or captured and executed, as threatened by the procla-

mation? If I make the attempt and succeed, possibly we may never meet again," he said with faltering
voice.

"Never meet again! Why not?"

Planning the Escape.

"I may be captured and hanged. If I reach the
army, I shall do what I can to drive the British from
Boston. If we do, the probabilities are that your
father, holding office under the crown, will be obliged
to leave the Colony; and his daughter "—

He could say no more. His lips were quivering, and tears coursing his cheeks. Her hand wiped them away; and her arm pillowed his bowed head.

"You are all the world to me. It is for you to say. Shall I go, or shall I stay?" he said.

The words were faintly spoken.

" Go, and God be with you. If it be his will, we shall meet again."

Oh brave heart! The world's redemption rests with such as you!

The busy brain of Berinthia planned the way. The British had seized all the boats along the wharves, and sentinels were guarding them, but there was an Indian canoe in the loft of the shipyard. Abraham Duncan would put it in trim and render all possible assistance.

No tears dimmed Ruth Newville's eyes when she bade him good-by and gave him a parting kiss. Not till she was in the seclusion of her own chamber were the fountains unsealed. Alone, she gave way to grief, to be comforted by her faith in One Unseen.

Many soldiers had deserted, so every night, at sundown, sentinels patroled the wharves, and boats manned by sailors and marines kept vigilant watch in Charles River and far down the harbor. Robert must go to the shipyard before sundown and remain secreted till well into the night. The new moon would go down at nine o'clock; the tide then would be half flood. What route should he take? Were he to go directly up the Charles River to join the army at Cambridge, he must run the gauntlet, not only of three or four of the war-ships, but of the marine patrol in the river and the sentinels on both banks. If he were to strike eastward toward the Mystic, he would encounter the guard in that direction and the warship Scarborough anchored in the channel. The route up the Charles was most direct and inviting, though beset with greatest danger.

During the day Abraham placed the canoe beneath the wharf of the shipyard. Bidding his friends good-by, with an overcoat to protect him from the cold, Robert made his way to the shipyard, secreting himself in one of the buildings just before the hour for placing the sentinels. The young tide was already setting up the bay, and a gentle wind blowing from the east, alike favorable for the execution of his plan; but with the sea-breeze came the fog, thick and dense, shrouding ship and shore. He rejoiced in the thought that it would cover all his movements and hide him from observation. But upon reflection there was another serious and disquieting aspect; how should he make his way and by what objects could he mark out his course? Would he not run upon the boats of the marine patrol and be hailed by the sentinels on the Boyne, Somerset, and other vessels of the fleet? He must run the chances and do the best he could.

The sentinels had been set along the wharves. The soldier guarding the shipyard was pacing his beat immediately in front of Robert's hiding-place. A thought came; why not seize his musket and have a weapon of defense? Noiselessly Robert opened the door: stealthy his step; one wrench, and the weapon was his, greatly to the astonishment of the surprised and frightened soldier, who saw his own bayonet pointed at his breast and heard the click of the gun-lock.

" Don't fire! Don't fire!" stammered the soldier.

" Take off that belt and cartridge box!"

The soldier obeyed the peremptory order.

" About face!"

Accustomed to obey orders, he faced as directed.

" March!"

Again he obeyed, taking the regulation step as if at drill, Robert following a short distance, then halting while the soldier continued the march. With the musket and cartridge box well filled, Robert seated himself in the canoe. He knew the Boyne with seventy guns, Preston with fifty, Phœnix, Lively, Scarborough, Empress of Russia, and several other smaller vessels of the fleet were anchored at different points. He had noted their positions during the day. but in the darkness and fog could make no calculations in regard to them. The flowing tide would be his only guide. By drifting with it, he would be borne to the Cambridge shore of the Charles, to General Washington's army, providing he could dodge the ships, floating batteries, and picket boats. Using the paddle, he struck out from the wharf, peering into the mist, his ears open to catch the faintest sound.

" Boat ahoy!"

The startling shout seemed to come from the sky. Looking up he saw the great black hull of the Boyne, recognizing the vessel by her triple tier of guns. He was almost beneath the bowsprit.

" Round to under the stern or I 'll fire," said the voice.

" Aye, aye, sir! " Robert replied.

While drifting past the ship, so near that he could touch the hull with his hands, he was deciding what to do. Reaching the stern, with a stroke of the paddle the canoe whirled under it, then shot up the other side of the ship into the teeth of the tide, back once more to the stern, and while the puzzled sentinels on the deck were wondering what had become of the canoe he was disappearing in the fog, the success of his strategy giving zest to his enterprise. He had kept his bearings as best he could, but was not quite certain of his position, as he drifted once more.

" Boat ahoy! Who goes there? "

The challenge came, not from overhead, but from the fog before him. A backward stroke arrested his movement. Again the hail and no reply.

" Up with the anchor! Out with your oars! "

Evidently he had drifted upon one of the boats anchored in the ferry-way. Paddling away, he suddenly heard the swash of waves, and found himself approaching a wharf, but on which side the river he could not say.

" Boat ahoy! Halt, or I 'll fire," the hail that came to him.

Peering into the mist, he saw the dim outline of a soldier raising his musket.

" Hold on. Don't fire. Please point me in the direction of the Boyne," said Robert.

The sentinel lowered his musket as if saying to himself, " This must be one of the officers of the frigate who has been on shore having a good time."

" The Boyne is right out in that direction," said

the sentinel, pointing with his musket, "but my orders are not to let any one pass along the wharf after ten o'clock without they give the countersign."

" All right; always obey orders. I'll come to the wharf."

Robert could hear the dip of oars in the fog, and knew it must be the patrol boat pursuing him. He paddled towards the wharf as if to give the countersign, but the next moment shot under it as the other boat approached.

" Boat ahoy! " he heard the sentinel shout.

" Ahoy yourself! We are the patrol. Have you seen a canoe?"

" Yes, and the man inquired where the Boyne was lying, and disappeared quicker than greased lightning when he heard you coming."

Robert was making his way, the while, amid the piles of the wharf. He knew the tide must be near its full flood, for he had to crouch low in the canoe, and the barnacles upon the piles were nearly covered with the water. He doubted if the patrol could follow him. Should he remain secreted? No. They might light a torch and discover him. Noiselessly he paddled amid the piles to the farther side of the wharf, and then glided from its shelter along the shore, screened from the patrol by the projecting timbers, and was once more in the stream. He could no longer be guided by the tide or drift with it. The wind had died away. It was blowing from the east when he started, but now only by waving his hand could he ascertain its direction. Whether it had changed he could not know. It was a welcome sound that came to his ears — the clock on the Old Brick Meetinghouse striking the hour.   He thought of Ruth, asleep in her white-curtained chamber so near the bell, and of her goodness, her brave heart, that bade him go.   The tones came to him over his right shoulder, when they ought to be over the left.   He must be headed in the wrong direction.   It was not easy for him to reason it out; yet, if he would reach Cambridge, he must turn squarely round.   It was plain that he had not made much progress.   He knew that several warships and floating batteries and picket-boats must be lying between his position and the Americans, but he must go on.   Suddenly a dark object loomed before him, and a hail as before came from the deck of a ship.

"Come alongside, or I 'll fire."

What should he do?   He saw a blinding flash.   A bullet whizzed over his head, and the report of the musket awoke the echoes along the shore.   It was from the stern of the ship.   Again, a flash from the bow, and a bullet pattered into the water.   Suddenly the light of a torch brought into full view a marine holding it over the side of the vessel.   Another marine by his side was reloading his musket.   A thought came — they had opened fire upon him; why not pay them in the same coin.   Dropping the paddle, he raised the musket he had wrenched from the sentinel.   The torch revealed the form of him who held it, — a man with weather-beaten features, hard and cold.   He was so near that it would be easy to send a bullet through his heart.   Should he do it? Why not?   Had he not been down to death's door through brutal treatment from the redcoats?   Why not take revenge?

No, he could not quench life forever, bring sorrow, perchance, to some household far away; but he would put out that torch. He ran his eye along the gun-barrel, pulled the trigger, and sent the bullet through the upraised arm. The torch fell into the water, and all was dark.

"We are attacked! Beat to quarters," was the shout on the ship.

He heard the roll of drums. Men leaped from their hammocks. There was hurrying of feet, rattling of ropes, and shouting of orders. Again a musket flashed and a bullet pierced the canoe, reminding him he was near enough to the ship to be seen. A few strokes of the paddle and he was beyond their aim. Suddenly he discovered the canoe was filling with water through the hole made by the bullet. Several minutes passed before he could find it, in the darkness; the canoe gradually sinking the while. When found, at last, he thrust in his finger and reflected what next to do. It was plain that the leak must be stopped, but how? He could not sit with his finger in the hole and drift wherever the tide might take him. Removing his finger, he would soon be sinking.

"Ah! I have it," he said to himself. It was but the work of a moment to cut a bit of rope from the coil at his feet and thrust it into the opening, stopping the leak.

But the canoe was water-logged; how should he get rid of it? To scoop out with the paddle would attract attention and bring the whole patrol to the spot; there was a better way.

"I'll use my hat for a bucket," he said to himself.

He bailed the canoe and reloaded the musket, drifting the while. Where he was he could not determine. Suddenly a musket flashed, high up in the air, and a bullet fell into the water by his side. He could see the faint outline of topmasts and yardarms, and the figure of a man upon the shrouds. He aimed as best he could and pulled the trigger.

" I 'm shot ! " were the words that came to him through the mist.

" Give 'em the six-pounder with grape," said a voice, followed by a blinding flash, a swish in the water, the roar of a cannon. It had been fired at random, and he was unharmed. Once more he used the paddle, wondering what next would happen.

What the meaning of that flash in the distance? What that plunge in the water not far away? What that deep, heavy roar reverberating along the shore? Surely it must be a shot from General Washington's cannon. And now all around he heard voices, and boatswains' whistles. Soon the great guns of the warships were flashing; shot were plunging into the water, and shells bursting in the air.

" I have kicked up a big racket," said Robert to himself as he listened to the uproar.

What should he do? The tide was beginning to ebb. Why not go with it down the harbor, reach one of the islands, wait till daylight, and then shape his course, instead of attempting to pass the pickets patrolling the river with everybody on the alert. While the cannon were flashing he drifted with the ebbing tide. Another dark object suddenly loomed before him, but no hail came from its deck. Plainly it was one of the transports. Another, and still no hail. The cannonade was dying away; suddenly, bells all around him were striking. He must be in the midst of the fleet of transports; it was four o'clock, the hour to change the watch. He heard once more the bell of the Old Brick, — he could tell it by its pitch. Wind, tide, and the meetinghouse bell enabled him to calculate his position : he could not be far from the Castle ; he resolved to make for Dorchester Heights.

Day was breaking and the fog lifting. In the dawning light he shaped his course. No patrol challenged him. Through the rising mist he discerned the outline of the shore and heard the gentle ripple of waves upon the beach. To leave the canoe was like bidding good-by to a faithful friend, but with cartridge-box and musket he stepped ashore and soon found himself upon the spot which he had scanned with the telescope from the Brandon home.

It was plain that he had not miscalculated its value as a military position, — that cannon planted there could plunge their balls upon the great fleet of transports, or upon a vessel attempting to enter or depart from the harbor. He descended the western slope of the hill, reached a narrow path leading across the marsh land, and made his way to Roxbury, to be warmly welcomed by General Nathanael Greene.

" You must tell General Washington about Dorchester Heights. I am going to dine with him to-day, and you must go with me," said General Greene, who informed Robert that Lieutenant Robert Walden was supposed to have been killed about the same time that Doctor Warren fell.

" But I am here and ready to give an account of myself," Robert replied.

It was a pleasure to be in the saddle once more, — to ride with General Greene along the works which his troops had constructed. They dismounted at the house of Mr. Vassall in Cambridge, where General Washington had established his headquarters. The

Washington's Headquarters.

commander-in-chief was pleased to welcome him and listen to his story.

" I think, General Washington, that if cannon could be planted there the British fleet could be driven from the harbor. It is a high hill and very commanding. Troops ascending it would do so in the face of a plunging fire from those on the summit. It occurred to me while standing there, that if hogsheads were to be filled with stones and sent rolling upon an assaulting force, it would be an effective means of defense."

" You must dine with me to-day, Lieutenant Walden. I want Colonel Knox, who commands the artillery, and who is to be here with his estimable wife, to hear what you have to say."

It was a pleasure to meet Colonel Henry Knox and Mrs. Knox.

" We all thought you went down in the mêlée at Bunker Hill, and yet here you are," said Colonel Knox.

" Yes, and ready to do what I can to drive the redcoats into the sea."

Mrs. Knox was delighted to hear from her old-time associate, Berinthia Brandon. She said that Tom was giving a good account of himself. There were tears in the eyes of all when he told them how Miss Ruth Newville had used her influence, she the daughter of a Tory, to save him.

" That is the noblest type of womanhood," said General Washington. " Perhaps," he added, " you may wish to visit your parents for a few days, but a little later I shall desire you to assist Colonel Knox in executing an important trust."

" I am ready to do what I can in any capacity for which I am fitted," Robert replied.

A flag of truce went out from the headquarters : among the letters to people in Boston was one directed to Miss Ruth Newville. The red-coated officer who inspected the letters read but one word.

" Safe."

To her who received it the one syllable was more than a page of foolscap.

XXII.

THE king's plan to punish Boston because the East India Company's tea had been destroyed was not working very satisfactorily. Ten thousand troops were cooped up in the town with little to eat. They could obtain no fresh provisions. Lord North was sending many ships, and the ship-owners were asking high prices for the use of their vessels; for the Yankee skippers of Marblehead, Captain Manly and Captain Mugford, were darting out from that port in swift-sailing schooners, with long eighteen-pounders amidships, and the decks swarming with men who had braved the storms of the Atlantic and knew no fear, capturing the ships dispatched from England with food and supplies for the army. The ministers had paid twenty-two thousand pounds for cabbages, potatoes, and turnips; as much more for hay, oats, and beans; half a million pounds for flour, beef, and pork. They purchased five thousand oxen, fourteen thousand sheep, and thousands of pigs, that the army three thousand miles away might have something to eat. There were plenty of cattle, sheep, and pigs within fifty miles of Boston, but General Howe could not lay his hand on one of them. The winter storms were on, and the ships sailing down the Thames or from Bristol Channel had a hard time of it before losing sight of the hills of Devon. The people along the Cornwall shores beheld the seashore strewn with carcasses of cattle, sheep, and pigs, tossed overboard from the decks of foundering vessels. The few cattle that survived the six weeks' tossing on the sea were but skin and bones when the ships dropped anchor by Castle William.

In contrast, Tom Brandon and the soldiers under General Washington had plenty of good food. It was a tantalizing handbill which Benjamin Edes printed on his press at Watertown.

Tom Brandon, on picket at Charlestown Neck, hailed the Britisher a few rods distant.

" How are you, redcoat ? "

" How are you, rebel ? "

" Say, redcoat, if you won't pop at me, I won't at you."

" Agreed."

" Would n't ye like a chaw of tobacco, redcoat ? "

" I would n't mind."

" All right. Here 's a plug with my compliments; 't ain't poisoned. Ye need n't be afraid of it," said Tom, tossing it to him.

The Britisher opened the paper and read : —

American Army.	*English Army.*
1. Seven dollars a month.	1. Three pence a day.
2. Fresh provisions in plenty.	2. Rotten salt pork.
3. Health.	3. The scurvy.
4. Freedom, ease, affluence, and a good farm.	4. Slavery, beggary, and want.

Other pickets besides Tom were tossing the handbills to the Britishers. Abraham Duncan, going here and there along the streets, saw the redcoats reading them, and night after night soldiers disappeared, never again to shoulder a musket in the service of the king.

Shut up in the town with nothing to do, the troops became lawless, breaking into houses and plundering the people. In vain were the efforts of General Howe, by severe punishments, to prevent it; giving one soldier four hundred lashes on his bare back; another six hundred; hanging a third.

Hard times had come to the people of Boston. In the autumn, General Howe had issued a proclamation, threatening with execution any one who should attempt to steal away from the town without his consent; but now he would gladly have them go, only they must obtain permission. He could not supply them with food, neither with fuel. He gave the soldiers leave to rip the boards from the Old North Meetinghouse, and cut its timbers into kindlings. After much hacking they leveled the Liberty Tree, not only to obtain the wood, but to manifest their hatred of the tree. Not being able to feed the people, he sent three hundred and fifty from the town, landing them at Point Shirley, to make their way over the marshes to Lynn as best they could. Others were directed to go.

"We shall not go. I do not propose to let the redcoats make themselves at home in this house," said Berinthia to the sergeant who asked if the family would like to leave the town.

"What will you live on? Butcher Thurbal, whom

General Howe has appointed to take charge of all the cattle, says he has but six left, and here it is December, with winter only just begun. You will starve before spring," the sergeant replied.

" We have a little flour, and there is a kit of mackerel; a layer of pork is still left in the barrel. We will not go till the last mouthful of food is gone," Berinthia said resolutely.

The knocker rattled.

" One of Massa Genral Howe's ossifers," said Mark Antony.

A young lieutenant entered; but seeing a fair-faced young lady he removed his cap.

" I would like to see the mistress of the house," he said.

" I am mistress. What is it you wish? "

" I come to inform you that Colonel Hardman desires to occupy these premises for himself and staff, of which I have the honor to be a member. I am directed to inform you that you can have twenty-four hours to effect your removal." [1]

" Colonel Hardman desires to take our house, does he? "

" That is his wish."

" Has he ordered you to take possession of it for him? "

" No, he has directed me to inform you of what he intends to do, that you may make preparations at once for your removal."

---

[1] Under date of September 13, 1775, is the following from the letter of Reverend Andrew Eliot to S. Eliot: " Every house is now taken as the officers please. General Clinton is in Mr. Hancock's, Burgoyne in Mr. Bowdoin's."

" You will please say to Colonel Hardman that we cannot accede to his wish."

It was said with such firmness and quiet dignity that the lieutenant was amazed. He waited to hear some reason why she would not comply with the demand. She stood silent before him, composedly looking him in the face. Not being able to find words to reply, the lieutenant bowed stiffly and departed.

" You have n't got through with Colonel Hardman," said Abraham. " He likes the looks of this house, evidently. He is a new officer just arrived."

" He will find that an American girl can make some resistance to force," Berinthia replied.

Once more the knocker rattled, and the lieutenant entered.

" I believe I have the honor to address Miss Brandon," he said, bowing.

" That is my name."

" I am extremely sorry, Miss Brandon, to be obliged to execute an order of this kind, but I am directed by Colonel Hardman to take possession of these premises, as you will see by this order," he said, handing her a paper.

" By what right does Colonel Hardman seize these premises?"

" Well, really — I suppose — because you are a — a rebel, you know," the lieutenant replied.

" How does he know that I am a rebel?"

" I don't mean exactly that. Of course, you are not in arms personally against his majesty, King George, but then, the people are, you know."

" You mean, that because the king's troops began

a war, firing upon the people at Lexington and Concord, your colonel proposes to turn me, my invalid father and mother, out of our home, that he may take possession and live in comfort."

"It is awfully bad business, Miss Brandon, but I can't help it, you know."

"I do not doubt, sir, that it is mortifying to you, personally, to be compelled to execute an order of this sort. Please say to Colonel Hardman that this is our home, and we shall not leave it voluntarily. If he desires to occupy it, he will do so only by force of arms."

The lieutenant took his hat, not knowing what to make of a young lady so calm and self-possessed, who did not cry or wring her hands.

"Oh, Ruth, you are just the one I want to see," said Berinthia, as Miss Newville entered a few minutes later. "Just look at this! Colonel Hardman proposes to turn us out of doors, that he may take possession of our home."

"Aren't you going to protest?"

"I have protested."

"Aren't you going to do something?"

"What can I do?"

"We will see. General Howe is to dine with us this afternoon, and I have come to get you to help me entertain him and the others. We will ask him what he thinks of such arbitrary action on the part of his subordinate officer."

"I will be there to hear what he has to say," Berinthia said.

The hard times and the want of fresh provisions

ruffled the temper of Phillis in the Newville kitchen. No longer could she baste a fat turkey roasting by the fire, or a joint of juicy beef, and yet the dinner she was preparing for his excellency General Howe, and Mr. Newville's other guests, was very appetizing, — oysters raw and fried, clam soup, broiled halibut, fresh mackerel, corned beef and pork, plum-pudding and pie.

Lord William Howe, commander-in-chief of his majesty's forces in America, was a gentleman, polite, affable, who delighted to make himself agreeable to beautiful ladies. At Bunker Hill he had shown the army that he could be brave on the battlefield. The other guests were Brigadier-General Timothy Ruggles, appointed commander of the militia, loyal to the king, and Captain John Coffin of his staff. General Howe solicited the honor of escorting Miss Newville to the dinner-table; Captain Coffin, possibly preferring the society of the girl with whom he often had romped to that of the mother, offered his arm to Berinthia, leaving to General Ruggles the honor of escorting the hostess.

"The state of the times," said Mr. Newville, "does not enable me to provide an elaborate repast, but Phillis has done her best with what she had."

"I am sure your dinner will be far more elaborate than anything I have upon my own table," said General Howe. "There being no fresh provisions in the market, I have to put up with salt junk."

"Do you think the present scarcity of food will continue long?" Ruth inquired.

"I trust not. It will be some time before the government supplies reach me from England, but I have dispatched vessels to Halifax and the West Indies, which, with fair winds, ought to be here in the course of a week."

" It is tantalizing to know there are abundant supplies of vegetables in the farmers' cellars, not twenty miles away, that droves of cattle and sheep come to Mr. Washington, and we cannot get a joint of mutton or a cabbage," said Mr. Newville.

" If the provincial pirates do not intercept the vessels, we shall have fresh provisions soon ; but they are a daring set of rebels who live down towards Cape Ann. A schooner darted out the other day from Marblehead, and captured the brig Nancy and a rich cargo which I could ill afford to lose, — two thousand muskets, one hundred thousand flints, thirty thousand cannon-balls, and thirty tons of musket-balls, and a thirteen-inch mortar. I understand Mr. Washington is greatly elated by the capture, as well he may be."

" Cannot Admiral Graves protect the transports ? " Mr. Newville asked.

" Perhaps a little more enterprise on the part of the marine force would be commendable. The provincials, I must admit, show far greater zeal than is seen in the king's navy."

" It is commonly remarked that the navy is not doing much," said General Ruggles.

" The army, although it is not marching into the country, is far more active, judging from the firing which I hear through the day," Berinthia remarked.

General Howe scanned her face, wondering if there was not a trifle of sarcasm in the words. He knew he was being criticised by the Tories for his inactivity; that Admiral Graves and the officers of the navy were asking when the army was going to scatter Mr. Washington's rabble.

" I was relying upon the muskets captured in the. Nancy," said General Howe, " to supply the gentlemen in General Robertson's command; also the loyal Irish Volunteers under Captain Forest, and the Fencibles under Colonel Graham, and those whom Colonel Creen Brush, a loyalist from New York, expects to raise. I am greatly gratified by this exhibition of loyalty on the part of the citizens. Doubtless other vessels will soon be here with arms, provided that audacious Captain Manly does not slip out from Marblehead and nab them while the warships are getting up their anchors. I have sent several ships along the shore to obtain supplies if possible, but it seems the madness of the people in revolting against our gracious sovereign is widespread. I learn there are many who are still loyal, but who do not dare to sell provisions through fear of their neighbors."

" I do not doubt it," General Ruggles remarked. " If it were not for the presence of the troops, we who are loyal would have a rough time. Even as it is, I see scowls upon the faces of my old-time friends whenever I go along the street."

" Since I accompanied your excellency to Bunker Hill and manifested my loyalty," said Captain Coffin, " and especially since I have taken part in organizing the loyal citizens to aid in upholding the government, I find some of my former friends, notably some of the young ladies, shutting their doors in my face."

"I suppose you can hardly wonder at it?" Ruth remarked.

"Why should they? I have not changed. Everybody knows how I have stood from the beginning," the captain replied.

"It is not that Captain Coffin is not as agreeable and entertaining as ever, but they regard the king as attempting to deprive the people of their rights and liberties; the appeal to arms has been made; if you actively support his majesty, do you not cut yourself off from their society? Can you expect them to be as gracious as in former days?" said Berinthia.

"Perhaps not, from the standpoint you have taken; but it is rather uncomfortable, to have a young lady who has welcomed you to her fireside pass you by on the street as if you were a cold-blooded villain."

"It comes to this," said Ruth. "One cannot be loyal to the king, neither to liberty, without suffering for it. Miss Brandon's brother Tom had to give up his lady-love because he sided with the provincials. Young ladies shut the door in Captain Coffin's face because he adheres to King George. If his majesty only knew the disturbance he is making over here in love affairs, perhaps he would withdraw the army."

"Of course he would," exclaimed General Howe. "I don't believe that side of the question has ever been laid before him. I am sure, Miss Newville, if you were to go as special envoy and present the case, showing him how the sword is cutting young heart-strings asunder, he would at once issue an order for us to pack up and be off, that the course of true love might run smoothly once more."

The company laughed heartily.

"Perhaps," continued General Howe, "we may have to pack up any way, for want of something to eat. Before I succeeded to the command, General Gage seriously thought of evacuating the town, but had not enough vessels to transport the troops. I could not, when I was invested with the command, send a portion away; to do so would invite an attack upon those remaining."

Berinthia saw a startled look upon Mr. Newville's face.

"Do you think, your excellency, the time will ever come when his majesty's troops will take their departure?"

"I trust not; but this rebellion, which we thought would be confined to this Province, has become a continental question. Neither the king nor his ministers anticipated it, but it is upon us, and we shall be obliged to treat it in all its vastness. Large reinforcements are to be sent. An agreement is being made to employ several thousand Hessian troops, and everything will be done to put down the rebellion."

"I expect to see," said General Ruggles, "the army of Mr. Washington crumble to pieces very soon. I hear that the Connecticut troops demanded a bounty as the condition of their staying any longer, and when it was refused, broke ranks and started for their homes."

"So I am informed," General Howe remarked, "though, to tell the truth, two thousand fresh men came from the New Hampshire province to take their places. I must say the provincials, thus far, have shown commendable zeal and persistence in maintaining the rebellion. They have constructed formidable earthworks on Cobble Hill, so near my lines that they have compelled the warships to drop down the river to a safer anchorage."

"If by any chance the town should be evacuated, what think you, your excellency, those of us who are loyal to the king ought to do?" Mr. Newville asked.

"That is really a very difficult question to answer. Your loyalty and that of all ladies and gentlemen who stand by the king undoubtedly will make you obnoxious to the rebels. The bitterness is increasing. I fear you will not be shown much leniency."

"Would you think it strange, your excellency, if they were not lenient?" Ruth inquired.

"Why should they not be, Miss Newville?"

"Would they not be likely to regard those who support the king as their enemies?"

"Why should they? You have not taken up arms. Of course, General Ruggles and Captain Coffin might be regarded as obnoxious, and would have to take care of themselves."

"But will they not say we have given moral support to their enemies, and is not moral support likely to be as heinous in their sight as the taking of arms? If we ask them to be lenient, will they not inquire if the king's troops were merciful when they set Charlestown on fire?" Ruth asked.

A flush came upon the face of General Howe. Although he commanded the troops at Bunker Hill, he had not ordered the burning of the town. General Gage was responsible for that act. He felt a little uncomfortable over the question, for the latest newspapers from London told him the people of England condemned the destruction of the homes of so many inhabitants.

"I am free to say it was rather hard on them thus to have their homes destroyed without a moment's notice," he replied.

"Will not," Ruth inquired, "the provincials think his majesty's forces were wanting in leniency when they recall- what was done at Falmouth a few days ago, where the inhabitants were given only two hours to remove from the town? Not one minute over that would Captain Mowatt grant them, though women went down on their knees before him. Was it not inhuman for him to fire bombs among the panic-stricken multitude, setting the buildings on fire, destroying the homes of five hundred people? If his majesty's officers do these things, what may we not expect from the provincials, should it ever come our turn?"

"We will do what we can, Miss Newville, not to have it your turn."

"I do not doubt it, my lord; but I was thinking of possible contingencies."

Again Berinthia noticed a flush upon the face of General Howe.

"I will admit, Miss Newville, that in war the unexpected may sometimes happen, and possibilities are not comforting subjects for contemplation. I do not anticipate disaster to the troops under my command."

"Shall we drink the health of our gracious sovereign?" said Mr. Newville.

The others drained their glasses, but Miss Newville's and Berinthia's were not lifted from the table.

" What, daughter!   What is the meaning of this? Not drink the health of the king!" Mr. Newville exclaimed.

" No, father.   I could drink to his own personal welfare, wish him health, happiness, and long life, but our drinking to the sentiment means approval of his government.   I cannot do that.   I never can think it right to burn the homes of innocent people without a moment's warning, as was done at Charlestown. The people of Falmouth never had done anything against the king except to prevent Captain Mowatt from loading masts and spars on board his ship for the use of the king's navy.   That was their offense, and yet the town was wantonly destroyed.   I cannot think such a course is likely to restore the alienated affections of the people to the king.   More, I fear the contingencies of war may yet compel us to suffer because of these unwarranted acts."

Mr. Newville sat in silence, not knowing what to say.   He had been outspoken in his loyalty.   He never had contemplated the possibility of failure on the part of the king to put down the rebellion, but if General Howe were to evacuate Boston, what treatment could he expect from the provincials?   The words of Ruth brought the question before him in a startling way.

" Those are my sentiments, also," said Berinthia.

" I see, Miss Brandon, that you are of the same opinion, which, of course, I expected in your case, but hardly from Miss Newville," said Captain Coffin.

" Yes, I am of the same way of thinking," Berinthia replied.

" You will not, ladies, decline to drink the health of the queen, I trust?" said General Howe, as Pompey refilled the glasses.

" Oh no, I will drink it with pleasure. The queen, of course, does not stand for mismanagement, as does the king, and we will not spoil our dinner by talking about the sad events," Ruth replied.

General Howe entertained them with an account of his boyhood days, his service with General Wolfe at Quebec, how the troops climbed the steep river bank at night and won the battle on the Plains of Abraham. Captain Coffin laughed with Berinthia and Ruth over good times he had enjoyed with them. Yet all were conscious that spectres unseen had come to the banquet. The ghost confronting General Howe was whispering of starvation, of possible humiliation through forced evacuation; the one glaring at Mr. and Mrs. Newville told of a possible departure from their home, to become aliens in a foreign land.

" May I ask Miss Newville to favor us with music?" said General Howe, when they were once more in the parlor.

" With pleasure, your excellency," said Ruth, seating herself at the harpsichord and singing " The Frog he would a-wooing go," " The Fine Old English Gentleman," and then with a pathos that brought tears to the eyes of the commander-in-chief, " True Love can ne'er forget."

During the dinner, and while Ruth was singing, they could hear the deep reverberations of the cannonade.

The provincials in Roxbury were sending their shot at General Howe's fortifications on the Neck, and his cannon in reply were thundering towards the works at Cobble Hill.

"Miss Newville," said General Howe, "I cannot express my thanks to you for your entertainment. While listening to your charming melodies I have been thinking of the strange, incongruous accompaniment, the uproar of the cannonade, but I have, in a measure, been able to forget for the moment the worries and perplexities that surround me. I trust I may be able to do something to add to your happiness some day." He rose to take his departure.

"Thank you, your excellency; I am glad if I have been able in any way to make it a pleasant hour to you and General Ruggles, and my old acquaintance, Captain Coffin. Your excellency can add much to my happiness and that of Miss Brandon. One of your subordinate officers, who I think has not been long here, Colonel Hardman, has notified Miss Brandon that he is going to take possession of her home to-morrow and turn her and her invalid parents out of doors. Berinthia, you have the colonel's order, I think?" [1]

Berinthia took the document from her pocket and handed it to General Howe, who ran his eye over it and seemed to be thinking.

"Is your father loyal to the king, Miss Brandon?" he asked.

---

[1] "I am by a cruel necessity turned out of my home; must leave my books and all I possess, perhaps to be destroyed by a licentious soldier." Andrew Eliot to Thomas Hollis. *Proceedings Mass. Hist. Society,* vol. xvi.

"In the same sense that I am, your excellency. You know that I did not drink the health of the king because I protest against the course he is pursuing towards the Colonies ; my father does the same."

"You have a brother, I think, in the provincial army?"

"I suppose that Tom is there. He did what he could to defeat your excellency at Bunker Hill. Possibly it was his bullet that went through your excellency's coat. He attempted to defeat the king's troops just as they attempted to defeat him, and succeeded. You give your allegiance to the king; he gives his to liberty, and is fighting for it just as conscientiously as your excellency is fighting for King George and the crown."

"As your father sides with the provincials, and as your brother is in arms against our most gracious sovereign, may I ask if you can give any good reason why my subordinate officer should not take possession of your home?"

"Pardon me, may I ask if your excellency will kindly favor me with any good reason why my parents should be driven from their beds in midwinter, that one of the king's officers may have comfortable quarters? Does your excellency think such a course of conduct will tend to restore to the king the alienated affections of his late subjects?"

"Then, Miss Brandon, you do not consider yourself, at this moment, one of his subjects?"

"I do not. I cannot own allegiance to a sovereign who burns the homes of an inoffensive community, standing for their rights and ancient liberties."

"I admire your frankness, Miss Brandon, as I do that of Miss Newville. Have you a pen at hand?"

Ruth brought a pen and ink-horn; General Howe wrote upon the document, and handed it to her.

"I cannot go back on my promise to do something for you, Miss Newville, to add to your happiness and Miss Brandon's, and I trust I never shall do anything that will lead you to think I am insensible to the claims of humanity," he said, bowing and taking his departure.

Berinthia read what he had written : —

It is hereby ordered by the general-in-chief commanding his majesty's forces, that Miss Brandon shall be allowed to remain in possession of her home till this order shall be countermanded.

HOWE, Major-General.

In bright uniform, with stars upon his breast, Colonel Hardman, accompanied by the members of his staff, knocked at the door of the Brandon home. Mark Antony was unceremoniously pushed aside, and the officers entered the hall.

"You can inform the lady of the house, nigger, that Colonel Hardman and staff have come to take possession of the premises and " —

The sentence was not finished, for Berinthia, queenly in her dignity, stood before him. Colonel Hardman, obedient to etiquette, removed his hat. It was not an old woman, wrinkled and toothless, but a young lady, calm and self-possessed, confronting him.

"Is this Colonel Hardman?"

" I have the honor to bear that name, lady."

" You have come to take possession of my house?"

" That is my errand. I trust it will not greatly inconvenience you. I see you have my order of yesterday in your hand, and so are not unprepared for my coming."

" It is your order, and I am not unprepared, as you will see," she said, handing him the paper.

He read the writing, bit his lips, grew red in the face, returned the document, bowed stiffly, and left the hall, followed by his astonished suite.

" Outwitted by a petticoat," he muttered, with an oath, as he passed down the street.

XXIII.

SUNDERING OF HEARTSTRINGS.

It was as if one had risen from the dead, when Robert Walden once more entered the old home. Father, mother, Rachel, all, had thought of him as lying in a grave unknown, — having given his life for liberty. It was a joyful home. All the town came to shake hands with him. His father and mother were older, the gray hairs upon their brows more plentiful, and sorrow had left its mark on Rachel's face; but her countenance was beautiful in its cheerful serenity.

A few days at home, and Robert was once more with the army, commissioned as major upon the staff of General Washington. Colonel Knox the while was transporting the cannon captured by Ethan Allen at Ticonderoga across the Berkshire Hills to Cambridge — fifty guns mounted on sleds, drawn by one hundred oxen.

The commander of the army had not forgotten what Major Walden had said about the military value of Dorchester Heights. The cannon were placed in position, but not till winter was nearly over were the preparations completed for the bombardment of Boston.

When the sun set on the afternoon of March 2d

little did Lord Howe and the ten thousand British soldiers imagine what was about to happen. Suddenly from the highlands of Roxbury, from Cobble Hill, from floating batteries in Charles River, cannon-balls were hurled upon the town. Bombs exploded in the streets; one in a guard-house, wounding six soldiers. The redcoats sprang to their guns, to give shot for shot. Little sleep could the people get, through the long wearisome Saturday night. During Sunday the lips of the cannon were silent, but with the coming of night again they thundered. General Howe was wondering what Mr. Washington was intending to do, not mistrusting there was a long line of ox-carts loaded with picks and spades, bales of hay, and casks filled with stones; the teamsters waiting till Major Walden should give a signal for them to move.

While the cannon were flashing, General Thomas, with two thousand men, marched across the marshes along Dorchester Bay and up the hill overlooking the harbor. Major Walden gave the signal, and the farmers started their teams, — those with picks, and spades, and casks following the soldiers; those with hay halting on the marsh land, unloading, and piling the bales in a line so as to screen the passage. Major Walden, General Rufus Putnam, and Colonel Gridley hastened to the summit of the hill in advance of the troops. Colonel Gridley marked the lines for a fortification; the soldiers stacked their arms, seized picks and spades, and broke the frozen earth. The moon was at its full. From the hill, the soldiers could look down upon the harbor and see the warships and great fleet of transports, with masts and yardarms outlined in the refulgent light. Robert expected to see a cannon flash upon the Scarborough, the nearest battleship; but the sentinel pacing the deck heard no sound of delving pick or shovel. Walden piloted the carts to the top of the hill, and placed the casks in such position that they could be set rolling down the steep at a moment's notice. The soldiers chuckled at the thought of the commotion they would make in the ranks of the redcoats, were they to make an assault and suddenly see the casks rolling and tumbling, sweeping all before them!

General Howe was astonished, when daylight dawned, to see an embankment of yellow earth crowning the hill overlooking the harbor.

" The rebels have done more in a night than my army would have done in a month," he said, after looking at the works with his telescope. What should he do? Mr. Washington's cannon would soon be sending shot and shell upon the warships, the transports, and the town. The provincials must be driven from the spot at once; otherwise, there could be no safety for the fleet, neither for his army. He called his officers together in council.

" We must drive the rebels just as we did at Bunker Hill, or they will drive us out of the town. There is nothing else to be done," said General Clinton.

General Howe agreed with him. A battle must be fought, and the sooner the better. Every moment saw the fortifications growing stronger. But what would be the outcome of a battle? Could he embark his army in boats, land at the foot of the hill, climb the steep ascent, and drive the rebels with the bayonet? At Bunker Hill there was only a rabble, — regiments without a commander ; but now Mr. Washington was in command; his troops were in a measure disciplined. That he was energetic, far-seeing, and calculating, he could not doubt. Had he not transported heavy cannon across the country from Lake Champlain to bombard the town? Evidently Mr. Washington was a man who could bide his time. Such men were not likely to leave anything at haphazard. One third of those assaulting Bunker Hill had been cut down by the fire of the rebels. Could he hope for any less a sacrifice of his army in attacking a more formidable position, with the rebels more securely intrenched? It was not pleasant to contemplate the possible result, but an assault must be made.

From the housetop, Berinthia saw boats from the vessels in the harbor, gathering at Long Wharf. Drums were beating, troops marching. Abraham Duncan came with the information that four or five thousand men were to assault the works and drive the provincials pell-mell across the marshes to Roxbury. At any rate, that was the plan. He was sure it would be a bloody battle. Possibly, while General Howe was engaged at Dorchester Heights, Mr. Washington might be doing something else.

Neither General Howe nor any one within the British lines knew just what the provincial commander had planned, — that the moment the redcoats began the attack, General Israel Putnam, on Cobble Hill, between Charlestown and Cambridge, with four thousand men, would leap into boats, cross the

Charles, and land on the Common; that General Nathanael Greene with a large force would advance from
Roxbury, and together they would grind the British
to powder, like corn in a mill.

It was mid-forenoon when Major Walden escorted
General Washington across the marsh land and along
the path to Dorchester Heights. The troops swung
their hats and gave a cheer when they saw their commander ascending the hill. He lifted his hat, and
thanked them for having constructed such strong in-
trenchments in so short a time.

"It is the fifth of March," he said, "and I am
sure you will remember it is the anniversary of the
massacre of the Sons of Liberty."

In Boston drums were beating, regiments marching;
but suddenly the wind, which had blown from the
west, changed to the east; and the sea waves were
rolling up the bay, making it impossible for the Somerset, Scarborough, Boyne, and the other ships, to
spread their sails and take position to bombard the
works of the rebels; neither could General Howe embark the troops upon the dancing boats. The clouds
were hanging low, and rain falling. Not till the wind
changed and the sea calmed could there be a battle;
General Howe must wait.

Night came; the rain was still pouring. The provincials wrapped their overcoats closely around them,
kindled fires, ate their bread and beef, told stories,
sang songs, and kept ward and watch through the
dreary hours.

Morning dawned; the wind was still east, and the
waves rolling in from the sea. With gloom upon

his brow, General Howe with his telescope examined the fortifications. Could he hope to capture them? Doubtful. Exasperating, humiliating, the reflection that Mr. Washington was in a position to compel him to evacuate the town. Only a few days before, he had written Lord Dartmouth he was in no danger from the rebels; he only wished Mr. Washington would have the audacity to make a movement against him; but now he must pack up and be off, give up what he had held so long, and confess defeat. What would the king say? What the people of England? He did not like to think of what had come. But he must save the army. What of the citizens who had maintained their loyalty to the king? Should he leave them to the tender mercies of the exasperated provincials whose homes had been burned? He could not do that. If Theodore Newville, Nathaniel Coffin, or any of the thousand or more wealthy citizens were willing to remain loyal, if they were ready to become aliens and fugitives and exiles, he must do what he could for them.

" What is it, husband?" Mrs. Newville asked as Mr. Newville entered his house, and she beheld his countenance, white, haggard, and woe-begone.

" What has happened, father?" Ruth asked, leading him, trembling and tottering, to his chair.

" It has come," he gasped, resting his elbows on his knees and covering his face with his hands.

" What has come?" Mrs. Newville inquired.

" The end of the king's authority in this town."

" What do you mean?"

"The army is going, and we have got to go."

"Go where?"

"I don't know; only we have got to leave this home, never to see it again, and be aliens the rest of our lives," he said, groaning and sobbing.

"Why must the army go?" Mrs. Newville exclaimed.

"Because General Howe cannot stay. The provincials are in a position to sink his ships and set the town on fire with their bombs."

"Can't General Howe drive Mr. Washington from the hill just as he did at Charlestown?"

"He was going to do it yesterday, but the sea wouldn't let him, and now it is too late."

"He must do it, and I will go and tell him so. Leave our home and become wanderers and vagabonds? Never!" she cried with flashing eyes.

"It is decided. Orders have been issued. The fear is that the provincials may open fire upon the fleet and sink the ships before the army can get away."

"Why didn't General Howe take possession of the hill, and prevent the provincials from doing it?"

"The Lord knows, and perhaps General Howe does, but I don't. I have seen for some time what might happen, and now we have it. We have got to go, and God help us."

Mrs. Newville, overwhelmed, tottered to a chair.

"So this is what Sam Adams and John Hancock have done. I hate them. But why must we go? Why not stay? We have as good a right to stay as they. Give up our home? Never! Never!"

With flashing eyes, and teeth set firmly together,

she rose, and took a step or two as if ready to confront a foe.

"We cannot stay," said Mr. Newville. "We have given our allegiance to the king; I have held office under the crown, and the Great and General Court will confiscate my estate, and we shall be beggars. More than that, I probably shall be seized and thrown into jail. There's no knowing what they will do. Possibly my lifeless body may yet dangle from the gallows, where murderers have paid the penalty of their crimes."

Mrs. Newville wrung her hands, and gave way to sobs and moans. Ruth had stood a silent spectator, but sat down now by her mother, put an arm around her, and wiped away the tears coursing down her cheeks.

"I haven't told you all," said Mr. Newville. "General Howe threatens to burn the town if Mr. Washington opens fire upon the ships."

"General Howe threatens that?" exclaimed Mrs. Newville.

"Yes; John Scollay and several of us have asked General Robertson to intercede with Howe. He has done so, but Howe will make no promise. He has permitted a flag of truce to go out to Mr. Washington to let him know if the British are molested he will set the town on fire. If Mr. Washington is the kind-hearted man they say he is, probably he will not make an attack. He wants to compel Howe to get out and to have the town spared. We are not the only ones who will suffer, but everybody who has stood for the king will have to go or take the consequences when the provincials march in. They will be implacable in their retaliation for the burning of Charlestown and Falmouth, and for the destruction of the Old North Meetinghouse, the desecration of the Old South, and the pulling down of hundreds of houses. They will confiscate the property of every one who has adhered to the crown, and make them beggars, or send them out of the Province, or perhaps do both. We may as well look the matter squarely in the face, for we have got to face it."

It was spoken with quivering lips. Several vessels had been designated on which the friends of the king might embark for Halifax, the only port near at hand where they could find refuge. He looked around the room, gazed mournfully at the portraits of his ancestors on the walls, at the rich mahogany furniture, the mirrors above the mantel reflecting the scene. In the dining-room was the buffet with its rich furnishings. Upon the stairs was the clock, its pendulum swinging as it had swung since the days of his boyhood. Upon the sideboard were the tea-urns used on many convivial afternoons and evenings. Whichever way he turned he saw that which had contributed to his ease, comfort, and happiness. Looking out of the window, he saw the buds were beginning to swell upon the trees under the genial rays of the sun. The bluebirds and robins had arrived and were singing in the garden. A few more days and the grass would be springing fresh and green, the asparagus throwing up its shoots, the cherry-trees white with blooms, the lilacs and roses perfuming the air; but never again was he to sit beneath the vine-clad arbor as he had sat in former years, listening to Nature's symphony rehearsed by singing birds; never again was he to see the coming of ecstatic life in bud and blossom. He must bid farewell forever to all the enchanting scenes, pull up by the roots, as it were, all cherished things. What should he take? What leave behind? There would be little room on shipboard for the richly carved mahogany chairs, sideboard, sofa, portraits of his ancestors. What use would he have for them in exile? How dispose of them? Who would purchase them? No one. How would he live in a foreign land? How occupy his time? His mansion was his own; he was possessor of other houses and lands, but all would be seized. He could take his silver plate, his gold and silver coin; not much else.

"Oh dear! oh dear! has it come to this!" Mrs. Newville exclaimed, "when we might have been far away, having everything heart could wish!"

She cast a reproachful look upon Ruth.

"Oh, if you had only done as I wanted!"

A gentle hand wiped the tears from the mother's face.

"Mother, dear, the past is gone, never to return. If it were to come again, bringing Lord Upperton, my answer to him would be as it was. We will let that pass. I know your every thought has been for my welfare and happiness. I trust I have not been ungrateful for all you have done for me and for all you thought to do. I have not seen things as you have seen them. You have been loyal to King George; you could hardly do otherwise with father holding an office under the crown. I have given my sympathies to the provincials, because I believe they are standing for what is right. My heart has gone out to one who, I doubt not, is over on yonder hill in arms against the king. I know the greatness of his love, that he will be always true to me, as I shall be to him."

The hand was still wiping away the tears; she was sitting between her father and mother, and laid the other hand upon the father's palm.

"Through these winter nights, dear father and mother, while hearing the cannon and the bursting shells, I have been looking forward to this hour which has come at last."

Tears stood in her eyes, and her voice became tremulous.

"We have come to the parting hour. You will go, but I shall stay, — stay to save the house, so that, by and by. when the heat of passion has cooled, and the fire of hate is only ashes. when the war is over and peace has come. as come it will, you can return to the old home."

"Leave you behind. Ruth!"

"Yes. mother."

"To be insulted and abused by the hateful rebels! Never!"

"I shall not be insulted. I am sure I shall be kindly treated. Do you think my old friends will do anything to annoy me? Why should they, when they know that I myself am a rebel? Mr. Sam Adams has always been my good friend. Have I not sat in his lap in my girlhood? Are not Lucy Flucker Knox, Dorothy Quincy. and Abigail Smith Adams my friends? Has not Mr. John Hancock danced with me? Have I done anything that should cause them to turn against me? Pompey and Phillis will be here to care for me. And now, dear father, I have one or two requests to make. This is your house, but I want you to give it to me, — make out a deed and execute it in my name; and one thing more, I want you to give me a bill of sale of Pompey and Phillis, so that I shall be absolute mistress here. When the Colonies, by their valor and the righteousness of their cause, have become independent of the king, when the last cannon has been fired, in God's good time you will come back and find me here in the old home."

Mr. Newville sat in silence a moment, then put his arm around her and drew her to him.

"Oh Ruth, daughter, you are dearer to me this moment than ever before. Your clear vision has seen what I have not been able to see, — till now, — the possible end of this conflict. The provincials are stronger than I supposed them to be, the disaffection wider, and the king is weaker than I thought. It never seemed possible that an army of ten thousand men could be forced to evacuate this town, but so it is, and I must go. I will not be so selfish as to ask you to go. I know your love has gone out to Robert Walden. I have no right to ask you to thrust a sword into your own loving heart. I do not doubt he will protect you with all the strength of a noble manhood. This house shall be yours, together with Pompey and Phillis, who will be as dutiful to you as they have been to your mother and me. You speak of our coming back, but when we once leave this house we never shall behold it again; nor shall we ever look again upon your face unless you come where we may be. Where that will be, God only knows; we shall be fugitives and wanderers without a home. Your mother and I will not long need an earthly home. Such a wound as this goes down deep into our souls, Ruth."

He could say no more, but hid his face in his hands to hide the agony of a breaking heart.

"Father, have you forgotten who it is that feeds the ravens and cares for the sparrows? Will He not care for you? Of one thing you may be sure, so soon as it is possible to do so I shall seek you wherever you may be: and now we will prepare for your going."

She kissed the tears from his face, cheered the desponding mother, and began to select whatever would most contribute to their comfort.

Abraham Duncan, as he walked the streets, beheld men with haggard faces and women wringing their hands and giving way to lamentations. In their loyalty to the king, they never had dreamed that the provincials could compel a disciplined army to quit the town. They had been informed that with the opening of spring the rebels would be scattered to the winds. In their loyalty they had organized themselves into militia and received arms from General Howe to fight for King George. As by a lightning flash all had been changed. Those who had thus organized knew they would be despised by the provincials and hardly dealt with: that houses and lands would be seized and sold to make restitution for the burning of Charlestown and buildings torn down in

Boston. They who had lived in affluence, who had
delightful homes on the slopes of Beacon Hill, must
leave them. All dear old things must be sacrificed
and family ties ruthlessly sundered. Fathers had
sons whose sympathies were with the provincials;
mothers, other than Mrs. Newville, had daughters
whose true. loves were marshaled under flags floating
on Dorchester Heights. Had not Colonel Henry
Knox sighted the cannon which sent the ball whirling
towards the early home of his loving wife, the home
where her father and mother and sisters were still
living, which they must leave? The sword drawn on
Lexington Common was severing tender heartstrings.

There was a hurly-burly in the streets, — drums
beating, soldiers marching, a rumbling of cannon
and wagons, the removal of furniture. Eleven hundred men and women were preparing to bid farewell
to their native land and homes.

The final hour came. Pompey had seen the trunks
and boxes safely stowed upon the ship in which Mr.
and Mrs. Newville, Nathaniel Coffin, the king's
receiver-general, and Thomas Flucker were to find
passage. With a cane to steady his tottering steps,
Mr. Newville took a last look of the home where his
life had been passed; the house in which his eyes first
saw the light; where a mother, many years in her
grave, had caressed him; where a father had guided
his toddling steps; the home to which he had brought
his bride in the bloom of a beautiful maidenhood;
where Ruth had come to them as the blessing of God
to make the house resound with prattle and laughter,

and fill it with the sunlight of her presence; make it attractive by her grace and beauty, — the soul beauty that looked out from loving eyes and became, as it were, a benediction. He was to go, she to stay. God above would be her guardian.

Mrs. Newville walked as in a daze from parlor to chamber, from dining-room to hall and kitchen. Was she awake or dreaming? Must she leave her home, — the home that had been so blissful, so hospitable? Was she never again to welcome a guest to that table, never hear the merry chatter of voices in parlor or garden? Oh, if Sam Adams and John Hancock had only been content to let things go on as they always had gone! If Ruth had only accepted Lord Upperton's suit! Why could n't she? What ought she to take, what would she most need? What sort of accommodations would they find at Halifax? Why could n't Ruth go with them? It was the questioning of a mind stunned by the sudden stroke; of a spirit all but crushed by the terrible calamity.

"I have put in everything I could think of that will in any way make you comfortable, mother dear," said Ruth, mentioning the articles.

"I've put up some jelly and jam for ye, missus," said Phyllis.

Berinthia Brandon and Abraham Duncan came to bid them farewell, and to help Ruth prepare for their departure.

It was Ruth's strong arm that upheld her mother as they slowly walked the street on their way to the ship. It was a mournful spectacle. Not they alone, but Mr. Shrimpton and Mary, Nathaniel Coffin and wife and John, and a hundred of Ruth's acquaintances were on the wharf preparing to go on board the ships.

"This is what has come from Sam Adams's meddling," said Mr. Shrimpton. "May the Devil take him and John Hancock. They ought to be hanged, and I hope King George will yet have a chance to string 'em up — curse 'em! I'd like to see 'em dangling from the gibbet, and the crows picking their bones," he said, smiting his fists together, walking to and fro.

He was bidding farewell to home, — to the house in which he was born. He had farms in the county, wide reaches of woodland, fields, and pastures. The provincials would confiscate them. In his declining years all his property was to slip through his fingers, and he was to totter in penury to his grave.

" I shall enlist in the service of the king and fight 'em," said John Coffin, who had shown his loyalty by accompanying General Howe to the battle of Bunker Hill.

" And I hope you 'll have a chance to put a bullet through the carcass of Sam Adams," said Mr. Shrimpton.

It was his daughter's hand that guided him over the gang-plank to the deck of the Queen Charlotte.

" Let me put this muffler round your neck ; the air is chill and you are shivering," said Mary, gently leading him.

With chattering teeth and curses on his lips for those whom he regarded as authors of his misfortunes, Abel Shrimpton, led by his daughter, descended the winding stairs to the cabin of the ship.

" Here are the rugs and shawls, mother, and here

is the wolf-skin, father, to wrap around you," said Ruth.

They were in the stifling cabin, the departing loyalists sitting as in a daze, stupefied, stunned by the sudden calamity, wondering if it were not a horrid dream.

To Mary Shrimpton and Ruth Newville it was no phantom, no hallucination, but a reality, an exigency, demanding calm reflection, wise judgment, and prompt, decisive action. They had talked it over, — each in the other's confidence.

" You must go and I will stay; you will care for them all ; I will look after things here. This war will not last always. You will all come back some time," said Ruth, her abiding faith rising supreme above the agony of the parting.

" I will care for them," had been the calm reply of Mary.

" Oh, missus! I can't bear to have ye go, you 's been good to me always. I 'se packed a luncheon for ye," said Phillis, kneeling upon the floor, clasping the knees of her departing mistress, crying and sobbing.

" Oh, massa and missus, old Pomp can't tell ye how good ye 've been to him. He 'll be good to Miss Ruth. He 'll pray for de good Lord to bless ye, every night, as he always has," — the benediction of the slave kneeling by Phillis's side.

Long and tender was the last embrace of the mother and daughter, — of the father and his beloved child. With tears blinding her eyes, with tottering steps, Ruth passed across the gang-plank. A sailor drew it in, and unloosed the cable. The vessel swung with the tide from its moorings, the jib and mainsail filled with the breeze, and glided away. The weeping crowd upon its deck saw Ruth standing upon the wharf, her countenance serene, pure, and peaceful, with tears upon her face, gazing at the receding ship. Those around her beheld her steady herself against the post which had held the cable, standing there till the Queen Charlotte was but a white speck dotting the landscape in the lower harbor, then walking with faltering steps to her desolate home.

XXIV.

IN THE OLD HOME.

"Here, Miss Ruth, I has a cordial for ye. Drink it, honey," said Phillis as Ruth sank into a chair.

"Don't be down-hearted, Miss Ruth; old Pomp will take keer of ye."

"I do not doubt it. You and Phillis have always been good to me, and now I have something to say to both of you. Would you like to be free, Pompey?"

"Would I like to be free, Miss Ruth?" the negro asked, hardly knowing what to make of the question.

"Yes, would you like to be free, to own yourself, to come and go as you please?"

"'Deed I would, Miss Ruth. Massa and missus was always very good to old Pomp, but 'pears I would like to be myself."

She rose and took Pompey and Phillis by their hands.

"Your old master has given you both to me, and now I give you to yourselves. You are both free now and forever," said Ruth.

"Free! Miss Ruth! Did you say we is free?"

"Yes, you are no longer slaves; you can go and come, now and always; you are your own."

"Oh, Miss Ruth, old Pomp never will leave ye, never. Old Pomp free! 'Pears like de New Jerusalem has come," said the negro, sinking upon his knees, kissing her hand and bathing it with tears.

"Oh, Miss Ruth, honey, I has held ye in my arms when ye was a little baby, toted ye in de garding when de flowers was bloomin', rocked ye to sleep when ye was pinin'; I've seen ye grow to be a woman, and now ye is my missus tellin' me I'm' free. I'll cook de chicken and de johnny-cake for ye till I can't cook no more," said Phillis, clasping Ruth in her arms, with tears rolling down her cheeks and laughter bubbling from her lips.

The foresight that had seen the probable departure of the British troops was forecasting the immediate future; that the interval before the arrival of General Washington's army would be one of peril, from vagabonds, camp-followers, and the ragamuffins enlisted by Crcen Brush, commissioned by General Howe to organize a battalion of Tories. Through the day the British regiments were sullenly taking their departure. Pompey informed Ruth that the vagabonds had begun to plunder the stores and break into houses.

"Dey won't git into dis yeer house, honey. I'se got de water b'ilin' hot in de kitchen for 'em," said Phillis.

Ruth did not doubt a mansion like hers would attract the villains, and determined to defend herself against all intruders. General Howe was going on shipboard; no longer would she recognize his authority or that of any subordinate officer. Years before, her father had been member of a battalion of horsemen. The pistols he carried then were in a closet. Pompey brought them, fixed the flints, oiled the locks, and found a horn of powder, but no bullets.

" Perhaps it is just as well, Pompey, for if I were to have a bullet, I might kill somebody, and I would not like to do that," she said.

" If ye are goin' to shoot, better shoot to kill, Miss Ruth," said Pompey.

" I never have fired a pistol, Pompey; how do you do it?"

" I 'll show ye, missus," said the negro, putting some powder in the pan and cocking the pistol.

" Now, Miss Ruth, you jes' pull de trigger and it will flash."

They were in the kitchen. Ruth pointed the weapon toward the fireplace and pulled the trigger. There was a flash and a bang.

" O Lord! Missus!" shouted Phillis, dropping on the floor.

" 'Pears, Miss Ruth. like she 's been loaded all dese years," said Pompey, his eyeballs rolling in astonishment.

" It appears I have found out how to fire," said Ruth, laughing. " But how do you load it?" she asked.

Pompey poured a charge of powder into his hand, emptied it into the barrel, and rammed it down with a wad of paper.

" We have n't any bullets. but we can use gravel-stones or dried peas or a tallow candle. I 've seen a candle fired right through a board, Miss Ruth," he said.

" We 'll load them with powder now; perhaps we shan't need anything else." Ruth replied.

In the gathering darkness Phillis saw a redcoat reconnoitring the grounds. He rapped upon the door leading to the kitchen. She did not unloose the chain, but opened it sufficiently wide to talk with the fellow.

" What d' ye want ? " she asked.

" I want to come in."

" What d' ye want to come in for ? "

" To see if ye have anything belonging to the king. People have seized the king's property and taken it into their houses."

" We have n't anything belonging to King George."

" Open the door or I 'll break it down."

" Go away. Dere can't no lobster come into dis yeer kitchen," said Phillis, attempting to close the door. But she saw the muzzle of a gun thrust into the opening. Her hands grasped it. One vigorous pull and it was hers, and the villain was fleeing.

" I 'se got it ! I 'se got de villin's gun. Wid de pistils, de musket, and de b'ilin' water we 'll fight 'em ! " she shouted.

Ruth, keeping watch, saw a squad of men. One of them rattled the knocker.

" What do you wish ? " she asked, raising a window.

" I am commissioned to search for property belonging to the crown."

" Who are you ? "

" I am a lieutenant in the command of Colonel Brush."

" I do not recognize your authority, neither that of Colonel Brush nor General Howe, who has taken his departure."

" I shall be under the necessity of entering by force if you do not open the door."

" You will do so at your peril."

" Break down the door, men ! "

The soldiers pounded with the butts of their muskets, but the panels did not yield.

" Smash a window ! "

A bayonet was thrust through a pane, and the glass rattled to the ground ; the butt of a musket smashed the sash, and a pair of hands grasped the window-sill. Memory recalled a day when two soldiers assaulted her ; from that hour a redcoat had been hateful. She seized one of the pistols. Remembering what Pompey had said, she picked the lighted candle from its socket and thrust it into the weapon. The ruffian was astride the window-sill. There was a flash, a loud report, and he dropped with a thud to the ground.

From the balcony came a flood of boiling water upon the astonished ruffians.

" I 'll give it to ye, b'ilin' hot ! " shouted Phillis. The ruffians saw the muzzle of a gun pointed towards them from the window, and the stalwart form of Pompey as he raised it to take aim. The astonished villains fled, leaving Ruth, Pompey, and Phillis victors in the encounter.

Morning dawned fair and beautiful. The robins and bluebirds were singing in the garden. Ruth heard again the beating of drums, the blast of bugles. General Washington was entering the town. By his side rode Major Robert Walden.

What surprise ! A white handkerchief was waving from the balcony of the Newville home. She was there, more beautiful and queenly than ever before !

Not an alien, not an exile, but loyal to liberty, to
him! He must leap from his saddle and clasp her
in his arms! No. He must accompany his great
commander in the triumphal entry. That accomplished, then the unspeakable joy.

There came an evening when the Newville home
was aglow with lights, and Pompey was bowing low
to General and Mrs. Washington, Generals Greene,
Putnam, Thomas, to colonels, majors, captains, councilors, the selectmen of the town, Reverend Doctor
Cooper, Colonel Henry and Lucy Knox, Captain and
Mrs. Brandon, Berinthia, Abraham Duncan, Major
Tom Brandon, Rachel Walden ; young ladies in the
bloom of maidenhood, matronly mothers, fathers resolute of countenance, — all rejoicing that the redcoats
were gone.

Down from the chamber, passing the old clock on
the stairs, came Major Robert Walden, in bright,
new uniform, and Ruth Newville in satin, white and
pure.

Reverend Doctor Cooper spoke of the bravery of
the bridegroom in battle, the manliness of character
that fitted him for fighting the battle of life. Tears
came to many eyes as he pictured the love of a
maiden who rescued her beloved, swept by life's ebbing tide far out towards a shoreless sea.

They who stood around beheld the countenance of
the bride transfigured as she pronounced the words,
" to love, to honor, and cherish him."

Amid the general joy, one heart alone felt a mo-
mentary pang. Never might Rachel whisper such

words to him whose last thought had been of her, who had given his life that liberty might live.

Once more food was to be had from the market-men around Faneuil Hall — joints of beef, pigs, sausages, chickens, turkeys, vegetables and fruit, brought in by the farmers of Braintree, Dedham, and Roxbury. Fishermen once more could sail down the harbor, drop their lines for cod and mackerel on the fishing ground beyond the Outer Brewster, and return to the town without molestation from a meddling town major.

With joyful countenance and conscious dignity, Pompey perambulated the market, inspecting what the hucksters had for sale.

"I want de juiciest j'int, de tenderest, fattest turkey, de freshest eggs right from de nest, 'cause de 'casion is to be Missus Ruth's weddin' dinner," he said.

Many banquets had Phillis prepared, but never one like the dinner for Miss Ruth on her wedding day.

"I've roasted de turkey and sparrib for Massa Ginerel Howe and Massa Ginerel Clinton, but dey ain't of no 'count 'side Massa Major Walden and Massa Ginerel Washington, 'cause dey drive de redcoats out of Boston. Miss Ruth fired de pistil and I scaldid dem with de b'ilin' water. He! he! he!" she laughed.

It was a pleasure to stuff the turkey, to turn the joint of beef roasting on the spit, mix the plums in the pudding, and mould the mince pies for Ruth and her friends.

"Miss Ruth told me to go free, and now she's Missus Ruth Walden. He! he! he!"

The laughter bubbled from her lips.

It was a joyful party that sat down to the dinner. The toasts drunk were not the health of George III. and Sophia Charlotte, but the health of General George Washington, the Continental Congress,

The Dinner-Party.

Major Robert Walden, and, more heartily than any other, long life and happiness to Ruth Newville Walden.

Years have gone by, — years of sorrow, privation, and suffering to those who, through their loyalty to King George, and their inability to discern the signs of the times, have been exiles from the land that gave them birth, whose property has been seized by the Great and General Court of Massachusetts. The days are long to Mary Shrimpton in the little cabin at Halifax. The great estates once owned by her father are no longer his. Her once beautiful home has been sold to the highest bidder. Only with her spinning-wheel can she keep the wolf from the cabin door. Parliament has been talking of doing something for the refugees in Nova Scotia, but the commoners and lords are three thousand miles away, and the people of England are groaning under the burden incurred by the fruitless attempt to subdue the Colonies. The struggle is over. Lord Cornwallis has surrendered his army to General Washington at Yorktown, and commissioners are negotiating a peace. Through the years Abel Shrimpton, unreconciled to life's changes, has been cursing Samuel Adams and John Hancock for having led the people to rebel against the king, not seeing that Divine Providence was using them as instruments to bring about a new era in human affairs. When the curses are loudest and most vehement. Mary's gentle hand pats his lips, smooths the gray hairs from the wrinkled brow, and calms his troubled spirit. Pansies bloom beneath the latticed windows of her cabin home. Morning-glories twine around it. Swallows twitter their joy, and build their nests beneath the eves. Motherly hens cluck to their broods in the dooryard. The fare upon the table within the cabin is frugal, but there is always a bit of bread or a herring for a wandering exile. When women pine for their old homes, when

homesickness becomes a disease, it is Mary Shrimpton who cheers the fainting hearts. As she sits by
her wheel, she sings the song sung by the blind old
harper Carolan, who, though long separated from his
true love, yet recognized her by the touch of her gentle
hand : —

> "True love can ne'er forget.
> Fondly as when we met,
> Dearest, I love thee yet,
> My darling one."

Tom Brandon said he would be true to her. The
war is over; surely if living he will come. Though
the thick fog at times drifts in from the sea, shutting
out the landscape and all surrounding objects, though
the rain patters on the roof, and the days are dark
and dreary, her face is calm and serene, glorified by
a steadfast faith and changeless love.

The time has been long to the occupants of the
cottage across the way. Though little gold is left in .
the purse, there is ever room for hungry refugees at
the table of the king's former commissioner of imposts. The locks beneath his tie-wig are whiter than
they were, the furrows on his brow have deepened.
Officers of the army and navy in Halifax, once guests
in his home on the slope of Beacon Hill, sometimes
call upon him, but the great world has passed him by.
Old friends, fellow exiles, at times gather at his fireside, talk of other days, and of what Parliament may
possibly do for them.

Time has left its mark upon the face of her who
sits by his side. The soft, brown hair, has changed
to gray. Plans of other days have not come to pass.

Disappointment and grief have quenched ambitious fire. Father and mother are separated from a daughter beloved. How could Ruth ever become a rebel, disloyal to her rightful sovereign? What possessed her to turn her back upon Lord Upperton, upon the opportunity to become a peeress of the

Home of the Exiles.

realm? Oh, the misery that has come from such waywardness! What has become of her? Will they ever again see her?

With the flag of the new nation — the banner of crimson stripes and fadeless stars — flying at her mast-head, the ship Berinthia Brandon, Major Tom Brandon owner, comes proudly sailing into Halifax harbor. The anchor dropped, he makes his way to the vine-clad cabin, listens a moment by the latticed window to hear a sweet voice singing words that thrill him.

> " Dearest, I love thee yet,
> My darling one."

He lifts the latch. There is a cry of delight, and Mary springs to his arms.

" I said I would come, and I am here."

" I knew you would, Tom. Ever since a ship arrived bringing the news from Yorktown that Cornwallis had surrendered, I have been expecting you."

" How do you do, father ? " said Major Tom, holding out his hand to Mr. Shrimpton.

" I ain't your father," the surly reply.

" But you are to be, as soon as I can find a minister. The past is past. I 've come to take you and Mary to your old home. When it was sold, I bought it ; you are to go back to it and live there. It is to be our home."

There is astonishment upon the cold, hard face, which relaxes its sternness; the chin quivers, the lips tremble, tears roll down the cheeks of the grayhaired exile. Through the years he has nursed his hate. But there is no sword so sharp, no weapon so keen to pierce the hardened human heart, as kindness. He has hated Samuel Adams, John Hancock, and Tom Brandon ; and this is Tom's revenge. His old home to be his own once more! No longer an exile ! To sit once more by the old fireside, through the kindness of him whom he had turned from his door! His head drops upon his breast; he sobs like a child, but reaches out his arms to them.

"Take her, Tom. I've hated you, but God bless you; you were right, and I was wrong."

No longer hard-hearted, cold, and animated by hate, but as a little child he enters the doorway leading to the Kingdom of Heaven.

A man of stalwart frame, a woman radiant and beautiful, with a little boy and girl, are standing by the door of the humble home across the way; fellow-passengers with Major Tom on the Berinthia Brandon. Mr. Newville opens the door in answer to the knock, to be clasped in the arms of Ruth. Great the surprise, unspeakable the joy, of father, mother, and daughter, meeting once more, welcoming a worthy son, taking prattling grandchildren to their arms.

"We have come for you, and we are all going home together. You will find everything just as it was when you left," said Ruth.

Once more there were happy homes in Boston, — that upon Copp's Hill, where Berinthia and Abraham Duncan cared for the father and mother; that where Tom and Mary Shrimpton-Brandon made the passing days pleasant to Abel Shrimpton, loyal no longer to King George, but to the flag of the future republic; and that other home, where Major Robert Walden and his loving wife, with queenly grace, dispensed unstinted hospitality, not only to those distinguished among their fellow-men, but to the poor and needy, impoverished by the long and weary struggle for independence of the mother land. Abel Shrimpton and Theodore Newville were no longer exiles, but citizens, acknowledging cheerful allegiance to the flag of the confederation, through the fealty to liberty by the Daughters of the Revolution.